JUDAISM IN ISLĀM

By the Same Author

TOLDOT HA-YAḤASUT SHEL EINSTEIN

•

HEBREW IN AMERICAN HIGHER EDUCATION

•

HEBRAIC CONTRIBUTIONS TO AMERICAN LIFE

•

HEBREW LANGUAGE, LITERATURE AND CULTURE
IN AMERICAN INSTITUTIONS
OF HIGHER LEARNING

•

HEBRAIC FOUNDATIONS
OF AMERICAN DEMOCRACY

•

NACHMAN KROCHMAL
AND THE GERMAN IDEALISTS

The Opening
(*Al-Fātiḥah*)

JUDAISM IN ISLĀM

BIBLICAL AND TALMUDIC BACKGROUNDS OF THE KORAN AND ITS COMMENTARIES

Suras II *and* III

ABRAHAM I. KATSH
CHAIRMAN
DEPARTMENT OF HEBREW CULTURE AND EDUCATION
NEW YORK UNIVERSITY

NEW YORK UNIVERSITY PRESS · 1916

PUBLISHED FOR
NEW YORK UNIVERSITY PRESS
BY
BLOCH PUBLISHING COMPANY
1954

Library of Congress Catalogue Card Number: 53-10662

PRINTED IN THE UNITED STATES OF AMERICA
PRESS OF MAURICE JACOBS, INC.
PHILADELPHIA, PENNA.

TO MY WIFE

ESTELLE

AND OUR CHILDREN

ETHAN AND SALEM

שי בחבה

CONTENTS

PREFACE

This book grew out of a doctoral dissertation submitted in 1943 to the Dropsie College for Hebrew and Cognate Learning. In the intervening years the incorporation of a large amount of source material has resulted in what is to all intents a new work. The original comparative study dealt, on the Moslem side, only with the Koran, whereas the present greatly expanded treatment also encompasses the work of Moslem commentators and exegetes.

I wish to express my gratitude to my late teacher and friend, Professor Solomon L. Skoss, who guided me during my years at Dropsie College. His critical evaluations, scholarly suggestions, and above all his kindness and personal interest were of inestimable value to me. Professor Skoss prepared the Foreword to this volume only a short time before his sudden death — a tragic loss not only to me personally, but to scholarship as well. A great teacher and scholar, he was greater still as a human being.

I am also grateful to President A. A. Neuman and Professor Solomon Zeitlin of Dropsie College, and Professor Philip K. Hitti of Princeton University, all of whom have been inspiring teachers and true friends.

It is a pleasure to acknowledge my indebtedness to Drs. M. M. Bravmann, David Rudavsky, Moshe Zucker and Mr. Jacob Moshief for reading the page proofs of *Judaism in Islām* and offering valuable criticism and constructive suggestions. Mr. Moshief was extremely helpful to me in verifying Arabic sources and in the preparation of the indices. To them and to the staff of Maurice Jacobs, Inc. — Mr. David Skaraton and Drs. Samuel Kurland and Menahem G. Glenn — my heartfelt thanks for their unfailing co-operation and painstaking efforts. From the New York University Press and its editors, Mr. Fillmore Hyde, Mr. Allan Angoff, and Mr. Wilson Follett, from Mr. Edward H. Bloch and Mr. Solomon Kerstein of the Bloch Publishing Company, now celebrating its centennial year, and from Dr. Maurice Jacobs, I have had every kind of inspiring encouragement.

For the many courtesies I have received, let me thank the Dropsie College Library and its Librarian, Dr. Joseph Reider; the Library of Congress and particularly Dr. Lawrence Marwick, Chief of its Hebraic Section; the Library of the Jewish Theological Seminary; the Oriental Section of the New York Public Library; and the New York University Library of Judaica and Hebraica.

My everlasting gratitude goes to my wife for her tireless labor in preparing the manuscript for publication. The dedication of this book to her and to our children is but a small expression of my appreciation for their devotion, patience, and infinite forbearance.

The publication of this volume has been materially assisted by the generosity of Mr. William Rosenthal, a friend and supporter of Jewish scholarship, of Mr. Louis M. Rabinowitz, eminent patron and benefactor of Hebrew letters, and of Mr. Harry Starr, President of the Lucius Littauer Foundation. I shall always be grateful for their assistance, vision, and keen appreciation of scholarship.

April, 1954 A. I. K.

FOREWORD

It is indeed a pleasure to write a few words in preface to the book *Judaism in Islām*, by my friend and former student, Professor Abraham I. Katsh.

Even a cursory reading of the Koran, the Bible of Mohammedan religion, reveals frequent references to various stories and episodes from the Old Testament, occasionally embellished by familiar Jewish legends and later customs. However, it exhibits at times such discrepancies and confusion in handling and presenting this material that it is often difficult to trace the various channels through which Mohammed obtained his information.

A number of general works have been written on the Jewish background of various topics in the Koran. But Professor Katsh's study undertakes to present a clear picture of Mohammed's indebtedness to Judaism, a picture which could not be obtained from previous sporadic topical studies or general discussions.

He presents a verse by verse study of two of the most important chapters of the Koran, tracing its background in the Old Testament, rabbinic lore and Jewish legends. He likewise traces the various Koranic allusions and metaphorical expressions which may have some Jewish background. Its significance, therefore, for every serious student of the Koran, and of the origin of Islamic religion, is quite obvious. This book will be of much interest to scholars pursuing Koranic and Islamic studies, and its publication will be deeply appreciated by them.

SOLOMON L. SKOSS
Professor of Arabic, Dropsie College

May 10, 1952

INTRODUCTION

Nature of Study

Ever since Abraham Geiger wrote his book, "Was hat Mohammed aus dem Judenthume aufgenommen?",[1] a number of scholars have tried to corroborate his view that Islām owes a tremendous debt to Hebraic writings and traditions. "The Koran," according to R. B. Smith, "teems with ideas, allusions, and even phraseology, drawn not so much from the written as from the oral Jewish law, from the traditions that grew round it, and the commentaries on it . . . It (the Talmud) is the meeting point of the three Monotheistic creeds of the world; and, even with the imperfect information that the Eastern scholars have given respecting it, it has done much to throw light upon them all. Mohammed was never backward to acknowledge the intimate connection between his faith and that of the Jews. And in more than one passage of the Koran he refers with equal respect to their oral and to their written law."[2]

On the other hand, there are scholars like Brockelmann, who claim that Muḥammad's "acquaintanceship with biblical material was, to be sure, extremely superficial and rich in errors. He may have owed some of its (Koranic) characteristics to the Jewish legends of the Haggadah, but more to the Christian teachers who, in addition,

[1] Abraham Geiger, *Was hat Mohammed aus dem Judenthume aufgenommen?* Bonn, 1833; translated into English by F. M. Young under the name *Judaism and Islam,* Madras, 1898. The references here will be to the German original (Leipzig, 1902 edition) unless otherwise indicated. Cf. S. Krauss, "Talmudische Nachrichten über Arabien," *ZDMG,* LXX (1916), pp. 325–53; Rudolph Leszynsky, *Mohammedanische Tradition über das Jüngste Gericht,* Berlin, 1909, also *Die Juden in Arabien zur Zeit Mohammeds,* Berlin, 1910; M. Maas, *Bibel und Koran,* Leipzig, 1893.

[2] R. B. Smith, *Mohammed and Mohammedanism,* London, 1889, p. 146; cf. Julian Obermann, "Islamic Origins," *The Arab Heritage,* ed. N. A. Faris, Princeton, 1944, pp. 58–120; I. Gastfreund, *Mohammed nach Talmud und Midrasch,* Berlin, 1875; J. Barth, *Midraschische Elemente,* Berlin, 1903 and *Studien zur Kritik und Exegese des Qorans,* Strassburg, 1915; J. J. Rivlin, *Gesetz im Koran,* Jerusalem, 1934; Heinrich Speyer, "Von den biblischen Erzählungen im Koran," *Korrespondenzblatt,* Berlin, (1923–24), pp. 7–26; M. Grünbaum, *Neue Beiträge zur semitischen Sagenkunde,* Leiden, 1893; I. Ben-Zeeb, *Hayehudim Ba'arab,* Tel-Aviv, 1931.

acquainted him with the Gospel of the Infancy, the legend of the Seven Sleepers, the saga of Alexander, and the other recurrent themes of medieval world literature."[3]

The same opinion is maintained by Wellhausen[4] and H. P. Smith,[5] who feel that "the impulse came from Christianity." However, no conclusive research has been done thus far to determine how much of Jewish and how much of Christian tradition went into the making of Islām.

The lack of unanimity among these scholars is due primarily to the character of the literature with which they deal. Though Muḥammad never disclosed the sources of his information, the Koran suggests that he obtained much of his knowledge from both Jewish and Christian scholars. "With Judaism," writes Torrey, "on the contrary, his acquaintance is intimate and many-sided. He learned his lessons well; and when a thorough-going comparison is made of the Koranic material, of all sorts, with the standard Hebrew-Jewish writings then current, we must say with emphasis that his authorities, whoever they were, were men well versed in the Bible, in the oral law, and the haggada."[6]

[3] Carl Brockelmann, *History of the Islamic Peoples*, London, 1950, pp. 16–17; cf. K. Ahrens, "Christliches im Koran," *ZDMG*, LX (1930), pp. 15–16, 148–90; C. H. Becker, *Christentum und Islam*, Leipzig, 1907. Also, *Islamstudien*, 2 vols., Leipzig, 1924–32.

[4] "Es ist wahrscheinlich, dass Muhammed denselben durch jüdische Vermittlung zugeführt bekommen hat, wenngleich man dessen eingedenk bleiben muss, dass derselbe Sagenstoff auch bei den orientalischen Christen im Umlauf war, und dass die Haggada ihre Quelle grossenteils in apokryphen Schriften hatte, die wenn sie auch jüdischen Ursprungs, waren doch seit dem zweiten Jahrhundert immer ausschliesslicher in christlichen Besitz übergingen." J. Wellhausen, *Reste arabischen Heidentums*, Berlin, 1897, p. 205, quoted in Ch. C. Torrey, *The Jewish Foundation of Islam*, New York, 1933, p. 66. Cf. Tor Andrae, *Der Ursprung des Islams und das Christentum*, Uppsala, 1926; also, *Die Person Muhammeds in Lehre und Glauben seiner Gemeinde*, Stockholm, 1918.

[5] H. P. Smith, *The Bible and Islam*, New York, 1897, p. 315; cf. R. Bell, *The Origin of Islam in its Christian Environment*, London, 1926; E. Fritsch, *Islam und Christenthum im Mittelalter*, Breslau, 1930; Axel Moberg, *Über eine Christliche Legende in der Islamischen Tradition*, Lund, 1930; D. L. O'Leary, *Arabia Before Muhammad*, London, 1927; H. Lammens, *L'Arabie Occidentale avant l'hégire*, Beyrouth, 1928.

[6] Torrey, *op. cit.*, p. 61; cf. J. Horovitz, "Jewish Proper Names and Derivatives in the Koran," *HUCA*, Vol. II, 1925, pp. 145–227; Abraham I. Katsh, "Li-She'elat

The scholars who have written on the subject of Jewish influence on the Koran have dealt with this theme from a general point of view. They either discussed whole narratives or dealt with religious terms or Aggadic stories common to Islām and Judaism.

In this volume the author treats the subject by means of a verse by verse study of the Koran and at the same time utilizes the Moslem commentators and traditionalists, Zamakhsharī,[7] Baiḍāwī,[8] Bukhārī[9] and Ṭabarī.[10] "The Koran," correctly writes von Grunebaum, "is not the book as Mohammed revealed it. In fact, he never revealed a book; he revealed short visions, injunctions, parables, fables, or doctrinal discourses."[11] Our approach, therefore, is to relate, wherever possible, Muḥammad's single utterances to their rabbinic sources. The study does not deal, however, with the detailed theological and philosophical doctrines of the two religions. For this study Suras two and three[12] were chosen as the most representative in the Koran.[13] Sura two, entitled *al-Baqarah*, and described as the "Koran in miniature," is a summary of all the essential points of the Revelation, which are elaborated elsewhere.[14] Furthermore, it tells of

Hashpa'at ha-Talmud 'al ha-Ḳoran," *Hateḳufah*, New York, Vols. XXXIV–XXXV, 1950, pp. 834–38; H. Hirschfeld, *New Researches into the Composition and Exegesis of the Qoran*, London, 1902; *Jüdische Elemente im Koran*, Berlin, 1878; and *Beiträge zur Erklärung des Ḳorân*, Leipzig, 1886; I. Schapiro, *Die haggadischen Elemente im erzählenden Teil des Korans*, Leipzig, 1907.

[7] Zamakhsharī, *The Kashshaf 'an Ḥaqaiq al-Tanzīl* (ed. Lees), 2 vols., Calcutta, 1856.

[8] Baiḍāwī, *Tafsīr* (ed. Ministry of Interior), 2 vols., Cairo, 1355 A.H.

[9] Âbou Abdallah Mohammed ibn Ismaîl al-Bukhârî, *Recueil des Traditions Mahométanes* (Krehl ed.), Leyde, 1862–1908.

[10] Muḥammad ibn-Jarīr al-Ṭabarī, *Jāmi'u'l-Bayān fī Tafsīru'l-Qur'ān*, 30 vols., Cairo, 1331 A.H.

[11] G. von Grunebaum, *Medieval Islam*, Chicago, 1946, p. 80; cf. Baiḍāwī, *Anwāru-l-Tanzīl*, Lipsiae (ed. Vogel), 1848, p. 552: "we sent it down gradually piece by piece," 25:32; and compare with B. Giṭ. 60a.

[12] According to Bukhārī, Muḥammad once remarked: "whoever reads the last two verses of the chapter entitled *Baqarah* on any night, they are sufficient for him." M. M. Ali, *The Holy Qur-ān*, Lahore, 1935, p. xlvi; cf. Marmaduke Pickthall, *The Meaning of the Glorious Koran*, London, 1930, p. 23.

[13] Sura I, known as *Al-Fātiḥah* (the Opening), consists of seven verses only, and is essentially a prayer. It is used by every Moslem at least thirty-two times a day.

[14] References to other verses in the Koran are frequently cited when they are related to this study.

Muḥammad's experiences with Jews, his discussions with them and his efforts to convince them of his greatness. One is apt, therefore, to find more of rabbinic background in this Sura than in any other. Sura three complements Sura two and contains a number of references to the Jews and Christians. However, less of the Hebraic background is evidenced there. It is the hope of the author to publish other Suras by this method in the future.

Our study reveals that Muḥammad (570–632 C. E.) borrowed extensively from Jewish sources. He was fully aware of the importance of the Jewish religion and leaned heavily upon it. He used all sources, the Bible, the Talmud, as well as the Apocrypha. The Christian tradition, too, was an invaluable material for the development of his new structure.[15]

Early Stages of Islām

According to the Koran, Muḥammad alone possessed a true understanding of God. He stated that he did not come to abrogate the Old and New Testaments, but rather to fulfill the spirit and the letter of the Book. He maintained that Abraham was neither a Jew nor a Christian, but the true expounder of ethical monotheism, and that the Koran, as revealed to him by Allah through the angel Gabriel, embodied the true revelation which the Jews and the Christians had failed to follow. Tracing his genealogy to Abraham through his son Ishmael, Muḥammad claimed to be the rightful heir to Abraham's high rank.[16]

It was Muḥammad's contention that God could not have omitted the Arabs from the revelations with which He had favored the Jews and the Christians. Though he denied the divinity of Jesus, he

[15] A. Sprenger, *Mohammed und der Koran*, Hamburg, 1889; H. Lammens "Mahomet fut-il sincère," *RSR*, 1911, p. 22; D. B. Macdonald, *Aspects of Islam*, New York, 1911, pp. 72–74; Tor Andrae, *Muhammad: The Man and His Faith*, New York, 1936, pp. 63–70; Nöldeke-Schwally, *Geschichte des Qorâns*, Leipzig, 1909, Vol. I, pp. 4–6; W. C. Klein (tr.), *Al-Ibānah 'an uṣūl ad-Diyānah*, New Haven, 1940, p. 13; J. Horovitz, *HUCA*, Vol. II (1925), pp. 145 f.; D. S. Margoliouth, "Old and New Testament in Muhammedanism," *ERE* # IX, pp. 482 f.; C. F. Gerock, *Versuch einer Darstellung der Christologie des Koran*, Hamburg, 1839; John Walker, *Bible Characters in the Koran*, Paisley, 1931.

[16] William Thomson, "Muhammad: His Life and Person," *The Moslem World*, XXXIX, #2 (1944), pp. 96–137.

accepted the Nazarene as the last of the Hebrew prophets. Himself he considered the Messenger of God and "the Seal of all the Prophets." He accused the Jews of deleting from the Bible predictions of his advent. At the same time, however, he accepted most of the narratives of the Bible.

Muḥammad never intended to establish Islām as a new religion. He considered himself the rightful custodian of the Book sent by Allah to "confirm" the Scriptures. It is for this reason that in the beginning he saw no difference between Judaism and Christianity and believed that both Jews and Christians would welcome him. It is only later, when he realized that he could never gain support from either of them, that he presented Islām as a new faith. He accepted whatever of their traditions that came within the purview of his plan, making such changes as he saw fit. This accounts for the seeming discrepancies between the stories of the Bible and the Koranic version of the same narratives. However, in relating the Koranic version of the biblical story to the Aggadic source as indicated in our study, the discrepancies almost entirely disappear. For, astonishingly enough, the biblical narratives are reproduced in the Koran in true Aggadic cloak.

At the time of Muḥammad's appearance, a great number of Jews made their home in Arabia, where, indeed, they had lived for many centuries. The Hebrew Bible contains a number of references to the close relationship between Arabs and Jews.[17]

Arabic sources abound in incidents attesting to the friendly relations between the Jews and the Arabs in the pre-Islāmic period

[17] "Commercial relations on a large scale between Palestine and Arabia certainly go back to the days of Solomon; and many books of the Old Testament, particularly Job and Proverbs, which are strongly marked by the presence of Arabic words, show that the connexion was steadily maintained." Alfred Guillaume, "The Influence of Judaism on Islam" in the *Legacy of Israel*, edited by Bevan and Singer, Oxford, 1928, p. 132. About the exalted Jewish poet al-Samaw'al in the pre-Islamic period see R. A. Nicholson, *A Literary History of the Arabs*, Cambridge, 1941, pp. 84 f.; J. W. Hirschberg, *Yisrael Ba'arab*, Tel Aviv, 1946, pp. 245–69: "We may gather . . . that the Arab Jews possibly exercised a certain indirect influence on the construction of the Talmud. Some paragraphs in the Mishnâh refer exclusively to the Jews of the Peninsula. It was considered lawful for them to live in Bedouin tents, and their women were permitted to go out on Sabbath wearing a veil. The Talmud also alludes to the custom of circumcision among Arabs and twice mentions Arab foot-gear." Hirschfeld, *op. cit.*, p. 104; see also G. Levi Della Vida, "A proposito di as-Samaw'al" in *Rivista degli Studi Orientali*, XIII, pp. 53–72.

(*Jāhilīyah*).[18] The southwestern part of the Arabian peninsula, known as Yemen, was generally considered a Jewish state. The last Himyar king, Dhū Nuwās, who converted to Judaism, fell in battle in 525 C.E.[19] The Jews of Yemen wrought a tremendous change in the religious life of the Arab people, hundreds of years before the advent of Muḥammad. It is likely that had Islām not appeared, the Jews and the Christians would have absorbed all Arabia into their faiths.

The Arab tribes in the *Jāhilīyah* period who had accepted Judaism followed Jewish practices extensively. Jewish customs and traditions were known to and practiced by many Arabs, and Muḥammad who knew many of these laws and customs incorporated a considerable number of them into his religious teachings.[20]

The Koran

Like the Torah in Judaism, the Koran[21] is considered the fountainhead of all knowledge dealing with human life. Furthermore, the arrangement of the Suras, the nomenclature for the new religion, and the pillars of Islām seem to have Jewish backgrounds. The term Koran is probably derived from the Hebrew and, like the Bible, it is

[18] "Whole tribes seem to have gone over to Judaism and accepted monotheism before the rise of Muhammad," Guillaume, *ibid.*, p. 154; cf. D. S. Margoliouth, *Mohammed and Mohammedanism*, London, 1889, p. 36; R. Dozy, *Die Israeliten zu Mekka*, Leipzig, 1864, pp. 15 f.

[19] Ṭabarī, *Annales*, 1885–93, Vol. I (ed. M. J. de Goeje), Leiden, pp. 901–3; D. S. Margoliouth, *The Relations between Arabs and Israelites prior to the Rise of Islam*, London, 1924, pp. 65 f.; Th. Nöldeke, "Die Geschichte der Juden in Arabien" in *Beiträge zur Kenntniss der Poesie der Alten Araber*, Hannover, 1864, pp. 192 f.; Ilse Lichtenstädter, "Some References to Jews in Pre-Islamic Arabic Literature," *PAAJR*, Vol. X (1940), pp. 187 f.; J. Horovitz, "Judaeo-Arabic Relations in Pre-Islamic Times," *Islamic Culture*, Vol. III (1929), pp. 161–99.

[20] J. Finkel, "A Risāla of al-Jāḥiẓ," *JAOS* (1927), pp. 326–28 and "Old Israelitish Tradition in the Koran," *PAAJR*, Vol. II (1931), pp. 7–21. Also, "Jewish, Christian and Samaritan Influences on Arabia" in *D. B. Macdonald Presentation Volume*, Princeton, 1933, pp. 147–66; C. C. Torrey, *op. cit.*, pp. 42–45; A. Sprenger, *Das Leben und die Lehre des Mohammed*, Berlin, 1869, Vol. I, pp. 54–57; Gustav Weil, *The Bible, the Koran and the Talmud*, New York, 1846, also *Biblische Legenden der Muselmänner*, Leipzig, 1886, and *Das Leben Mohammeds nach Mohammed ibn Ishāq . . .*, Stuttgart, 1864, Vol. I, p. 143.

[21] I. Goldziher, *Muhammedanische Studien*, Halle, 1899, Vol. II, pp. 40–45.

known as "The Book." The division of the Koran into 114 Suras follows similar divisions of the Hebrew Scriptures. The veneration of the Koran by the Moslems, as well as the practice of reading it at Friday Assemblies and other religious holidays, follows the Hebrew pattern.

Fundamental Tenets of Islām

Islām is built on Imān (religious belief) and Dīn (religion or practice). Imān involves six major principles, i. e. belief (a) in God, (b) in His angels, (c) in His "scriptures," (d) in the prophets, (e) in the Last Day and (f) in predetermination of good and evil. The religious duties of the Moslem center upon five canonical obligations: the *shahādah*, or the affirmation that there is no God but Allāh and that Muḥammad is His messenger; the observance of prayer; the payment of *zakāh* (legal alms); the pilgrimage to Mecca; and fasting in *Ramaḍān*.[22]

The canonical obligations or the pillars of Islām as well as a great number of names or narratives in the Koran have their biblical and Aggadic counterparts. Adam, Noah, Abraham are mentioned 70 times each; Ishmael, Lot, Joseph, Saul, David, Solomon, Elijah, Job and Jonah figure prominently.[23] Moses' name occurs in 34 Suras. The story of the Creation and the Fall of Adam is cited five times and the Flood and Sodom eight times.

The Unity of God

Like the Jew, the Moslem affirms the unity of God. God is one, eternal, merciful, compassionate, beneficent, almighty, all-knowing, just, loving and forgiving. Like Judaism, Islām does not recognize saints serving as mediators between the individual and his Creator. In both the Jewish and Moslem religions any learned man of good character may conduct the prayer service. Like the Jew, the Moslem believes in the immortality of the soul and in personal accountability for actions on earth and negates the doctrines of original sin and redemption. And like the Jew, the Moslem believes that each individual is to follow a righteous path and secure atonement by improving his conduct and by sincere repentance.

[22] Cf. Bu., Vol. I, p. 21.

[23] Philip K. Hitti, *History of the Arabs*, 3rd ed., London, 1946, p. 125.

Gabriel

According to Islām, Muḥammad is the Apostle of God to whom God revealed his will through the angel Gabriel. The latter is of the same stature in the Koran as the angel Michael in the Bible. Scholars have been puzzled by Muḥammad's selection of Gabriel and have indicated that in his break with the Jews he probably substituted Gabriel for Michael. They claim that in Islām Gabriel is considered an adversary of the Jews and a friend of the Moslems who brings them prosperity and good tidings. Jewish tradition, however, does not substantiate this view. On the contrary, in numerous instances Gabriel occupies a position almost similar to that of Michael.[24]

To the writer, it appears that the primary reason for designating Gabriel as the angel of Muḥammad's revelations is to be found in the role Gabriel played in the lives of the two outstanding personages in Judaism, Abraham and Moses. Gabriel is described in rabbinic literature as having been the guardian angel of Abraham and Moses, and he is generally more prominent than Michael in the careers of these great Jewish leaders. Hence, Muḥammad selected Gabriel as the angel of Revelation, because he believed him to be closely associated with Abraham, the "father of Islām,"[25] and with Moses, the exalted of all prophets.[26]

Prayer

Every Moslem is obligated to pray five times daily (at sunrise, mid-day, mid-afternoon, sunset and at night before retiring). "While Muhammad and his followers," writes Brockelmann, "prayed twice a day in Mecca, and according to Jewish example three times a day in Medina, subsequent ritual, under Persian influence, makes five prayer periods obligatory."[27] Goldziher in his article on *Islām* in the Jewish Encyclopedia, regards the five daily prayers as of Persian influence. On the other hand, we find the famous rabbinic scholar Simon Duran (1361–1444) of Algiers attributing the Moslem custom of five prayers to the Jewish practice on *Yom Kippur*, the Day of Atonement. Similarly, Professor Torrey states that in their anxiety to surpass the Jew in devotion, the followers of Muḥammad

[24] B. Sanh. 44b; cf. notes to 2:91.

[25] 2:125.

[26] 2:91.

[27] Brockelmann, *op. cit.*, p. 39.

adopted the *five* daily prayers, "and it is not clear that they were instituted by Mohammed. It is not like him to ordain a five-fold service even for *one* day in the week."[28]

However, in addition to the sunrise prayer, the mid-day prayer and the night prayer, which Torrey cites from the Koran, we also find references to the mid-afternoon prayer in 20:130 and to the sunset prayer in 11:116. Islāmic tradition also claims that it was the Prophet who told his followers that "Allah has made obligatory upon them the five prayers every day and night."[29]

It would appear, however, that in regard to worship, as in so many other Moslem practices, Islām has followed a Jewish pattern. The late Professor Louis Ginzberg, the eminent authority on Talmud, claimed that the Arabian Jews actually prayed five times daily; but this number was reduced to three, by combining two prayers in the morning and two in the evening, in order not to make the burden upon the congregation too onerous. The five daily prayers were undoubtedly ordained by Muḥammad as a result of this early Jewish practice of gathering five times daily for prayer.[30]

Among the Moslems, the hours of prayer are announced by a crier (*Mu'adhdhin*) from the tower of the mosque. Muḥammad was under the impression that the Jews used the blowing of the horn (*Shofar*) for summoning the Jewish people to worship. For the Moslems, however, he ordained that a man sound the call for prayers. This Moslem practice may be traced to an ancient custom followed in the Temple in Jerusalem. According to a talmudic passage an appointed crier used to announce: "Arise, ye priests to your service, ye Levites to your platforms, and ye Israelites to your stands."[31] The crier's voice was heard at a distance of three miles.

Muḥammad chose Friday to take the place of the Jewish Sabbath and the Christian Sunday. Now we know that the practice of the Jews in Arabia was to begin the observance of the Sabbath early on Friday. It is quite possible that Muḥammad took this pattern as a model for his day of rest, although the notion of a complete day of rest was alien to him. Though he considered the day of rest as a

[28] Torrey, *op. cit.*, p. 40.

[29] Bu., Vol. I, p. 354.

[30] Louis A. Ginzberg, *A Commentary on the Palestinian Talmud*, New York, 1941, Vol. I, p. 73.

[31] Hirschberg, *op. cit.* p. 197; cf. Georges Vajda, "Jeûnes Musulmans et jeûnes Juifs," *HUCA*, XII–XIII (1937–38), pp. 367–79 and "Juifs et Musulmans selon le Ḥadīt" in *Journal Asiatique*, Paris, 1937.

burden imposed upon the Jews and the Christians, nevertheless he followed the Jewish practice of making Friday a day of special congregational services, including a sermon.

Almsgiving

The giving of alms is another fundamental pillar of Islām. The Koran is studded with verses and aphorisms extolling the importance of and the reward for the giving of *ṣadaqah* (alms) to the poor, the widow, and the orphan. This doctrine is of Jewish origin.[32] The Bible and the Talmud regard the giving of charity (*Ẓedaḳah*) as an act of righteousness and not merely as an act of generosity or philanthropy. All wealth is the Creator's and man is merely the custodian who must share it with the less fortunate of God's children.

Ḥajj (Pilgrimage)

It is incumbent upon every Moslem to make a pilgrimage to Mecca at least once in a lifetime unless he is physically and financially unable to do so. The idea of the pilgrimage is well known in the Bible, which prescribes that the Israelites make a pilgrimage to Jerusalem three times a year. After the destruction of the First Temple in 586 B. C. E. when the Jews were no longer able to travel to Jerusalem, the synagogue was instituted, out of which the church and the mosque developed. Like the synagogue, the mosque is a house of worship without any images or figures. The purpose of prayer in the case of the Moslem is comparable to that in the case of the Jew, i. e. self-examination, training to be humble, exalting the Almighty, offering thanksgiving and receiving God's mercy and guidance.[33]

Ramaḍān

Muḥammad at first accepted the Day of Atonement as a day of fast. It was known as '*Ashūrā*' ("the fast of the tenth"), a synonym for the Jewish Day of Atonement, which falls, according to the Hebrew calendar, on the tenth of *Tishri*. Only later when he turned his back on Judaism did Muḥammad institute the fast of the month of *Ramaḍān* which occurs during the ninth month of the Moslem lunar

[32] Cf. notes to 2:1–2, 172; G. Weil, "Oral Tradition in Judaism and in Islam" (Hebrew), *Magnes Anniversary Book*, Jerusalem, 1938, pp. 132–48.

[33] 2:193.

year. However, '*Ashūrā*' has been retained as a voluntary fast and observed not on the original tenth of *Tishri* but rather on the tenth of the Moslem Muḥarram.

Ramaḍān has been held by scholars to be a Moslem counterpart of the Christian Lent, but it also resembles the Jewish observance of the month of '*Elul* as a period of *Teshubah* or penitence. To this day, pious Jews still keep the forty days from the beginning of '*Elul* until *Yom Kippur* as a season for fasting and prayer. The rabbinical explanation for this observance is that it commemorates the forty days which Moses spent on Mount Sinai before giving the Torah to Israel.[34]

Jihād

The duty of *Jihād*, the waging of a Holy War, has been raised to the dignity of a sixth canonical obligation, especially by the descendants of the Khārijites.

To the Moslem, the world is divided into regions under Islāmic control, the *dâr al-Islâm*, "and regions not subjected as yet, the *dâr al-ḥarb*. Between this 'area of warfare' and the Muslim-dominated part of the world there can be no peace. Practical considerations may induce the Muslim leaders to conclude an armistice, but the obligation to conquer and, if possible, convert never lapses. Nor can territory once under Muslim rule be lawfully yielded to the unbeliever. Legal theory has gone so far as to define as *dâr al-Islâm* any area where at least one Muslim custom is still observed."[35]

Thanks to this concept the Moslem is required to subdue the infidel, and he who dies in the path of Allāh is considered a martyr and assured of Paradise and of unique privileges there.[36]

Other Precepts discussed in the study

Muḥammad found guidance for his legislation in Hebraic tradition and in rabbinic lore. Cleanliness plays a tremendous role in Jewish life. Cleanliness is part of godliness, and the individual, made in the image of God, must always be pure in mind as well as in body. He must always be charitable, love mercy, be kind and walk humbly with his

[34] 2:179–181.

[35] Grunebaum, *op. cit.*, p. 9.

[36] 2:125, 187.

God and fellow men. Similar concepts are found in Islām. "The key to paradise is prayer and the key to prayer is purification."[37]

The Koran prescribes the need of at least two witnesses to a formal business transaction. However, in ordinary loans or transactions no evidence in writing is required; it is assumed as in Jewish law that no man will go back on his word. Regarding usury, the Moslem, following biblical law, is duty-bound not to engage in usury with a fellow believer. It is permissible, however, in dealing with infidels (non-Moslems).

Muḥammad regarded many of the precepts given to the Jews as a punishment from God and for that reason a Moslem is not obligated to observe them. Thus, the Koran disregards the Jewish concept of a day of rest, inheritance laws, and dietary laws, but prescribes the rite of circumcision and prohibits the use of blood and of the meat of a pig or of an animal that "dieth of itself" for culinary purposes.

The Koranic stories of the Creation, life in Paradise, the question as to whether earth or heavens came first, the objection of the angels to the creation of man, Adam's remarkable wisdom, Satan's rejection of Adam, Adam and Eve in the garden of Eden, Adam's universal lesson for repentance, stem from biblical and midrashic elements. The stories about Israel's covenant with God, the travails in Egypt, the miracles at the Red Sea, the making of the golden calf after Moses went up the mountain, the Israelites' request to see God manifestly in order to believe in Him, the restoration of the stricken dead to life, the pillar of cloud, the manna and the quails, Moses' smiting of the rock, the objection to the taste of the manna, the giving of the Torah by "raising the mountain," the breakers of the Sabbath, the red heifer — all these stories in the Koran are traceable to Jewish origins. Likewise, the concepts of ethical monotheism, the unity of God, prayer, consideration for the underprivileged, reverence for parents, fasting, penitence, the belief in angels, the stories about Abraham, the Patriarchs, Samuel, Saul, David, Solomon, the injunction of a pilgrimage to Mecca, waging war against the enemy, the status of women, and the position of prophets, all have their antecedents in Jewish tradition.

In tracing the rabbinic background of each Koranic verse and in relating it to the comments by authoritative Moslem exegetes, the author feels that he has succeeded in shedding new light upon the debt Islām owes to Judaism. Many biblical stories and sayings (especially

[37] Cf. 2:1–2, notes 45–64.

from the Pentateuch and the Psalms), intertwined with an inexhaustible amount of talmudic and midrashic tales, weave the structural core of the Koran and its exegeses.

Conclusion

Our findings negate the theories of many historians who claim that the Arabian Jews were uncultured and ignorant and were severed from traditional Judaism that had been flourishing in Palestine and in Babylonia. The abundance of Jewish thought and ideas contained in the Koran and in its early authoritative commentaries testify to the profound knowledge of Judaism possessed by Arabian Jews. They may even help us to restore some Aggadic concepts lost in the course of time and unknown to Jewish scholarship today, as well as to gain much-sought data about the life and practices of the Jews in Arabia. From the literature of the Moslem exegetes we may rightfully surmise that had Islām not appeared on the scene, Judaism would have extended its faith throughout all of Arabia or at least through an extensive part thereof. Many Arab communities accepted the Jewish faith and practices and even Muḥammad himself was almost Judaized.

The knowledge of the Jews and Judaism displayed in Islāmic literature reflects not only upon the excellent relationship between the Jews and the Arabs but also shows that Arabian Judaism was not different from that of other Jewish communities. The Arabian Jews abided by the laws and traditions that prevailed among Jews everywhere who, steadfast in their faith, resisted Muḥammad's attempt at Islāmizing them. The unusual number of Aggadic stories quoted in the writings of Zamakhsharī, Baiḍāwī, Bukhārī and Ṭabarī testify to the fact that the Arabian Jews took an active part in Jewish spiritual life, erected many synagogues, schools and other institutions, and succeeded in maintaining strong permanent ties with the Jews of Palestine and Babylonia. The Moslem commentators used in our study are thus excellent source material for reconstructing Jewish traditions hitherto unknown and forgotten.

SURA II

VERSES 1–2

> That is the book![1] there is no doubt therein; a guide to the pious, who believe in the unseen, and are steadfast in prayer, and of what we have given them expend in alms.

The word "Koran" is either a genuine Arabic term signifying "reading" or "reciting," or a word borrowed from the Hebrew or Aramaic, which was used by the rabbis to describe Scripture or Torah.[2]

The division of the Koran into 114 Suras (Chapters) follows the type of arrangement found in the Hebrew Scriptures. The veneration of the Book by the Moslems, as well as their practice of reading it on holy days and of reciting certain verses therein for prayers, also appears to emulate a Jewish pattern.[3]

Muḥammad considers the Koran the fountainhead of all knowledge

[1] Ali in *The Holy Qur-ān*, p. 12, translates *Dhālika 'l-Kitāb* as "This book," and claims that Palmer's rendition as "That is the book" is erroneous, for *Dhālika* does not refer here to a remote thing, but indicates "the high estimation in which the Qur-ān is held"; Pickthall, Rodwell, and Wherry also translate *Dhālika* as "this". Cf. Gen. 5:1, "This is the Book" (זה ספר).

[2] *Miḳra'* מקרא. This term was used by the Jews for the Scriptures, שנים מקרא ואחד תרגום. Th. Nöldeke claims that the word *Sura* is derived from the Hebrew *Shurah* (row), *Geschichte des Qorâns*, Göttingen, 1860, pp. 24–25; cf. his *Neue Beiträge zur semit. Sprachwissenschaft*, Strassburg, 1910, p. 26, as well as Nöldeke-Schwally, *op. cit.*, Vol. I, pp. 31 f. Just as Judaism claims that the Bible was written in the Holy Tongue (Hebrew), (שניתנה תורה בלה"ק (בראשית רבה פי"ח, ו so Muḥammad, too, claimed the Koran to be an "Arabic Koran" (20:112; 42:5; 43:2–3); cf. Jallālein 29:27; J. Horovitz, *Koranische Untersuchungen*, Berlin-Leipzig, 1926, p. 75; Baiḍāwī 3:98; Zamakhsharī 3:6. See also Arthur Jeffery, *The Qur'ān As Scripture*, New York, 1952, pp. 9 f. and notes 2:48–50; 3:2 on *furqān*.

[3] Hirschfeld conjectures that "the disfigurement of many Biblical names and words mentioned in the Qorân is due to misreadings in his (Muḥammad's) own notes made with unskilled hand . . . Sura, written in square characters (סורה) could easily be misread from *Sidra* (סדרה)." *New Researches* . . . p. 13 n.; cf. F. Buhl, "Sura," *EI*, Vol. 4, pp. 560 f. See also Bu., Vol. IV, p. 400.

dealing with human life, and refers to it as "the Book" (*al-Ḳitāb*).[4] Similarly the Bible[5] promises its followers: "When thou walkest, it shall lead thee, When thou liest down, it shall watch over thee; And when thou awakest, it shall talk with thee." Referring to this verse in Proverbs (6:22), the Talmud explains: "When thou walkest, it shall lead thee (in this world); when thou liest down, it shall watch over thee (in the grave); and when thou wakest, it shall talk[6] with thee (in the world to come)."[7]

The Koranic emphasis on the significance of prayer has its antecedent in Jewish tradition.[8] We find in the Talmud that the injunction, "And ye shall serve the Lord your God," refers to the reciting of the *Shema*' (Israel's confession of faith, recited twice daily, in the morning and the evening), and to *Tefillah* (Prayer, the Eighteen Benedictions, i. e. "the main constituents of the regular prayers which are recited three times daily"). Both the *Shema*' and the Moslem *Shahādah* express identical ideas.[9] As with the

[4] 2:171. Synonyms for the Koran are: *al-Furqān* (the "Distinguisher between right and wrong" or "Divine help"), 25:1; *al-Tadhkira* (the Reminder), 15:9; *al-Tanzīl* (Revelation), 26:192; *al-Hudā* (the Guidance), 72:13; *al-Raḥmah* (the Mercy), 17:84; *al-Khair* (the Goodness), 2:103; *al-Rūḥ* (the Spirit of Life), 42:52; *al-Bayān* (the Explanation), 3:133; *al-Ni'mah* (the Blessing), 93:11; *al-Burhān* (the Argument), 4:175; *al-Qayyim* (the Maintainer), 18:2; *al-Muhaimin* (the Guardian), 5:48; *al-Nūr* (the Light), 7:156; and *al-Ḥaqq* (the Truth), 17:83. In a similar vein, Judaism speaks of the Torah as "Tree of Life," "Maintainer," "Guide," "Light," "The Wisdom," "Truth," etc. Cf. M. M. Ali, *The Religion of Islām*, Lahore, 1926, pp. 17–57; אדר"נ, פרקים א–ח; Mishnah Ab. 5:19 הפך־בה והפך־בה דכלא בה; B. 'Erub. 54b; and במדבר רבה פי"ד, כב.

[5] Cf. B. Meg., 16a; B. Ta'an., 7a; *Num. Rab.*, 3.

[6] *I. e.* "intercede on thy behalf."

[7] Mishnah Ab. 6:9; cf. *Yalḳuṭ Shim'oni*, *Prov.*, Vol. II, § 938.

[8] B. Ber. 32a: "Prayer is more efficacious even than good deeds, for there was no one greater in good deeds than Moses our Master, and yet he was answered only after prayer." Cf. תשובה עושה מחצה ותפלה עושה הכל (ויקרא רבה פ"י, ה), and *Deut. Rab.* 8:1: "Great is the efficacy of prayer before the Almighty." Cf. 2:239, note 3.

[9] The Koranic لا اله الّا الله, "There is no God but Allah (the God)," stresses the idea of Monotheism as expressed in שמע ישראל ה' אלהינו ה' אחד, "Hear, O Israel: the Lord our God, the Lord is One" (Deut. 6:4). The utterance of these phrases, according to Islām and Judaism, is tantamount to a confession of faith; cf. Zeph. 3:9 and Zech. 14:9 as well as Rashi's commentary on Deut. 6:4 that "He who now is our God and is not yet recognized by the nations as their

Shema',[10] the Moslem in reciting the *Shahādah* accepts the yoke of the kingdom of Heaven, and in uttering the famous *lā ilāhā illā 'llāhu* (there is no God but Allah), he repeats the biblical phrases, "For who is God, save the Lord,"[11] and "There is no God but the Lord."[12]

It is incumbent upon every Moslem to pray five times daily (at sunrise, mid-day, mid-afternoon, sunset and before retiring).[13] Goldziher[14] regards the five daily prayers as of Persian influence.[15] Rabbi Simon Duran (1361–1444), who lived in Algiers, maintains that Muḥammad borrowed the custom from the Jewish Day of Atonement.[16] Professor Torrey claims that, in their anxiety to surpass the

God, will yet be the ONE God of the whole world"; see also 21:107: "Say, I am only inspired that your God is one God," قل انما يوحى إلىّ أنما إلهكم اله واحد. According to *Khaṭīb Mishkāt al-Maṣābīḥ*, Vol. I, p. 12, "Whoever dies while he knows that there is no God but Allah enters paradise", من مات وهو يعلم انه لا اله الا الله دخل الجنّة.

[10] B. Ber. 13b; cf. "Israel, a nation unique on the earth, declares daily the unity of His great Name, saying, 'Hear, O Israel: The Lord is our God, the Lord is One'" (Deut. 6:4), P.R.E., p. 26. See also 3:16; 13:29; 112:1.

[11] מי אלוה מבלעדי יהוה (שמואל ב׳, כ״ב, ל״ב); מי אל מבלעדי יהוה (תהלים, י״ח, ל״ב); אני אל ואין עוד (ישעיה מ״ה, כ״ג).

[12] לית אלהא אלא יי (אונקלוס תהלים יח, לב); cf. Deut. 4:35, אין עוד מלבדו; and Is. 6:3; Ps. 98:2; 138:4; Hos. 13:4. Cf. Torrey, *op. cit.*, p. 134; and Hirschfeld, *op. cit.*, 29–31. Regarding the incorporeality of God in the Koran and the Bible see H. A. Wolfson, *Philo*, Cambridge, 1947, Vol. 2, p. 152.

[13] *Fajr* (morning); *Ẓuhr* (early afternoon); *'Aṣr* (late afternoon); *Maghrib* (sunset); *'Ishā'* (night). Cf. E. Mittwoch, *Zur Entstehungsgeschichte des islamischen Gebets und Kultus*, Berlin, 1913, p. 9 and A. J. Wensinck, *Mohammed en de Joden te Medina*, Leiden, 1908, pp. 106 ff. See also notes on 2:239, 240 and 3:7.

[14] J. E., "Islam," Vol. 6, New York, p. 653; "Islamisme et Parsisme," *RHR*, xliii (1901), p. 15. Cf. Nöldeke-Schwally, *op. cit.*, p. 151; Anton Baumstark, "Jüdischer und Christlicher Gebetstypus im Koran" in *Der Islam*, Vol. 16, Berlin, 1927, pp. 229–48.

[15] According to Pollack, the institution of five daily prayers is regarded by Islām as an integral part of the Sunna. חוקרים חדשים מייחסים את הגדלת מספר התפילות משלש לחמש להשפעה פרסית שלאחר זמנו של מוחמד, ואילו האיסלם רואה את עיתות התפילה כחלק הסונה. (א. נ. פולק, דברי ימי הערבים, ירושלים, תש״ו, ע׳ קל״ב)

[16] S. Duran, *Qeshet u-Magen* in *Ozar Ṭob*, ed. by Steinschneider, Berlin, 1881, p. 14: ולפי שידע שהיותר נכבד שבימי ישראל לתפלה ולתשובה הוא יום הכפורים ויש בו חמש תפלות תקן להם חמש תפלות בכל יום. However, it is questionable whether the *Musaf* (additional service) following closely upon the *Shaharit* (morning service) should be considered as

Jews in devotion, the followers of Muḥammad adopted the five daily prayers after his death. "There is in the Koran no prescription of the *five* daily prayers, and it is not clear that they were instituted by Mohammed. It is not like him to ordain a five-fold service even for *one* day in the week. What he commands in the Koran is characteristic. It is simple, reasonable, and like other features of the new legislation in its adaptation of an already existing ritual to Arabian conditions. The traditional Jewish prescription was three daily prayers, as e. g. in Dan. 6:11. In four passages (11:116, 17:80 f., 50:38 f., 76:25 f.), all from the Mekka period, the prophet directs his followers to pray three times in the day: in the morning, at eventide, and *in the night* — a time better suited to the Bedouin travelling under the stars than to the city-dweller."[17]

In addition to the four passages quoted by Torrey, we find several other passages in the Koran which give indications of the practice of five daily prayers. Thus, in 20:130 we read: "Bear patiently then what they say, and celebrate the praises[18] of thy Lord before the rising of the sun, and before its setting, and at times in the night celebrate them; and at the ends of the day; haply thou mayest please (Him)." Here Muḥammad directs his followers to pray at sunrise, sunset and "at the ends of the day," i. e., before retiring.[19] In 11:116 Muḥammad also directs his followers, "And be thou steadfast in prayer at the two ends of the day, and the (former and latter) parts of the night." Pickthall[20] renders the last phrase "and in some watches of the night," whereas Ali[21] translates it "in the first hours of the night." This would add, immediately after sunset, another prayer to the three prayers mentioned in 17:80, i. e., "from the declining of the sun until the dusk of the night, and the reading of the dawn." In 24:57 the Koran also talks about "the prayer of dawn, and when ye put off your

a separate service rather than as an extension of the *Shaḥarit*. Compare, however, Maimonides, *Hilkot Tefillah*, Ch. I., Halakah V, VI and B. Ber. 26 b. Rabbi Duran (*ibid.*, p. 14) also maintains that *Ramaḍān* is of Jewish influence: ולפי שהוא (יוה"כ) צום ותשובה תקן להם שלשים צומות (יום). See also Mittwoch, *op. cit.*, pp. 36 ff.

[17] Torrey, *op. cit.*, pp. 135–36.

[18] "Celebrate the praises" here refers to prayer, as shown by the context in 20:132: "Bid thy people prayer, and persevere in it." Cf. Ps. 68:20; ברוך אדני יום יום; Ps. 78:4: מספרים תהלות יהוה; Ps. 96:3: ספרו בגוים כבודו; Ps. 105:2: שיחו בכל נפלאתיו.

[19] Here the two evening prayers are spoken of together, while the sunrise prayer and mid-afternoon prayer are indicated.

[20] Marmaduke Pickthall, *op. cit.*, p. 234.

[21] *The Holy Qur-ān*, p. 474; cf. Ali, *The Religion of Islām*, pp. 406 f.

clothes at noon, and after the evening prayer." Thus, the sunrise prayer, the mid-day prayer and the prayer before retiring are referred to in 17:80, the mid-afternoon prayer in 20:30 and the sunset prayer in 11:116. According to Islāmic tradition,[22] it was the Prophet who told his followers: "Allah has made incumbent upon them the five prayers in every day and night."[23]

The rules and regulations concerning prayer in general in Islām would indicate that the five daily prayers originated with Jewish practices. Thus, a Moslem, like a Jew, is encouraged to pray often and as frequently as possible.[24] Prayers may be combined or curtailed when one is on a journey or in time of danger. If one unwittingly omits a prayer he may recite it when he becomes aware of the omission.[25] Prayers, too, must not be said in a loud voice nor in a whisper.[26] Nor may a drunken man pray.[27] Similarly, the rules with regard to prayers pertaining to the congregation, such as reading from the Book, special prayers for the community, petitions for rain, etc., are all traceable to Jewish practices.[28] Some authorities even claim that

[22] Bu., Vol. I, p. 354:
...فاعلمهم ان الله قد افترض عليهم خمس صلوات في كل يوم وليلة

[23] Cf. discussion on the five prayers by Baiḍāwī and Zamakhsharī *ad. loc.* According to Zamakhsharī and Baiḍāwī, صلوة الغدوة refers to the sunrise prayer, whereas صلوة العشى refers to the prayers of mid-day, mid-afternoon, sunset and before retiring. See also Ibn Hishām, *Life of Muhammad* (Arabic), Būlāq, 1877, Vol. I, p. 204: "It was Muḥammad who decreed the institution of five daily prayers."

[24] המרבה בתפלה נענה (תלמוד ירושלמי, ברכות פ"ד, ה"א); Bu., Vol. I, p. 181. "Frequent prayers are best for people to do." Cf. Bu., Vol. I, p. 144: "He who utters prayers, converses intimately with God" ان احدكم اذا صلّى يناجى ربّه; *Yalkuṭ Shim'oni,* Vol. II, § 847.

[25] 4:10; Bu., Vol. I, p. 157: .من نسى صلوة فليصلّ اذا ذكر

[26] 17:111, "And do not say the prayers openly, nor yet murmur them, but seek a way between these." Compare: "*But her voice could not be heard* (I Sam. 1:13): from this (we learn), it is forbidden to raise one's voice in the *Tefillah,*" B. Ber. 31b; cf. 23:3, "who in their prayers are humble," and Ecc. 5:1, "Be not rash with thy mouth, and let not thy heart be hasty to utter a word before God; for God is in heaven, and thou upon earth; therefore let thy words be few."

[27] 4:46. Compare B. Ber. 31 b, ". . . a drunken person is forbidden to say the *Tefillah.*"

[28] Hirschberg, *op. cit.*, pp. 196–7: גם בסידור התפילה ובתוכנה וכן בדיני תפילת יום הכניסה, אפשר להכיר את השפעת התפילות שהיו נהוגות אצל היהודים (קריאה בתורה ובנביא,

at the early stages of Islām, Moslems used to put on a *Ṭallit* (prayer shawl) at services in the mosque.[29] It seems logical that, since most of the rituals were derived in the main from Jewish usage, the five daily prayers should have originated from the same source.

That the Jews in Arabia prayed five times daily is substantiated by recent talmudic studies. In the Book of Daniel it is related that Daniel's windows were "open in his chamber in Jerusalem, (and) he kneeled upon his knees three times a day and prayed and gave thanks before his God as he did aforetime" (Dan. 6:11).[30] From this we may infer that the custom of three daily services included the morning (*Shaḥarit*), afternoon (*Minḥah*), and evening prayers (*Ma'arib*).[31] According to the Talmud, the Great Assembly[32] established the institution of daily prayers. Important portions of the morning

תפילה לשלום הצבור, תפילות לתענית גשמים וכול'). Cf. notes to 2:239. Muḥammad praising his followers for "reciting God's signs in the night-time" (3:109) recalls a Jewish practice (B. Ber. 3b; Mishnah Ber. 4:4; B. Sanh. 42b; also 3:188). Even the calling to prayer by a special person may be traceable to an old Jewish custom by which one man would assemble the entire congregation: עמדו כהנים לעבודתכם ולוים לדוכנכם וישראל למעמדכם! והיה קולו נשמע בשלש פרסאות (יומא כ, ע"ב) Hirschberg, *ibid.*, p. 197; see Ibn Hishām, Vol. II, p. 101, quoted in I. Ben-Zeeb, *op. cit.*, p. 29; Mishnah Yom. 1:8. The saying of *'Āmīn* at the close of a congregational prayer in the mosque also follows the Hebrew usage, *'Amen*. Similarly, امن has the same connotation as אמן. David Yellin, *Ḥiḳre Miḳra'*, Jerusalem, 1937, p. 33; and Is. 7:9; Ps. 44:14; 2:196. In Islām as in Judaism any learned man of good character may lead in the prayer service. Bu., Vol. I, p. 181:

كان يؤمهم سالم سولى ابن حذيفة وكان اكثرهم قرانا.

[29] Hirschberg, *ibid.*, p. 197: מסופר כי פעם התעטפו גם המוסלמים בטלית ביום הכניסה בהיותם במסגד, ואז נראו כיהודי ח'יבר. Cf. A. J. Wensinck, "Die Entstehung der Muslimischen Reinheitsgesetzgebung," in *Der Islam*, V (1914), pp. 62 ff.

[30] וכוין פתיחן לה בעליתה נגד ירושלם וזמנין תלתה ביומא הוא ברך על ברכוהי ומצלא ומודא קדם אלהה כל קבל די הוא עבד מן קדמת דנה (דניאל ו, יא).

[31] *Shaḥarit* — from sunrise to a third of the day; *Minḥah* — from high noon to sunset; and *Ma'arib* — the entire night. Cf. Ps. 55:18; Talmud Yer. Ber. 4, 1; *Numbers Rab.* 2,1.

[32] During the Second Commonwealth. Cf. Solomon Zeitlin, "An Historical Study of the First Canonization of the Hebrew Liturgy," *JQR*, *N.S.*, Vol. XXXVI (1946), 211–29 and Vol. XXXVIII (1948), 289–316; I. Elbogen, *Der jüdische Gottesdienst in seiner geschichtlichen Entwicklung*, Leipzig, 1913; L. J. Liebreich, "The Intermediate Benedictions of the Amida," *JQR*, *N.S.*, XLII (1952), # 4, 423–26; L. Zunz, *Die Gottesdienstlichen Vorträge der Juden*, 2nd ed., Frankfurt a. M., 1892; B. Ber. 33a; B. Meg. 17b.

prayer were recited in the Temple,[33] which would indicate that regular daily services were in existence during the greater part of the Second Commonwealth. From the time of the destruction of the Temple, the public recitation of the *Shemone 'Esre* (Eighteen Benedictions) or, as they are also known, the *'Amidah* became an important part of the three daily services, though the recitation of some of the benedictions must have been in vogue much earlier. It was Rabbi Gamaliel (c. 90 C. E.), of the Academy of Jabneh, who enacted that each worshipper should recite the *Shemone 'Esre* individually. In order not to deviate from the original public recitation, he ruled that the Reader should also repeat it in public. In the prayer book (*Siddur*), the *Shema'* and the *'Amidah* constitute the most important parts of the service, while the other parts are mainly supplementary. The *Shema'* is composed of verses from the following passages of the Pentateuch: Deuteronomy 6:4–9, dealing with the unity and love of God and observance of the precepts; Deuteronomy 11:13–21, emphasizing reward for the fulfillment of the laws and punishment for their transgression and the duty of the teaching of the Torah to the children; Numbers 15:37–41, embracing the law concerning the observance of the *ẓiẓit* (fringes on the garment) and an exhortation to submit to the laws of God in remembrance of the Exodus. The *Shemone 'Esre* is divided into three parts. The first three prayers contain praises of the Lord; the twelve middle ones, petitions; and the last three, thanks to the Lord. In the morning prayer as well as in the evening prayer there is also, between the *Shema'* and the *Shemone 'Esre*, a benediction for the deliverance from Egypt, which is called the *Ge'ullah*.

In the Talmud, we find a difference of opinion between Rabbi Joḥanan and Rabbi Joshua b. Levi as to whether the *Ge'ullah* should be attached to the *Shemone 'Esre* at the evening prayer or not. Rabbi Joḥanan holds that it should be attached to the *Shemone 'Esre*,[34] while Rabbi Joshua b. Levi maintains that it should not.[35] Unless the *Ge'ullah* is attached to the *'Amidah*, there are two separate prayers, that of the *Shema'* and that of the *Shemone 'Esre*. Otherwise there is only one. The majority opinion agrees with Rabbi Joḥanan and holds that the *Ge'ullah* should be attached to the *'Amidah* in the evening

[33] אמר להם הממונה ברכו ברכה אחת והם ברכו, קראו עשרת הדברות שמע והיה אם שמוע ויאמר ברכו את העם שלש ברכות אמת ויציב ועבודה וברכת כהנים ובשבת מוסיפין ברכה אחת למשמר היוצא (משנה תמיד ה, א).

[34] דא"ר יוחנן איזהו בן העולם הבא זה הסומך גאולה לתפלה של ערבית, רבי יהושע בן לוי אומר תפלות באמצע תקנום (ברכות ד, ע"ב).

[35] *Ibid.*, cf. משנה תמיד, ה, א; משנה תענית, ד, ג.

prayer. As for the *Shaḥarit* (morning prayer), all scholars agree that in it the *Ge'ullah is* attached to the *Shemone 'Esre*. Therefore, according to the Babylonian Talmud, we have only three daily prayers. However, Prof. Louis Ginzberg, in his monumental study on the Talmud Yerushalmi,[36] shows that the institution of Jewish prayer originally called for *five* daily prayers instead of the known three. Ginzberg maintains that *all* scholars in the Talmud Yerushalmi are of the opinion that the Jews in the talmudic period did not attach the prayer of Redemption to the *Shemone 'Esre* in the evening prayer.[37] Thus the *Shema'* and the *Shemone 'Esre* were *two* separate prayers.

In early times, the custom was to recite the *Shema'* at home before retiring and immediately upon arising. Before the institution of prayer, the people recited the *Shema'* in the morning at dawn and *before* the rising of the sun, i. e., between rising and the hours of work. This practice was based on the biblical verse, "and when thou liest down and when thou risest up."[38] Later on, when prayer became an institution, the morning prayer was held in the synagogue after the rising of the sun. The *Shema'*, too, was recited in the synagogue at the usual time. The hardship of congregating twice, once for the *Shema'* and once for the "prayer" (*Shemone 'Esre*), was eased by reciting the *Shema'* closer to sunrise, immediately before the "prayer" (*Shemone 'Esre*). Though there were still many who continued to recite the *Shema'* at home and joined the congregation for prayer later on, the general practice was to combine the two. This finally led to the assumption that it was obligatory to attach the prayer of *Redemption* to the *Shemone 'Esre*.

Thus, we learn that the Jews in Arabia during the talmudic period really met *five* times daily for prayer in the synagogue; twice for the recitation of the *Shema'*,[39] and three times for the three regular "prayers."[40] For practical reasons, the two prayers in the morning[41] were combined into one, as were the two prayers in the evening.[42]

[36] Louis Ginzberg, *op. cit.*, Introduction and Vol. I, pp. 68–75.

[37] *Ibid.*, Vol. I, 68. [38] Deut. 6:7; 11:9.

[39] Ginzberg, *op. cit.*, Vol. I, 64: שהרי לדעת הירושלמי ק"ש מן התורה.

[40] *Shemone 'Esre*; cf. 26:79–84 which recall some of the prayers in the Eighteen Benedictions.

[41] *I. e.* the *Shema'* and *Shemone 'Esre*. Moslem tradition, too, provides that when the days are short, the *Ẓuhr* and the *'Aṣr* prayers may be combined. Similarly when the nights are too short the *Maghrib* and the *'Ishā* may be combined. See Bu., Vol. I, pp. 141–60.

[42] Ginzberg, *op. cit.*, p. 63: ואולם רוב הצבור לא יכלו לדקדק כל כך וביחוד הפועלים

The five daily prayers may thus have been directed by Muḥammad as a result of the early Jewish practice of meeting five[43] times daily for prayer.[44]

One of the cardinal principles of Islām is that of giving alms.[45] The tradition is "Faith in Allah, and then the hope that 'prayer' would carry the true believer half-way to God, that 'fasting' would bring him to the door of His palace, and that 'alms' would gain him admittance."[46] Throughout the Koran one finds numerous utterances which emphasize the importance of charity,[47] feeding the poor,[48] emancipating slaves,[49] taking care of widows and orphans,[50] doing good to humanity in general,[51] as well as engaging in other benevolent enterprises.[52]

שהתחילו בעבודתם בהנץ ולכן הקדימו לקרא ק"ש בבה"כ זמן מה קודם הנץ החמה וכמו שאמרה המשנה א', ב, שמותר לקרא ק"ש משיכיר בין תכלת ללבן ואף שבמקום אחר במשנה עצמה הנץ החמה הוא זמנה של ק"ש; עיין פרק ג' ה', ובבלי כ"ה, ב'. וכבשחרית הקדימו גם בערבית וקראו ק"ש קודם צאת הכוכבים, שהיה קשה להם לבטל ממלאכתם וללך לבה"כ פעמים לתפלת מנחה ולתפלת מעריב ולכן התפללו שתי תפלות אלה זו אחר זו סמוך לשקיעה כלומר מנחה לפניה וערבית מיד לאחריה. . . . . . שהיו מקדימין להתפלל ערבית ולקרא ק"ש קודם זמנה.

[43] *Ibid.*, p. 74: ואם נניח שעוד בימי האמוראים לא סמכו גאולה לתפלה נמצא תשובה על דבר שנתקשו בו רבים והיא תקנת ה' תפילות שהתקין מחמוד מייסד דת האיסלמי, שכפי הנראה תקנתו זו יסודה במנהג יהודי ערב אלא שקשה והלא אין לנו אלא ג' תפילות. ואולם לפי דברינו הכל עולה יפה שיהודי ערב לא היו סומכין גאולה לתפילה וא"כ ה' תפלות (לא תפלה במובנה הטכני, י"ח ברכות אלא במובנה הכללי, ברכות בקשות ותחנונים) היו להן, פריסת על שמע בשחרית ובערבית וג' תפלות של י"ח ברכות.

[44] *Ibid.*, p. 75. See, however, Naphtali Wieder, *Islamic Influences on the Jewish Worship*, Oxford, 1947, p. 16; cf. Ibn Hishām, *op. cit.*, p. 72.

[45] 3:86: "Ye cannot attain to righteousness until ye expend in alms of what ye love. But what ye expend in alms, that God knows." Cf. Bu., Vol. I, p. 365: "Ṣadaqah is every Moslem's obligation" على كل مسلم صدقة.

[46] J. J. Pool, *Studies in Mohammedanism*, Westminster, 1892, p. 7 (quoting the historian Gibbon).

[47] 2:172, 255, 265, 266; 3:86; 5:12; 24:22; 91:15. Cf. note 55.

[48] 69:34; 76:8; 90:15; 93:9; Bu., Vol. IV, p. 114: "He who is not merciful receives no mercy" مَن لا يَرْحَمْ لا يُرحَم.

[49] Bu., Vol. I, p. 15. Cf. פדיון שבויים.

[50] 17:36; 76:8; 89:17; 90:15; 93:8; 107:2. "One who takes care of the widow and the poor is like the one who fights for the cause of God" (Bu., Vol. I, p. 485). الساعى على الارملة والمسكين كالمجاهد في سبيل الله

[51] 90:14; 107:6; cf.: Bu., Vol. I, p. 11.

[52] 2:272, 275, 278; 3:86, 110; 4:9; 57:10–14; 58:14. Cf. Bu., Vol. IV, pp. 117, 128.

The Koranic *zakāh* or *ṣadaqah* (righteousness)[53] signifies the supreme virtue obtainable by human beings. Through *ṣadaqah* "man becomes God-like and God's creditor."[54] All this is modelled after Jewish tradition.[55]

Giving alms was prevalent among the Hebrews long before the Mosaic laws of charity were promulgated. Jacob, following his famous dream, vowed to give one-tenth of all his possessions to God: "I will surely give the tenth unto thee" (Gen. 28:22). Moses later incorporated this principle into the biblical laws of charity (Deut. 14:22). The one-tenth of all the produce was to be given to the members of the tribe of Levi, who did not share in the tribal land division. Similar provisions were made for the poor, the needy, the landless and the foreigner (Lev. 19:9–10). According to Simeon the Just, "The world is based upon three things: the Torah, divine service, and the practice of kindliness."[56] The rabbis stipulate that "an individual's obligation to support charity was in direct proportion to his wealth; that every poor person must be supported; that even if he declined aid, he must be assisted through the subterfuge of a loan or a gift."[57] Rabbi Judah said: "Great is charity, in that it brings the redemption nearer."[58] "Give unto him of that which is his."[59] "He who is merciful to others, mercy is shown to him by Heaven."[60]

[53] Cf. צדקה; זכות (זכאה). See also Franz Rosenthal, "Sedaka, Charity" in *HUCA*, (1950–51) Vol. XXIII, Part I, pp. 411–30.

[54] 2:246; Torrey, *op. cit.*, p. 141, claims that the terminology and practice are of Jewish origin. Compare, however, K. Ahrens, *Muhammad als Religionsstifter*, Leipzig, 1935, p. 119, where he tries to show that though the terms are of Jewish origin, the practice is taken from Christianity. See also J. Horovitz, *HUCA*, pp. 206–8; Nöldeke-Schwally, *Geschichte des Qorâns*, Vol. II, p. 205, and notes to 2:172, 211, 246, 271, 272, 273, 280; 3:128, 136.

[55] B. B. B. 9b; B. Ket. 67b; B. Giṭ. 7b; B. Suk. 49b; cf. A. J. Wensinck, *Mohammed . . .*, p. 114.

[56] Mishnah Ab., 1:2. Cf. [B] אברהם הפריש תרומה גדולה (תנחומא, ראה, יב).

[57] A. A. Neuman, *The Jews in Spain*, Philadelphia, 1942, Vol. 2, p. 171; cf. כל המעלים עיניו מן הצדקה כאלו עובד עבודת אלילים (כתובות, סח, ע"א).

[58] B. B. B. 10a; cf. B. Giṭ. 7a: כל הגוזז מנכסיו ועושה מהן צדקה ניצל מדינה של גיהנם אפי' עני המתפרנס מן הצדקה יעשה צדקה (גיטין ז, ע"ב); שקולה צדקה כנגד כל המצות (ב"ב, ט, ע"א) and compare with Bu., Vol. I, p. 365, that even the poor are not excused from charity.

[59] Mishnah Ab. 3:8.

[60] B. Shab. 151b; cf. B. Suk. 49b: גדול העושה צדקה יותר מכל הקרבנות שנאמר עשה צדקה ומשפט נבחר לה' מזבח.

The attitude of Judaism towards charity is mirrored in all Koranic utterances and in the *ḥadīth*.[61] Technically, *zakāh* is a fixed portion of one's wealth which a Moslem is obliged to contribute annually for the benefit of the poor, and the giving of *ṣadaqah* in secret is praised.[62] According to Islām, the practical realization of the belief in the Unity of God, in Divine revelation and in the Hereafter, is through prayer and the service of humanity through charity. "But if they repent and are steadfast in prayer and give alms, then they are your brethren in religion."[63] This concept echoes the prayer of the Jew in the synagogue on the Holy Days: "Repentance, prayer and charity (righteousness) avert the (Divine) harsh decree."[64] e.g. avert a strenuous passage into the forthcoming Kingdom of God.

With repentance, prayer, & charity one remains like a child .... always ready for the Kingdom of God.

[61] The Koran prescribes: "and know that whenever ye seize anything as a spoil, to God belongs a fifth thereof, and to His Apostle, and to kindred and orphans, and the poor and the wayfarer" (8:42). The limit of one-fifth recalls B. Ket. 50a, that a man should not spend more than a fifth for charity. Torrey, *op. cit.*, p. 143; also Talmud Yer. Peah 1, 1.

[62] 2:275; Bu., Vol. I, p. 360: رجل تصدّق بصدقة فاخفاها حتى لا تعلم شماله ما تنفق يمينه; cf. B. B. B. 9b מתן בסתר.

[63] 9:11; cf. Bu., Vol. I, p. 354: "Allah has decreed . . . to bear witness that there is no God but Allah . . . prayers . . . and charity."

ان النبي .... بعث معاذا الى اليمن فقال ادعهم الى شهادة ان لا اله الا الله وانى رسول الله فان هم اطاعوا لذلك فاعلمهم ان الله قد افترض عليهم خمس صلوات ... فان هم اطاعوا لذلك فاعلمهم ان الله افترض عليهم صدقة...

[64] ג' דברים מבטלין את הגזירה קשה ואלו הן תפלה צדקה ותשובה ושלשתן בפסוק אחד (תלמוד ירושלמי, תענית, פ"ב, ה"א). Cf. *Rosh Hashanah* and *Yom Kippur* prayer books, . . . תשובה צדקה ותפלה; compare Tobit 12:8; Matt. 6:1–8.

VERSE 5

Verily, those who misbelieve, it is the same to them if ye warn them or if ye warn them not, they will not believe.

Baiḍāwī, referring to a similar verse in Sura 3:84,[1] comments that he who turns aside from the truth after it has been made clear to him is sunk in error and far from guidance.[2] A counterpart is found in the talmudic statement: "The wicked do not repent even at the gate of Gehenna."[3] Muḥammad's warning that those who pay no heed at all to him cannot benefit by his preaching, recalls the talmudic statement that the wicked man is as little able to learn from the righteous as the righteous man is able to emulate the behavior of the wicked: Rabbi Eleazar said, "A wicked man lived between two righteous men and did not learn from their ways."[4]

A similar thought is expressed in Jer. 13:23: "Can the Ethiopian change his skin, or the leopard his spots? Then may ye also do good, that are accustomed to do evil."

In compartmentalized Landscape Humanity Evil is as indigenous as Good is.
The Good wait for Judgement Day.
The Evil are praecox (precocious).
Historē is the passage of Man from the Good + Evil of First Judgement to Messiah and Dementia Praecox of Last Judgement.
With Israel consciousness has continuity: Torah, Talmud, and One Knows Everything.

[1] "Verily, those who misbelieve after believing, and then increase in misbelief, their repentance shall not be accepted; these are those who err," 3:84.

[2] Baiḍāwī, Vol. I, p. 80.

[3] B. 'Erub. 19 a.

[4] B. Yom. 38 b.

VERSE 6

> God has set a seal upon their hearts and on their hearing; and on their eyes is dimness, and for them is grievous woe.[1]

Zamakhsharī maintains that this sentence should not be taken literally but only to indicate that after man has wilfully turned away from the truth, his capacities for comprehension become dulled as if a partition existed between the man and the things to be comprehended by him. Zamakhsharī also states that this sentence does not contradict the idea of free will.[2] It is interesting to note that the very same problem posed by Zamakhsharī with regard to free will was also raised by Sa'adia Gaon (882–942 C. E.) in connection with the sentence in Isaiah 6:10.[3] Sa'adia, too, endeavors to harmonize the sentence in Isaiah with the principle of free will.[4] Likewise, Yellin[5] calls attention to the similarity of the roots used in the Bible[6] and in the Koran,[7] and claims that the Koranic verse is almost an exact translation of Isaiah 6:10.[8]

[1] Cf. Isaiah 6:10.

[2] Zamakhsharī, Vol. I, p. 27:

فان قلت ما معنى الختم على القلوب والاسماع وتغشية الابصار —
قلت لا ختم ولا تغشية ثَمه على الحقيقة وانما هو من باب المجاز
....تجعل قلوبهم لان الحق لا ينفذ فيها ولا يخلص الى ضمائرها
من قبل اعراضهم عنه واستكبارهم عن قبوله واعتقاده واسماعهم
لانها تمجّه وتنبو عن الاصغاء اليه وتعاف استماعه كانها مستوثق
منها بالختم وابصارهم لانها لا تجتلى ايات الله المعروضة ... كانها
غطى عليها وحجبت وحيل بينها وبين الادراك....
فان قلت فلم اسند الختم الى الله تعالى واسناده اليه يدلّ على
المنع من قبول الحق والتوصل اليه بطرقه وهو قبيح والله يتعالى عن
فعل القبيح علوّا كبيرا لعلمه بقبحه وعلمه بغناه عنه وقد نص على
تنزيه ذاته بقوله وما انا بظلام للعبيد .... وما ظلمناهم ولكن كانوا
هم الظالمين .... ونظائر ذلك مما نطق به التنزيل.

[3] השמן לב העם הזה ואזניו הכבד ועיניו השע (ישעיה, ו, י).

[4] *Kitāb al-Amânât wa'l-'itiqâdât*, ed. S. Landauer, Leiden, 1880, ch. 4, p. 160. Cf. *Beliefs and Opinions*, ed. S. Rosenblatt, New Haven, 1948, pp. 198 f.

[5] David Yellin, *op. cit.*, pp. 7, 32.

[6] השע.

[7] غشاوة is from the root غشا = עשה.

[8] "Make the heart of this people fat, And make their ears heavy, And shut their eyes."

VERSE 12

> And when it is said to them, 'Believe as other men believe,' they say, 'Shall we believe as fools believe?' Are not they themselves the fools? and yet they do not know.

The theory that he who disbelieves or transgresses is foolish is discussed extensively in Jewish tradition. "Resh Laḳish said: A person does not commit a transgression unless the spirit of folly (*sheṭut*) enters into him."[1] This deduction the Talmud makes from the Scripture: ". . . if any man's wife go aside" (Num. 5:12).[2] We also find in the Talmud that "sin dulls the heart of man."[3] In a similar vein Jeremiah (5:21) exclaims: "Hear now this, O foolish people, and without understanding, That have eyes, and see not, that have ears, and hear not."[4]

[1] B. Soṭ. 3 a.

[2] The Hebrew word *tisṭeh* is rendered "to act in folly." Hence the rabbinical saying: "No one sinneth unless the spirit of folly has entered into him." P.H., p. 589n.

[3] B. Yom. 39a. Cf. Lev. 11:43.

[4] Cf. Is. 3:11: אוי לרשע רע כי גמול ידיו יעשה לו.

VERSE 20

> Who made the earth for you a bed and the heaven a dome; and sent down from heaven water, and brought forth therewith fruits as a sustenance for you; so make no peers for God, the while ye know!

The concept of rain as a heavenly gift rewarding good deeds occupies a prominent place in rabbinic tradition.[1] Thus: "The clouds draw water from the depth, as it is said, 'He causeth the vapours to ascend from the ends of the earth' (Ps. 135:7), and in every place where the King commands them, there they cause rain (to fall), and forthwith the earth becomes fruitful and yields produce . . . But when the Holy One, blessed be He, desires to bless the produce of the earth and to give provision to the creatures, He opens the good treasuries in heaven and sends rain upon the earth, namely, the fructifying rain . . ."[2]

The phrase here, "make no peers for God," and the one in Sura 51:51, *ilāh ākhar*,[3] recall the Hebrew phrase *'Elohim 'aḥerim*[4] used in the Second Commandment (Exod. 20:3; Deut. 5:7).

The unity of God, which is a fundamental doctrine of Islām[5] as

[1] Cf. the phrase in the Eighteen Benedictions, מוריד הגשם. The Bible warns the people to "hearken diligently unto the voice of the Lord thy God" and the reward will be that "the Lord will open unto thee His good treasure the heaven to give the rain of thy land in its season, and to bless all the work of thy hand . . ." (Deut. 28:12); the fact that God alone, and not the idols, is capable of giving rain is clearly stated in Jer. 14:22: היש בהבלי הגוים מגשמים ואם השמים יתנו רבבים הלא אתה הוא יהוה אלהינו ונקוה לך כי אתה עשית את כל אלה. The *Targum* refers הבלי הגוים to idols: הא לית צרוך בטעות פלחי כוכביא לאחתא מטרא ואם שמיא לא יתנון רסיסין אלהין על מימרך הלא את הוא יי אלהנא ונסבר קדמך ארי את עבדת ית כל אלין (ירמיהו יד, כב). It would seem that the Koranic term for idolatry طاغوت (2:257) is a derivative of the Aramaic טעות used in the Targum and תלמוד ירושלמי ברכות, פ"ט, ה"א. See, however, Geiger, *op. cit.*, p. 55, who claims that this word for idolatry is not found in rabbinic literature.

The Talmud states that three keys has God "retained in His own hands and not entrusted to the hand of any messenger, namely, the Key of Rain, the Key of Childbirth, and the Key of the Revival of the Dead" (B. Ta'an. 2a). An identical view that God alone sends down water from heaven is expressed here by Muḥammad. See also [B] תנחומא, בחקתי, ג, and W. R. Taylor, "Al-Bukhārī and the Aggada," *The Moslem World*, XXXIII (1943), # 3, p. 196.

[2] P.R.E., p. 30. Cf. Jer. 5:24 הנתן גשם ויורה ומלקוש בעתו.

[3] اله آخر.

[4] אלהים אחרים.

[5] Cf. notes to 2:1–2, 256 and R. A. Nicholson, *op. cit.*, p. 225.

well as of Judaism, is expressed by Muḥammad as *Allāh 'aḥad* (God is One) (112:1).[6] The latter seems to be a replica of the Hebrew phrase *'Adonai 'Eḥad* (the Lord is One), which is from the *Shema'*.[7] The Koranic unity of God negates the idea of a plurality of gods and condemns the worship of the sun, the moon, and the stars. "And of His signs are the night and the day, and the sun and the moon. Adore ye not the sun, neither the moon; but adore God who created you, if it be Him ye serve" (41:37). The same admonition is found in Deut. (17:3): ". . . and hath gone and served other gods, and worshipped them, or the sun, or the moon, or any of the host of heaven, which I have commanded not."

Muḥammad frequently refers to God as *rabb* (Lord) (2:4; 2:19; 96:1) or, as in Al-Fātiḥah, *rabb al-'ālamīn* (the Lord of the world); *Raḥīm* Merciful); *Mālik* (Master or King) and *Raḥmān* (Beneficent) (1:2, 78:3). Exact counterparts for the Divine being are used in the Bible and in the Talmud: *ribbōn ha-'Olāmīn*; *ha-Raḥman*; *Melek*.[8] The same applies to the other names for the Deity mentioned in the Koran, which have their Hebrew equivalents, such as *'Aḥad* (One); *Quddūs* (Holy); *Bārī'* (Creator); *Salām* (Author of Peace); *'Aliyy* (Exalted); *Kabīr* (Great); *Ḥamīd* (Praiseworthy); *Ḥakīm* (Wise); and *Malik-al-mulk* (Master of the Kingdom).[9]

[6] Cf. *lā ilāha illa-'llāhu* (There is no God but Allah).

[7] שמע ישראל יהוה אלהינו יהוה אחד, Deut. 6:4.

[8] רבון העולמים, הרחמן, מלך, רחמנא. For a lengthy discussion of these terms see Horovitz, *HUCA*, pp. 198–204; Nöldeke, *op. cit.*, p. 93; Geiger, *op. cit.*, pp. 51–52; Obermann, *op. cit.*, p. 100.

[9] שבעים שמות להקב"ה אל, אלהים, הויה, אדני, אחד . . . ברוך, בורא, גדול, גואל, גבור . . . חי . . . חנון . . . חכם . . . נשגב . . . עליון . . . עזוז . . . צור . . . קדוש . . . רחום, ראשון, רב חסד, שומר, שלטון, שר, שוכן עד . . . (בבאר היטב, בהעלותך, ובתלפיות, ענף כנוים) cf. *Sefer Yeẓirah*, p. 10; *Num. Rab.* 14:10; אדיר הוא in הגדה של פסח.

VERSE 23

> But bear the glad tidings to those who believe and work righteousness, that for them are gardens beneath which rivers flow; whenever they are provided with fruits therefrom they say, 'This is what we were provided with before,' and they shall be provided with the like; and there are pure wives for them therein, and they shall dwell therein for aye.

The Muḥammadan promise for Paradise is that of a material world with gardens, rivers, fruits of various types, tastes and colors, wives or perpetual virgins of constant purity, wherein the God-fearing Moslem shall abide forever.[1]

Jallālain, approving of this sense, supposes the fruits of Paradise, though of various tastes, to be alike in color and outward appearance.[2] According to Zamakhsharī, however, the meaning is that the righteous will find there the kinds of fruits they tasted while on earth.[3]

In the liturgical epic *'Akdamut*, written in the Aramaic language and recited on the first day of Pentecost prior to the biblical reading of the Decalogue, it is stated: "Leviathan and the wild ox of the mountain will meet in battle . . . And the sea-monster will smite him with his powerful fins. His creator will then approach him with his mighty sword and prepare a banquet for the righteous. They will sit around tables made of precious stones and before them will flow rivers of balsam. They will regale themselves and drink full cups of the wine preserved for them from the time of the creation of the world."[4] The

[1] Zamakhsharī, Vol. I, p. 59. Cf. 2:34; 3:13, 127, 130, 197; 9:73. The "pure mates" (ازواج مطهّرة) are the wives of the faithful. This is clearly indicated in the Koranic verse: "Verily, the fellows of Paradise upon that day shall be employed in enjoyment; they and their wives, in shade upon thrones, reclining; therein shall they have fruits, and they shall have what they may call for. 'Peace!' — a speech from the merciful Lord!" (36:55).

[2] Quoted by E. M. Wherry, *A Comprehensive Commentary on the Qurān*, London, 1882, Vol. I, p. 298 n; cf. Is. 3:10: "Say ye of the righteous, that it shall be well with him: For they shall eat the fruit of their doings." Also, B. B. B. 11a; B. Ḥag. 12a; B. Yom. 38b.

[3] Zamakhsharī, Vol. I, p. 58. Cf. 77:41; 78:31–35; 88:5–14 and J. Horovitz, "Das Koranische Paradies," in *Scripta Universitatis*, Vol. I, article 6, Jerusalem, 1934.

[4] טלולא דלויתן ותור טור רמותא וחד בחד כי סביך ועביד קרבותא
בקרנוהי מנגח בהמות ברבותא יקרטע נון לקבלה בציצוי בגבורתא
מקרב לה בריה בחרביה ברברבותא ארסטון לצדיקי יתקן ושרותא

items in this poem were gathered from the Midrashim[5] and other rabbinic sources.[6]

Muḥammad does not mention here the number and quality of the rivers, but the idea is completed in 47:16 where he mentions four rivers. They are rivers of water, milk, wine and honey.[7] A parallel is found in *Yalkuṭ*,[8] where we read that there flow four rivers: milk, honey, wine and oil. It is to be noted, however, that meat is not mentioned in the Koranic paradise, though it frequently appears in the rabbinic sources.[9]

מסחרין עלי תכי דכדכד וגומרתא
ומתפנקין ורוו בכסי רויתא

נגידין קמיהון אפרסמון נהרתא
חמר מרת דמבראשית נטיר בי־נעותא
(אקדמות, מחזור שבועות)

[5] עתיד הקב"ה ליעשות ראש חולה (χορηγός) לצדיקים לעתיד לבוא . . . והצדיקין מראין אותו באצבע ואומר כי זה אלהים אלהינו עולם ועד הוא ינהיגנו עלמות עלמות בעלימות עלמות בזריזות עלמות כאלו עולמתא (ירושלמי מו"ק, פ"ז, ה"ז). Cf. S. Lieberman, הירושלמי כפשוטו, כרך א, Jerusalem, 1935, p. 9; Abraham S. Yahuda, עבר וערב, New York, 1946, p. 153; and: אמר רבי אלעזר עתיד הקב"ה לעשות מחול לצדיקים והוא יושב ביניהם בגן עדן וכל אחד ואחד מראה באצבעו (תענית לא, ע"א). Rashi, *ad loc.*, explains מחול as an "outer space." This interpretation is based on Mishnah Kil. 4:3 מקום הפנוי מן הכרם שאין שם גפנים.

[6] שבעה שערים יש בגן עדן וכל השערים בתים ועליות . . . וכל צדיק וצדיק מקומו מוכן לפניו, ושם מלאכי השרת ומלאכי החסד לפניו ומרקדים לפניו ומזמרים ואותם חופות מעוטרים בח' מאות וורדים וכשיבא הצדיק לפניהם בבגדיו אלו מפשיטים אותם הבגדים מעליו ומלבישין אותו ח' בגדים של משי וענני כבוד מקיפים אותו מכל צדדיו. ומשם מוציאין אותו לחופת ארבע נהרות של הוד מעדנים אשר שם היין והדבש ושותים הצדיקים מהם . . . וכל צדיק וצדיק יש לו חופה בפני עצמה ומלאכים משמשים לפניהם, וחמה ולבנה מרקדים לפניהם, וכל צדיק וצדיק יש לו כתר על ראשו לפי כבודו. (א. יעללינק, בית המדרש, חדר ה', ע' 42). אמר שלמה ברוח נבואה מן קדם יי עתיד מרי עלמא למימר לכל צדיקיא באנפי נפשיה אזיל טעום בחדוא לחמך . . . ושתי בלב טב חמרא דאצטנע לך בגן עדן. (תרגום, קהלת ט', ז')

[7] 47:16: "The similitude of Paradise which is promised to the pious, — in it are rivers of water without corruption, and rivers of milk, the taste whereof changes not, and rivers of wine delicious to those who drink; and rivers of honey clarified . . ."

[8] ומושכין ממנה ד' נהרות א' של חלב וא' של יין וא' של אפרסמון וא' של דבש (ילקוט שמעוני, בראשית, רמז כ). הקב"ה עושה לו למשיח שבע חופות של אבנים טובות ומרגליות וכל חופה וחופה מושכים מתוכה ארבע נהרות של יין ושל דבש ושל חלב ושל אפרסמון טהור (פסיקתא רבתי, פל"ז, ע' קסג, [F]). Cf. B. Sanh. 99a and V. Aptowitzer, "Die Paradiesesflüsse des Kurans," *MGWJ*, 1928, pp. 151–55.

[9] אריסטון עתיד הקב"ה לעשות לעבדיו הצדיקים לעתיד לבא וכל מי שלא אכל נבלות בעולם הזה זוכה לראות לעולם הבא. (ויקרא רבה, פי"ג, ג). Cf. B. B. B. 75a.

VERSE 26

How can ye disbelieve in God, when ye were dead and He made you alive, and then He will kill you and then make you alive again, and then to Him will ye return?

The idea that God destroys and restores life abounds in the Koran. In 53:45 Muḥammad states: "And that it is He who makes man laugh and weep and that it is He who kills and makes alive . . . ." Similarly, we find in 75:35: "Is not He able to quicken the dead?"

A comparable idea is found in the Talmud: ". . . the Holy One, blessed be He, restores the souls to the dead bodies . . ."[1] It also brings to mind the Jewish benediction, "Blessed art Thou, O Lord, who revivest the dead,"[2] and the biblical passages, "The Lord killeth, and maketh alive; He bringeth down to the grave, and bringeth up" (I Sam. 2:6) . . . "I kill, and make alive; I have wounded, and I heal" (Deut. 32:39).

Zamakhsharī associates the words of the Koran, "when ye were dead and He made you alive," with the emergence of living man out of a dormant sperm.[3] The same idea is expressed by Baiḍāwī.[4] In the Talmud we also find reference to the formation of a living soul out of the unfertilized seed:[5] "An emperor said to Rabban Gamaliel: 'Ye maintain that the dead will revive; but they turn to dust, and can dust come to life?' Thereupon his (the emperor's) daughter said to him (the Rabbi): 'Let me answer him: In our town there are two potters; one fashions (his products) from water, and the other from clay: who is the more praiseworthy?' 'He who fashions them from water,' he replied (this being far more difficult). 'If he can fashion (man) from water (sperm), surely he can do so from clay!' (the dust into which the dead are turned)."[6]

[1] B. Sanh. 108a.

[2] B. Ket. 8b. Cf. Bu., Vol. II, p. 201.

[3] Zamakhsharī, Vol. I, p. 65:
كانه قيل كيف تكفرون بالله وقصتكم هذه وحالكم انكم كنتم امواتا نُطَفا في اصلاب آباءكم فجعلكم احياء.

[4] Baiḍāwī, *ad loc.*

[5] Cf. Rashi to B. Sanh. 91a: א"כ הקב"ה אם מן המים הוא מצייר דמטפה סרוחה שהיא כמים הוא מוליד . . . והכי נמי הקב"ה יוצר את האדם מטפה קטנה שאין בה ממש וכ"ש שיכול לבראותו מן העפר אי נמי כל העולם כולו יצר בתוהו.

[6] Cf. B. Sanh. 90b–91a; Hirschfeld, *New Researches* . . . , p. 43, about "resurrection," and notes to Verse 2:53 about "the revival of the dead." Also notes to 2:52, 53.

VERSE 27

> It is He who created for you all that is in the earth, then he *made for* the heavens and fashioned them seven heavens; and He knows all things.

This verse dealing with the creation recalls 50:38: "We did create the heavens and the earth and what is between the two in six days and no weariness touched us." In the latter verse, "heavens" precedes "earth," whereas in our present text the order is reversed. In the Talmud, too, there is a controversy between the school of Shammai and that of Hillel, as to whether the heaven or the earth was created first. The former, maintaining priority for the heavens, bases its claim upon Genesis 1:1: "In the beginning God created the heaven and the earth." The school of Hillel in upholding the opposite view claims that the earth was created first, as is written: ". . . in the day that the Lord God made earth and heaven" (Gen. 2:4). Each school sets forth arguments to substantiate its claim by logical reasoning. The Sages, however, hold that both, heaven and earth, were created at the same time. They offer as evidence the Scriptural verse: "Yea, My hand hath laid the foundation of the earth, And My right hand hath spread out the heavens; When I call unto them, They stand up together" (Is. 48:13). The Talmud then quotes Resh Laḳish: "When they were created, He created heaven (first), and afterwards He created the earth; but when He stretched them forth He stretched forth the earth (first), and afterwards He stretched forth heaven."[1] The Midrash cites the above legend and adds that the controversy of the two schools lasted until the *Shekinah* rested on them and they both agreed that heaven and earth were created together.[2]

Moslem commentators also raise the question of sequence in the creation of heaven and earth. According to Zamakhsharī, the creation

[1] B. Ḥag. 12a. From the word *together* in Is. 48:13, "the inference is drawn that heaven and earth are coeval."

[2] נכנס תחרות ביניהם על הדבר הזה עד ששרתה שכינה ביניהם והסכימו אלו עם אלו ששניהם נבראו בשעה אחת וברגע אחד מה עשה הקב"ה פשט יד ימינו ונטה שמים ופשט יד שמאלו ויסד ארץ (פדר"א, פי"ח). איזה נברא תחילה תנינן רשב"י אומר שמים וארץ לא נבראו אלא כהדין אלפס וכסוי הדדי, ר"א בר"י אומר שניהם שוין שפעמים שמקדים שמים לארץ וארץ לשמים מלמד ששניהם שוין (מסכת אצילות באגדת בראשית, ע' קמ"ז). As to שמים נברא תחילה, consult Talmud Yerushalmi, Ḥag. 2, 1, and מדרש אבכיר, ed. A. Marmorstein, *Dvir*, Book I, 1923, p. 127.

of the earth preceded that of the heavens. Referring to the Koranic verse: "And the earth after that He did stretch out" (79:30), he explains that in the beginning the earth was created where Israel's sanctuary was later erected. This was in the form of a round rock surrounded by smoke. Later on the smoke ascended upward and the heavens emerged. Only then did the rock expand, and the earth assumed its final form.[3]

That the world was created (started) from the place of the sanctuary is also a rabbinic conception. Thus: "The world was created (started) from Zion . . . ;"[4] and: "When the Holy One, blessed be He, created the sea, it went on expanding, until the Holy One, blessed be He, rebuked it and caused it to dry up."[5] The Talmud also adds that the heavens were created from fire and water, rather than from smoke.[6]

The seven heavens mentioned in the Koran are: the Garden of Eternity, the Abode of Peace, the Abode of Rest, the Garden of Eden, the Garden of Resort, the Garden of Pleasure, and the Garden of Paradise.[7] The Koranic idea that God "fashioned them seven

[3] Zamakhsharī, Vol. I, p. 67:

....لان جرم الارض تقدم خلقهُ خَـلْق السماء .... وعن الحسن خلق الله الارض في موضع بيت المقدس كهيئة الفهر عليها دخان ملتزق بها ثم اصعد الدخان وخلق منه السموات وامسك الفهر في موضعها وبسط منها الارض ....

[4] Cf.: ושתיה היתה נקראת. תנא שממנה הושתת העולם . . . (יומא נ"ד, ע"ב); also: ללמדך שהמשכן שקול כנגד כל העולם וכנגד יצירת האדם שהוא עולם קטן כיצד כשברא הקב"ה את עולמו כילוד אשה בראו. מה ילוד אשה מתחיל מטבורו ומותח לכאן ולכאן לארבעה צדדין כך התחיל הקב"ה לבראות את עולמו מאבן שתיה תחלה וממנה הושתת העולם (תנחומא, פקודי קכז, ע"ב); and: ה' בחכמה יסד ארץ וגו' שברא הקב"ה את העולם כילוד אשה . . . מתחיל מטיבורו ומשם הוא מתחיל והולך כך העולם התחיל הקב"ה מטיבורו ומשם נמתח לכאן ולכאן. והיך טיבורו זו ירושלים . . . ולמה קרא שמו אבן שתיה שממנו הושתת העולם כולו . . . א. יעללינעק, בית המדרש, חדר חמישי, ע' 63. Cf. Aptowitzer, re מקדש in *Haẓofeh*, Budapest, 1926, p. 270.

[5] Cf. B. Ḥag. 12a; V. Aptowitzer, "Zur Kosmologie der Agada," *MGWJ* (Reprint), 1929, pp. 363–70.

[6] B. Ḥag. 12a; cf. *Gen. Rab.* 4, 7; *Num. Rab.* 12, 4.

[7] Muḥammad refers often to the seven heavens السموات السبع or سبع السموات. In 78:12 he calls the seven heavens "the seven strongholds" سبع شداد and in 23:17 he calls them the "seven paths" سبع طرائق, corresponding to the talmudic expression שבילי דרקיע. The Koran, however, stresses the fact that at the time of the creation "His throne was upon the water" كان عرشه على الماء,

heavens" and that the latter were made out of one of them is also Jewish. This tale is found in *Midrash ha-Ne'elam*: "Rabbi Joḥannan said: This *Raḳia'* (heaven) that was created on the second day (of creation) is the uppermost one . . . All the other heavens were made out of this one . . . The Scriptures call it both *Raḳia'* and *Shamayim* (Gen. 1:8) because *Shamayim* was made of *Raḳia'*. And that heaven bore all the other heavens which came out of it."[8]

Innumerable references to the heavens are found in rabbinic sources. Thus in Midrash *'Aseret Hadibrot* we find: "God created the heavens and he named the lowest one *Wilon*."[9] And elsewhere: "Rabbi Me'ir says: 'There are seven heavens';"[10] "Resh Laḳish said: There are seven heavens, named *Wilon*, *Raḳia'*, *Sheḥaḳim*, *Zebul*, *Ma'on*, *Makon* and *'Arabot*."[11] "Every seventh is loved by God. In the heavens, the seventh is loved: *Heaven*, *Upper Heaven*, *Raḳi'a*, *Sheḥa-ḳim*, *Zebul*, *Ma'on* and *'Arabot*, as the Psalmist (68:5) writes: 'Extol him that rideth upon 'Arabot.' "[12]

We find a similar treatment in the Midrash with both a change of sequence and a change of one name. "Rabbi Eleazar said: There are

11:9. The latter idea is found in Rashi who states that the throne of glory stands in the air, and hovers over the waters by the command of God כסא כבוד עומד באויר ומרחף על פני המים ברוח פיו של הקדוש ברוך הוא ובמאמרו (Rashi, Gen. 1:2). Cf. Geiger, *op. cit.*, pp. 64–65; Hirschberg, *op. cit.*, p. 219. The Arabic terms السموات والارض (heaven and earth) correspond to the Hebrew שמים וארץ. J. Obermann, *op. cit.*, p. 102.

[8] ת"ח כשברא הקב"ה את עולמו, עשאו מאותו האור הנאצל מלמעלה, וברא השמים מאותו הרקיע הראשון, שהכינו הקב"ה ובראו בתחלה, ואותו הרקיע הוליד כל שאר הרקיעים שנתהוו ממנו . . . וכשברא הקב"ה אותו הרקיע, נטל את המאורות והניחם באותו רקיע הנקרא רקיע השמים שאותו הרקיע נתהוה מן השמים (מדרש הנעלם בז"ח, יד), quoted in T.S., Vol. I, p. 130.

[9] Quoted in Jellinek, 60 בית המדרש, א, דף: עוד ברא הקב"ה שבעה רקיעים ותחתון שבכולן וילון שמו (מדרש עשרת הדברות, דבור ראשון).

[10] רבי מאיר אומר שבע רקיעין הן אלו הן וילון רקיע שחקים זבול מעון מכון ערבות (אדר"נ ל"ז, ט).

[11] B. Ḥag. 12b.

[12] כל השביעים חביבין. למעלה השביעי חביב, שמים ושמי שמים, רקיע, שחקים, זבול, מעון וערבות. סולו לרוכב בערבות (תהלים ס"ח, ה); פסיקתא, פסקא כג בחדש השביעי, קנ"ד, ע"ב [B]. According to *Lisān-'l-'Arab*, " 'The mention of *seven* and *seventy* and *seven hundred* is frequent in the Qur-ān and in the sayings of the Holy Prophet, and the Arabs use them to signify a large number and multiplicity' " (quoted in Ali, *The Holy Qur-ān*, p. 22). Cf. Sa'adia on Gen. 4:15 and 24, where שבעתים is rendered כת֗ירא and שבעים ושבעה — אכת֗ר ואכת֗ר.

seven heavens: *Heaven*, *Upper Heaven*, *Raḳia'*, *Sheḥaḳim*, *Ma'on*, *Zebul*, *'Araphel*."[13] The Midrash also cites a controversy between Rab and the Rabbis. The former says there are two heavens; the latter claim that there are three. R. Eliezer, however, says that there are seven.[14] The Koranic phrase that God "knows all things" is frequently mentioned in Jewish literature.[15]

[13] רבי אליעזר אמר ז׳ רקיעים הן: שמים ושמי שמים, רקיע, שחקים, מעון, זבול, ערפל (דברים רבה, ב, לב). Cf. שוחר טוב, קי״ד, ז; *Midrash ha-Gadol* to Gen. 24.

[14] רבנן אמרו שני רקיעין הן שנאמר לרוכב בשמי שמי קדם רבנן אמרי שלשה הן לד׳ השמים ושמי השמים. ר׳ אליעזר אומר שבעה הן (שוחר טוב, קיד, ה, ו, ז). In the explanatory remarks to *Leḳaḥ Ṭob* [B] (Gen. 1,7 note 94) רב is substituted for רבנן. In the same place the word גשמים mentioned in the Midrash Tehillim *Shoḥer Ṭob* is corrected to read ג׳ שמים (three heavens).

[15] In the prayer book of *Rosh Hashanah* the following is recited: לפניך נגלו כל תעלומות והמון נסתרות שמבראשית... הכל גלוי וידוע לפניך יי אלהינו, צופה ומביט עד סוף כל הדורות... (מחזור — מוסף ראש השנה, זכרונות).

VERSES 28–30

> And when thy Lord said unto the angels,[1] 'I am about to place a vicegerent[2] in the earth,' they said, 'Wilt Thou place therein one who will do evil therein and shed blood? we celebrate Thy praise and hallow Thee.' Said (*the Lord*), 'I know what ye know not.'

Rashi, on Gen. 1:26, sums up the Midrashim and states that when man was created God consulted the heavenly hosts in order to emphasize an ethical principle that "the greater should always consult and receive the permission of the lesser."[3] The general idea was that if there be none of God's likeness in the lower spheres, there would be

[1] The word used here for angel is *mal'ak* (pl. ملائكة) which corresponds to the Hebrew *mal'ak* מלאך meaning the bearer of messages; cf. Macdonald's article on *Malā'ika* in *E. I.*, Vol. 3, pp. 189–92. Also, S. S. Haas, "The 'Creation of Man' in the Qur'ān," in *The Moslem World*, XXXI (3), July 1941, pp. 268–73; Horovitz, "Muhammads Himmelfahrt," in *Der Islam*, Vol. IX, pp. 159 f.

[2] The term خليفة used here means that man is endowed with the gift of ruling the rest of the earthly creation. It is so stated in 45:11, 12: "God it is who subjects to you the sea that the ships may sail thereon at his bidding, and that ye may crave of His grace, and that haply ye may give thanks; and He has subjected to you what is in the heavens and what is in the earth — all from Him; verily, in that are signs unto a people who reflect." This idea is identical with the biblical statement that man was created in the image of God, "... after our likeness; and let them have dominion over the fish of the sea, and over the fowl of the air, and over the cattle, and over all the earth, and over every creeping thing that creepeth upon the earth ... and God said unto them: 'Be fruitful, and multiply, and replenish the earth, and subdue it; and have dominion over the fish of the sea, and over the fowl of the air, and over every living thing that creepeth upon the earth'" (Gen. 1:26–28). Cf. Zohar I, 47, Vilna edition: בצלמנו כדמותנו לאשתכללא דא בדא למהוי הוא יחידאי בעלמא שליט על כולא (זהר ח"א, מז). The latter echoes Sa'adia's idea that man like God may possess the power of governing: בצלמנו וכדמותנו — בצורתנא כשבהנא מס̈לטא (בראשית א, כו). Sa'adia, *Œuvres Complètes* . . ., ed. Dérenbourg, Vol. I, 1893. See also, תנחומא כת"י במבוא לתנחומא ישן ע"ז and אלא מה, בצלמנו וכדמותנו בגונינו שיהא שולט למטה כמו אנו למעלה, quoted in T. S., Vol. I, p. 159n.

[3] Rashi, *ad. loc.*: ענותנותו של הקב"ה למדנו מכאן לפי שהאדם בדמות המלאכים ויתקנאו בו לפיכך נמלך בהם וכשהוא דן את המלכים הוא נמלך בפמליא שלו . . . אעפ"י שלא סייעוהו ביצירתו. לא נמנע הכתוב מללמד דרך ארץ ומדת ענוה שיהא הגדול נמלך ונוטל רשות מן הקטן ואם כתב אעשה אדם לא למדנו שיהא מדבר עם בית דינו אלא עם עצמו ותשובתו כתב בצדו ויברא את האדם ולא כתב ויבראו.

jealousy among angels and man, and the earth would be jealous of the heavens.

In the Midrash, too, it is related that God consulted the angels concerning the creation of man.[4] The angels were not all of one opinion. Because man would be affectionate, his creation was favored by the angels of love. But the angel of truth opposed it on the ground that man would rarely be truthful. The angel of justice, however, knowing that man would practice justice, favored his creation, while the angel of peace opposed it.[5]

Moslem commentators also inquire how the angels could have known in advance what man's character would be like. Ṭabarī's[6] and Zamakhsharī's[7] statements that the ministering angels were informed by God himself are found in Aggadic sources. There the narrative reads: "Rab Judah said in Rab's name: When the Holy One, blessed be He, wished to create man, He (first) created a company of ministering angels and said to them: Is it your desire that we make a man in our image? They answered: Sovereign of the Universe, what will be his deeds? — Such and such will be his deeds, He replied. Thereupon

[4] ויאמר אלהים נעשה אדם. במי נמלך. רבי יהושע בשם ר' לוי אמר: במלאכת השמים והארץ נמלך . . . ר' שמואל בר נחמן אמר, במעשה כל יום ויום נמלך . . . ר' אמי אמר, בלבו נמלך . . . ר' חנינא לא אמר כן, אלא בשעה שבא לבראת את אדם הראשון נמלך במלאכי השרת (בראשית רבה, ח, ג–ד).

[5] א"ר סימון בשעה שבא הקב"ה לבראת את אדה"ר נעשו מה"ש כיתים כיתים וחבורות חבורות מהם אומרים אל יברא ומהם אומרים יברא הה"ד חסד ואמת נפגשו צדק ושלום נשקו, חסד אומר יברא שהוא גומל חסדים, ואמת אומר אל יברא שכולו שקרים, צדק אומר יברא שהוא עושה צדקות, שלום אומר, אל יברא דכוליה קטטה, מה עשה הקב"ה נטל אמת והשליכו לארץ הה"ד (דניאל ח) ותשלך אמת ארצה. אמרו מה"ש לפני הקב"ה רבון העולמים מה אתה מבזה תכסיס אלטיכסייה שלך תעלה אמת מן הארץ, הה"ד אמת מארץ תצמח . . . עד שמה"ש מדיינין אלו עם אלו ומתעסקין אלו עם אלו בראו הקב"ה אמר להן מה אתם מדיינין כבר נעשה אדם (בראשית רבה ח, ה).

[6] Ṭabarī, Vol. I, p. 157:

وذلك انه ذكر في اوله ان الملائكة سالت ربّها ما ذاك الخليفة حين قال لها اني جاعل في الارض خليفة فاجابهم انه تكون له ذرية يفسدون.... فقالت الملائكة حينئذ اتجعل فيها من يفسد فيها ... فكان قول الملائكة ما قالت من ذلك لربها بعد اعلام الله اياها ان ذلك كائن من ذرية الخليفة الذي يجعله في الارض....

[7] Zamakhsharī, Vol. I, p. 67:

فان قلت من اين عرفوا ذلك حتى تعجبوا منه وانما هو غيب — قلت عرفوه باخبار من الله.

they exclaimed: Sovereign of the Universe, *What is man that thou art mindful of him, and the son of man that thou thinkest of him*? (Ps. 8:5). Thereupon He stretched out His little finger among them and consumed them with fire. The same thing happened with a second company. The third company said to Him: Sovereign of the Universe, what did it avail the former (angels) that they spoke to Thee (as they did)? The whole world is Thine, and whatsoever that Thou wishest to do therein, do it. When He came to the men of the Age of the Flood and of the division (of tongues) whose deeds were corrupt, they said to Him: Lord of the Universe, did not the first (company of angels) speak aright? *Even to old age I am the same, and even to hoar hairs will I carry you* (Is. 46:4), He retorted."[8]

The motif of the angels envying man is also illustrated in the story of Moses' ascent to God in order to receive the Torah. " 'Sovereign of the Universe! What business has one born of woman amongst us?' 'He has come to receive the Torah,' answered He to them. Said they to Him. 'That secret treasure, which has been hidden by Thee for nine hundred and seventy-four generations before the world was created, Thou desirest to give to flesh and blood! . . .'"[9] Whereupon God told Moses to "return them an answer." When Moses had explained to the angels that the Torah is given to man and not to the angels who have no opportunity for fulfilling its precepts, each one of them was moved to love Moses. They had to agree that man's intellectual qualities were superb and they praised the Lord for the creation of man upon earth.[10]

As to the purpose of God's consulting the angels about creating man, Zamakhsharī gives various explanations. One is that it might serve as a moral lesson for His subjects to consult others before acting, though God, of course, with His infinite wisdom, needs no advice.[11]

[8] B. Sanh. 38b.

[9] B. Shab. 88b. Cf. [B] תנחומא, בחוקתי ו, where the angels' reply to God's inquiry, "Who will obey My laws, if I shall not create man?" is replaced by, "We shall follow your teaching." Here Muḥammad uses a similar expression, "we hallow Thy name."

[10] *Gen. Rab.* 17, 5; *Leḳaḥ Ṭob*, Gen. 2, 19. Cf. also 2:31 and Is. 6:3; *Yalḳuṭ Shim'oni*, Vol. II, § 404.

[11] Zamakhsharī, Vol. I, p. 67:
وقيل ليُعلّم عباده المشاورة في امورهم قبل ان يُقدموا عليها
وعَرضَها على ثقاتهم ونُصحائهم وان كان هو بعلمه وحكمته
البالغة غنيّا عن المشاورة.

The Midrash *Leḳaḥ Ṭob* also states that the reason why God said, "Let Us make man," is that God does nothing without consulting His heavenly court,[12] though He does not require their advice. Similarly, the Talmud states: "The Holy One, blessed be He, does nothing without consulting His heavenly Court."[13]

According to the Talmud, the Bible itself attests to the creation of man by God alone without assistance. This is deduced from the biblical verse: "And God created man in His own image" (Gen. 1:27). However, God wanted to teach man an ethical principle, always to ask the advice of others before doing something.[14]

Ṭabarī quotes the Moslem tradition that God gathered earth from all over the world and that, therefore, man's physiognomy differs in color as does the earth out of which he was formed.[15] In the same manner, Jewish tradition explains the various colors of the parts comprising the human body,[16] and that for the creation of man, God collected the dust from all parts of the world.[17]

[12] ...שאין הקב"ה עושה דבר אלא אם כן נמלך בפמליא של מעלה שנאמר בגזירת עירין פתגמא ובמימר קדישין שאילתא. (לקח טוב, בראשית פ"א, כ"ו [B])

[13] B. Sanh. 38b. ...שאם יבוא הגדול ליטול רשות מן הקטן ממנו אמר מה אני צריך ליטול רשות מן הקטן ממנו והם אומרים לו למוד מבוראך... (בראשית רבה, ח, ז)

[14] *Ibid.*

[15] Ṭabarī, Vol. I, p. 165:

ان الله خلق آدم من قبضة. قبضها من جميع الارض فجاء بنو آدم على قدر الارض جاء منهم الاحمر والاسود والابيض وبين ذلك ...

[16] התחיל לקבץ את עפרו של אדם הראשון מארבע כנפות הארץ, אדום שחור לבן ירוק. אדום זה הדם, שחור אלו הקרבים, לבן אלו עצמות וגידים, ירוק זה הגוף (פדר"א, פי"א). However, *Targum Jonathan* to Gen. 2:7 mentions three colors only, סומק, שחום וחיור.

[17] B. Sanh. 38a–38b: "Adam's trunk came from Babylon, his head from Ereẓ Yisrael, his limbs from other lands, and his private parts, according to R. Aḥa, from Aḳra di Agma." See also [Z] תוספתא סנהדרין ח, ד, and Talmud Yerushalmi, Sanh. 4, 9.

VERSES 31–32

And He taught Adam the names, all of them;[1] then He propounded them to the angels and said, 'Declare to me the names of these, if ye are truthful.' They said, 'Glory be to Thee! no knowledge is ours but what Thou thyself hast taught us, verily, *Thou* art the knowing, the wise.' Said *the Lord*, 'O Adam, declare to them their names;' and when he had declared to them their names He said, 'Did I not say to you I know the secrets of the heavens and of the earth, and I know what ye show and what ye were hiding?'

Adam's remarkable wisdom, according to Jewish tradition, was displayed by his ability to find names for all the animals:[2] "The ministering angels spake before the Holy One, blessed be He, saying: Sovereign of all Worlds! 'What is man, that thou shouldst take note of him?' (Ps. 144:3) 'Man (Adam) is like unto vanity' (*ibid.* 4), upon earth there is not his like. (God) answered them: Just as all of you praise Me in the heights of heaven so he professed My Unity on earth,

[1] Cf. 55:3: "He created man, taught him plain speech." Note, however, that in verse 31 "*Adam*" is used for *insān* as in biblical Hebrew בן־אדם; cf. S. Haas, *op. cit.*, p. 269; A. Jeffery, *The Foreign Vocabulary of the Qur'ān*, Baroda, 1938, p. 79.

[2] בשעה שבא הקב"ה לבראות את האדם נמלך במלאכי השרת אמר להן נעשה אדם בצלמנו אמרו לו אדם זה מה טיבו אמר להן חכמתו מרובה משלכם הביא לפניהם את הבהמה ואת החיה ואת העוף אמר להם זה מה שמו ולא היו יודעין כיון שברא אדם העבירן לפניו אמר לו זה מה שמו אמר זה שור זה חמור זה סוס וזה גמל ואתה מה שמך אמר לו אני נאה להקרא אדם שנבראתי מן האדמה ואני מה שמי א"ל לך נאה להקרא אדני שאתה אדון לכל בריותיך (בראשית רבה, בראשית י"ז, ד). The story is fully related in the Midrash cited below. According to *Midrash Leḳaḥ Ṭob*, the names Adam called were to remain forever because Adam designated those names by the heavenly spirit. ויחכם מכל האדם אדם הראשון מה היתה חכמתו את מוצא כשבקש הקב"ה לבראות את האדם נמלך במלאכי השרת אמר להם נעשה אדם בצלמנו אמרו לפניו מה אנוש כי תזכרנו א"ל אדם שאני רוצה לבראות חכמתו מרובה משלכם מה עשה כינס כל בהמה חיה ועוף והעבירן לפניהן א"ל מה שמותן של אלו לא ידעו כיון שברא אדם העבירן לפניו אמר לו מה שמותן של אלו אמר לזה נאה לקרות שור ולזה ארי ולזה סוס ולזה גמל ולזה נשר שנאמר ויקרא האדם שמות אמר לו ואתה מה שמך . . . אמר לו הקב"ה אני מה שמי אמר ליה ה' למה שאתה אדון על כל הבריות. (במדבר רבה, פי"ט, ג) Cf. אדם הראשון נרו של עולם היה, (תלמוד ירושלמי שבת פ"ב ה"ו); and: בשעה שבראה אדה"ר ואמרו לפניו רבש"ע מה אנוש כי תזכרנו וגו' באותה שעה אמר הקב"ה למלאכי השרת בואו וראו שבני אומרין לפני אף הן כיון שראו אמרו שירה מה שירה אמרו ה' אדוננו מה אדיר שמך בכל הארץ. (תוספתא, סוטה ו, ה) [Z] See also (Sch. ed.) אדר"נ, י"ב and [B] פסיקתא דרב כהנא פרשת פרה, פסקא ד, ע' ל"ד.

nay, moreover, are you able to stand up and call the names for all the creatures which I have created? They stood up, but were unable (to give the names). Forthwith Adam stood up and called the names for all His creatures, as it is said, 'And the man gave names to all cattle' " (Gen. 2:20).[3]

God also assembled all the angels and requested them to name the animals according to their kind. But they were not equal to the task. God then called upon Adam, and he spoke without hesitation.[4]

A direct parallel to this Aggadic source may be found in Zamakhsharī who writes that God showed Adam the various species he created and taught him to name the horse, the camel, etc. God also informed Adam about their characteristics and their usefulness in secular and religious matters in this world.[5]

[3] *P.R.E.*, p. 91.

[4] *Leḳaḥ Ṭob*, Gen. 2,20 [B]; cf. *Gen. Rab.* 17,5.

[5] Zamakhsharī, Vol. I, p. 68:
آراه الاجناس التي خلقها وعلّمه ان هذا اسمه فرس وهذا اسمه بعير وهذا اسمه كذا وهذا اسمه كذا وعلّمه احوالها وما يتعلق بها من المنافع الدينيّة والدنيويّة.

VERSE 33

> And when we said to the angels, 'Adore Adam,' they adored him save only Iblîs, who refused and was too proud and became one of the misbelievers.[1]

Geiger claims that this "legend bears unmistakable marks of Christian development." He goes on to say that "it is true that in Jewish writings great honour is spoken of as shewn by the angels to Adam, but this never went so far as adoration; indeed when this was once about to take place in error, God frustrated the action."[2]

This claim of Geiger is refuted if we assume that the word *sajada*, literally meaning "bow down" (before him), does not refer to the deification of man by the angels, but merely to tribute and honor. Such an interpretation is actually given by Zamakhsharī and Baiḍāwī, who agree that the command to the angels to "bow down before Adam" is not to be understood as a command to adore or deify him.[3]

It is worth mentioning that quite apart from the Moslem commentaries, Torrey recognizes that "the Koran does not speak of *worshipping*, however, but merely of approaching a personage of high rank in a truly oriental way."[4] To the interpretation of the Moslem commentators, the rabbis offer an abundance of parallels and counterparts.[5] We find in the Midrash: "On the day when the first man was

[1] Cf. 38:71–75 and E. J. Jurji, *Illumination in Islamic Mysticism*, Princeton, 1938, pp. 84 f.

[2] Geiger, *op. cit.*, p. 98 and p. 77 (English edition). He also quotes a source (found in Zunz, "Die Gottesdienstlichen Vorträge der Juden," p. 291 n.) that shows a striking resemblance to this Koranic verse. It is found in the ms. Midrash of Rabbi Moses Haddarshan, who, however, lived in the eleventh century. M. Grünbaum, *Neue Beiträge zur semitischen Sagenkunde* (p. 60), follows Geiger in that worshipping any other than God would be inconceivable in Jewish tradition. The same view is upheld by Hirschberg, *op. cit.*, p. 224. See also H. Speyer, *op. cit.*, p. 16: "Diese Vorstellung is typisch christlich."

[3] Zamakhsharī, Vol. I, p. 69:

[السجود] لله تعالى على سبيل العبادة ولغيره على وجه التكرمة
كما سجدت الملائكة لآدم وآبَوا (وأبو) يوسف واخوته له.

[4] Torrey, *op. cit.*, p. 71; according to Ali, *op. cit.*, p. 25 n., *sajada* means "saluted."

[5] כיון שנברא אדם קם על רגליו והיה מתואר בדמות אלהים והיה קומתו מן המזרח למערב
וראו אותו כל הבריות ונתיראו מפניו סבורים שהוא בוראם ובאו להשתחוות לו, אמר להם

created, as it is said, 'In the day when thou (Adam) wast created they were prepared,' the Holy One, blessed be He, said to the ministering angels: Come, let us descend and render loving service to the first man . . . ."[6]

That the angels adored Adam "save only Iblîs," is also discussed in the Talmud and other rabbinic sources. R. Judah says: "Adam reclined in the Garden of Eden, whilst the ministering angels roasted flesh and strained wine for him;"[7] thereupon the serpent[8] looked in, saw him, and became envious of him.[9] "In the hour when the Holy One, blessed be He, created man, the ministering angels mistook him for the Deity and wished to proclaim him as the Holy One. God then made man to fall into a deep sleep, and all knew that he was human."[10]

מה אתם באים להשתחוות לי בואו אני ואתם ונלביש גאוה ועוז ונמליך עלינו למי שבראנו באותה שעה פתח אדם את פיו וענו כל הבריות אחריו ה' מלך גאות לבש (ילקוט שמעוני, תהלים, רמז תתמז).

[6] *P.R.E.*, p. 89.

[7] The Talmud, repeating the Aggada that the angels were serving roast meat to Adam in the Garden of Eden, states that this was "flesh that descended from heaven" (B. Sanh. 59b).

[8] *I. e.* Satan; cf. *Gen. Rab.* 17 and L. Ginzberg, *Legends of the Jews*, Vol. 5, p. 84. Re the term *Iblīs* (Satan: Iblīs — diabolos; Shaiṭan — Ethiopic), see Horovitz, *Kor. Unt.*, p. 87; also (*ash-shaiṭān*) *ibid.*, pp. 120 f.; cf. A. N. Pollack, *op. cit.*, p. 130; and Ibn Ezra to Gen. 3:1: הנחש . . . שטן. See also L. Jung, *Fallen Angels*, Philadelphia, 1926, pp. 59–61; and 7:22 as well as Ṭabarī, Vol. I, p. 179.

[9] *Yalkuṭ Shim'oni*, Vol. I, § 15 and B. Sanh. 59b: הציץ בו נחש וראה בכבודו ונתקנא בו.

[10] בשעה שברא הקב"ה אדם הראשון טעו מלאכי השרת ובקשו לומר לפניו קדוש . . . מה עשה הקב"ה הפיל עליו תרדמה וידעו הכל שהוא אדם (מדרש בראשית רבה, ח, ו); cf. *Ecc. Rab.* 6, 10.

VERSE 34

> And we said, 'O Adam dwell, thou and thy wife, in Paradise, and eat therefrom amply as you wish; but do not draw near this tree or ye will be of the transgressors.' And Satan made them backslide therefrom and drove them out from what they were in, and we said, 'Go down, one of you the enemy of the other, and in the earth there is an abode and a provision for a time.'

Equivalent phrases are found in Gen. 2:16–18; 3:4,13–23. The Arabic term for the devil (*Shaiṭān*) is the same as the Hebrew *Saṭan*.[1] Likewise the Arabic *Jannātun* (Paradise) (68:32) (98:7) is undoubtedly borrowed from the Hebrew *Gan* or *Gan 'Eden*.[2]

Grünbaum claims that the identification here of Satan with the snake is not to be found in Jewish literature and should therefore be attributed to Christian influence.[3] However, in Jewish lore of the post-Koranic period, Satan is definitely identified with the serpent.[4] According to Zamakhsharī and Baiḍāwī, Satan hid himself in the mouth of the snake in order to be able to enter Paradise.[5] A similar idea is expressed by Sa'adia Gaon, who states that an angel spoke out of the mouth of the snake and not the snake himself.[6]

[1] Ibn Ezra to Gen. 3:1; Maimonides, מו"נ, ח"ב, פ"ל.

[2] Geiger, *op. cit.*, pp. 46–47; "'Eden," עדן, is the proper name of a region signifying bliss, and גן עדן is the garden of pleasure." See also Torrey, *op. cit.*, p. 71; *Gen. Rab.* 17, 18; Ginzberg, *Legends of the Jews*, Vol. 5, p. 84. Though the term جنة is used in the Koran in connection with other gardens and is also found in the pre-Islamic literature, there is no doubt that its derivation is from the Hebrew. S. Fränkel, *Die Aram. Fremdwörter im Arabischen*, Leiden, 1886, p. 148. The Koranic expression here recalls the biblical "And the Lord God planted a garden eastward, in Eden." Compare 18:107; 23:10; B. Ḥag. 14a and U. Cassuto, מאדם עד נח, Jerusalem, 1953, p. 70.

[3] *Neue Beiträge* . . ., p. 61.

[4] וסמ"אל הוה ואתחזי על נחש וצולמיה דנחש דא איהו שטן וכלא חד . . . והנחש היה ערום דא יצר הרע דא מלאך המות ובגין דנחש איהו מלאך המות גרם מותא לעלמא (זהר ח"א, ל"ה), quoted in T. S., Vol. II, p. 252.

[5] Zamakhsharī, Vol. I, p. 69:

وروى انه اراد الدخول فمنعته الخَزَنة فدخل في فم الحية حتى دخلت به وهم لا يشعرون.

Baiḍāwī, *ad loc.*

[6] Ibn Ezra's commentary, Gen. 3:1: ויאמר רב סעדיא גאון . . . כי הנחש גם האתון לא

Ṭabarī elaborates on the sadistic acts of the snake as well as on the punishment inflicted by God on the snake and on Adam and Eve. He writes that when Satan wanted to enter Paradise he entered the body of the snake, which was a quadruped and had the appearance of a camel. In Paradise he came out of the snake, took the fruit from the forbidden tree, brought it to Eve and enticed her by pointing out the greatness of its beauty, the sweetness of its taste and fragrance. Eve tasted it and came to Adam and persuaded him, too, to follow her example. Adam also ate it and then they began to realize their nakedness and hid themselves in the tree. God came and called: "Adam, where art thou?" And Adam replied, "Here I am. I hid because I am ashamed to stand before Thee." God replied: "The earth out of which thou wert created will be afflicted because of thee, cursed shall be the fruits it shall bear, and no tree, whether in Paradise or on earth, shall surpass in beauty the cedar and the lote trees in the Garden of Eden." And to Eve He said: "Painful (like death) shall be thy giving birth." And to the snake He said: "Because thou misled My servant, be thou condemned. Upon thy belly shalt thou go and dust shalt thou eat all the days of thy life. Enmity shall prevail between thee and man."[7]

בשביל' דבר מלאך רק .דברו. This idea is also found in פדר"א פ' י"ג; cf. Geiger, *op. cit.*, p. 100.

[7] Ṭabarī, Vol. I, p. 181:

... فلما اراد ابليس ان يستزلهما دخل في جوف الحية وكانت للحية اربعة قوائم كانها بختية من احسن دابة خلقها الله فلما دخلت الحية الجنة خرج من جوفها ابليس فاخذ من الشجرة التى نهى الله عنها آدم وزوجته فجاء به الى حواء فقال انظرى الى هذه الشجرة ما اطيب ريحها واطيب طعمها واحسن لونها فاخذت حواء فاكلت منها ثم ذهبت بها الى آدم فقالت انظر الى هذه الشجرة ما اطيب ريحها.... فأكل منها آدم فبدت لهما سوآتهما فدخل آدم في جوف الشجرة فناداه ربه يا آدم اين انت... الا تخرج قال استحي منك يا رب قال ملعونة الارض التى خلقت منها لعنة يتحول ثمرها شوكا قال ولم يكن في الجنة ولا في الارض شجرة كان افضل من الطلح والسدر ثم قال يا حواء انت التى غررت عبدي فانك لا تحملين حملا الا حملته كرها فاذا اردت ان تضعي ما في بطنك اشرفت على الموت مرارا وقال للحيّة انت التى دخل الملعون في جوفك... تتحول قوائمك

This narration in its entirety is drawn from Jewish sources. That the snake was like a camel is related in the Midrash.[8] Similarly, the Midrash speaks of Adam's sin and of thorns and thistles that would grow from the earth instead of trees because of man's unworthiness.[9] The same applies to the story about Adam hiding from God because he was ashamed of his wrong doings.[10]

As for the curses inflicted upon the earth, Adam, Eve and the snake, Ṭabarī's words duplicate the story in Genesis 3:14–19: "... cursed art thou (snake) from among all cattle, and ... beasts of the field ... I will put enmity between thee and the woman ... 'I will greatly multiply thy (woman's) pain and thy travail; in pain thou shalt bring forth children ... cursed is the ground for thy (man's) sake; in toil shalt thou eat of it all the days of thy life ...' ".

Ṭabarī also mentions that the menstruation of woman is a punishment inflicted originally upon Eve because of her sin.[11] This, too, appears in several rabbinic sources: "Eve was cursed with ten curses, since it is written: *Unto the woman He said, and I will greatly multiply* (Gen. 3:16), which refers to the two drops of blood, one being that of menstruation and the other that of virginity."[12]

According to Baiḍāwī, the prohibition to "draw near this tree" was a means of precaution. For the proximity of a thing stirs up a desire for it.[13] The Aggada, too, relates that when Adam told Eve that

في بطنك ولا يكون لك رزق الا التراب انت عدوة بنى آدم
وهم اعداؤك...

[8] רבי שמעון בן אלעזר אמר כגמל היה (בראשית רבה, פי"ט א).

[9] ר"י אמר: אלו זכית היתה מעלת לך מכל אילני גן עדן, עכשו שלא זכית קוץ ודרדר וכו' (בראשית רבה, פ"כ, י).

[10] ישב לו בדין אמת שופט צדק ואמת, קרא לאדם ואמר לו: למה ברחת מפני. אמר לפניו שמעך שמעתי ורעדו עצמותי שנאמר את קולך שמעתי בגן ואירא כי עירום אנכי ואחבא, ואחבא מפועלי, ואירא ממעשי, כי עירום אנכי ... (פדר"א, פי"ד). Cf. בראשית רבה, פי"ט, ו.

[11] Ṭabarī, Vol. I, p. 182:

... فقال الله فان لها على ان ادميها في كل شهر مرّة .... لولا
الثلاثة التى اصابت حواء لكان نساء الدنيا لا يحضن ....

[12] B. 'Erub. 100b; cf. T. S., Vol. II, p. 273 n.

[13] Baiḍāwī, Vol. I, p. 20. On God's command "do not draw near this tree" he writes:

فيه مبالغات تعليق النهى بالقرب الذي هو من مقدمات التناول
مبالغة في تحريمه ووجوب الاجتناب عنه وتنبيها على ان القرب

God commanded not to eat from the tree of knowledge, he added the prohibition of "not touching" the tree as a preventive measure.[14]

Muḥammad leaves us in the dark as to the nature of the prohibited tree. Zamakhsharī and Baiḍāwī, however, do raise the question of "the nature" of the tree and state that opinions about it are divided among Moslem commentators. Some hold that it was a "wheat (tree)," others claim it was a "vine (tree)," still others maintain it was a "fig tree."[15] All three opinions mentioned above are found in the Talmud. "That (forbidden) tree from which Adam ate was a vine, for nothing else but wine brings woe to man. R. Judah said: It was the wheat plant, for an infant cannot say 'father' and 'mother' until it has tasted of wheat (thus, wheat is the first thing to induce knowledge). R. Nehemiah said: It was the fig tree, for whereby they transgressed, they were taught to make amends as it is written, *And they sewed fig leaves together*. (Gen. 3:7)"[16]

Around the Koranic statement, "one of you the enemy of the other," the counterpart of which is found in the Bible (Gen. 3:16), Ṭabarī weaves an Islamic legend: Muḥammad was once asked whether it was permitted to kill a snake. He replied: "Man and snake are eternal enemies. When the snake sees man he frightens him and bites him and inflicts pain upon him."[17] In the Talmud, too, we find that "only an ox that killed (is tried) by twenty-three, but any other animal or beast who killed, whoever is first to kill it acquires merit in

من الشيء يورث داعية وميلا يأخذ بمجامع القلب ويلهيه عما هو مقتضى العقل والشرع.

Cf. 7:18, "but draw not nigh unto this tree or ye will be of the unjust."

[14] איזהו סייג שעשה אדם הראשון לדבריו הרי הוא אומר ויצו ה' אלהים על האדם... לא רצה אדם הראשון לומר לחוה כדרך שא"ל הקב"ה אלא כך אמר לה ועשה סייג לדבריו יותר ממה שאמר לו הקב"ה ומפרי העץ אשר בתוך הגן אמר אלהים לא תאכלו ממנו ולא תגעו בו פן תמותון שרצה לשמור את עצמו ואת חוה מן העץ אפילו בנגיעה (אדר"נ, פ"א).

[15] Baiḍāwī, Vol. I, p. 21: والشجرة هي الحنطة او الكرمة اوالتينة; cf. Zamaksharī, *ad loc.*

[16] B. Sanh. 70a–70b; B. Ber. 40a; *Gen. Rab.* 15, 7: "the forbidden tree was a fig tree." As to the nature of the tree of knowledge in Jewish and Christian sources see L. Ginzberg, *Die Haggada bei den Kirchenvätern und in der Apokryphischen Literatur*, Berlin, 1900, pp. 38 ff. and Judah Rosenthal, שאלות עתיקות בתנ"ך, *HUCA*, XXI, 1948, p. 56.

[17] Ṭabarī, Vol. I, p. 181.

the sight of Heaven . . . . . . Is not R. Akiba's opinion identical with that of the first Tanna (of the Mishnah)? — (No;) they differ in the case of a serpent (which, according to R. Akiba, can be killed even without trial)."[18]

[18] B. Sanh. 15b: אחד שור שהמית ואחד בהמה וחיה שהמיתו בעשרים ושלשה ר׳ אליעזר אומר שור שהמית בעשרים ושלשה ושאר בהמה וחיה שהמיתו כל הקודם להרגן זכה בהן לשמים . . . ר׳ עקיבא . . . היינו תנא קמא איכא בינייהו נחש: אין דנין כו׳. The rabbis also discuss the reason why the carcass of a snake is not contaminating like that of other creeping animals. Their opinion is that it was deliberately done so in order that the man should be eager to kill him and use his skin and thus fulfill God's command, Gen. 3:15, "and I will put enmity between thee and the woman . . .": למה לא טימא נבלתו כשאר כל השרצים אחר שהוא בזוי, שלא יעכב אדם להורגו מפני הטומאה ויקוים בו ואיבה אשית (מדרש תדשא, פ״ז, ט,) quoted in T. S., Vol. II, p. 270. Cf. מסכת סופרים, פט״ו, where it is stated that טוב שבנחשים רצוץ את מוחו. According to *Targum Yerushalmi* (Gen. 3:21), "the garments, (כתנות עור) which God made for man were made of the skin of the snake."

VERSE 35

> And Adam caught certain words from his Lord, and He turned towards him, for He is the compassionate one easily turned.

The Arabic expression of *tāba-‘alayhi*, if used in the religious sense, implies returning to a state of obedience, i. e., repentance.[1]

According to Baiḍāwī, the phrase, "and He turned towards him," refers to the Lord turning to Adam mercifully and accepting his repentance.[2] This idea is also found in rabbinic sources, where it is related that God showed Adam the way to repent.[3] The Midrash derives its explanation from the biblical phrase, "In the sweat of thy face shalt thou eat bread, till thou return unto the ground" (Gen. 3:19).[4]

We also find that when Adam met Cain and inquired about his penalty for killing Abel, the latter replied that he had repented and his punishment was mitigated.[5] Thereupon Adam realized the importance of repentance.[6] The Midrash also states that when Adam violated the prohibition of eating from the forbidden fruit, he implored God not to mete out the punishment of death on the very same day,

[1] توبة having the same meaning as the Hebrew term תשובה (repentance), from the root שוב, "return".

[2] Baiḍāwī, Vol. I, p. 21.

(فتاب عليه) رجع عليه بالرحمة وقبول التوبة وانما رتبه بالفاء على تلقى الكلمات لتضمنه معنى التوبة وهو الاعتراف بالذنب والندم عليه والعزم على ان لا يعود اليه.

Cf. Mahdi Allam, "The Theory of Forgiveness as expressed in the Qur'ān," in *Manchester Literary and Phil. Society*, Warrington, 1939, Vol. LXXXIII, pp. 63–79.

[3] ויקרא ה' אלהים אל האדם . . . הקדים לו מדת רחמים למדת הדין . . . וכשחזר אצל האדם, לא חייבו אלא רמז לו לעשות תשובה, מנין, אמר ר' ברכיה בשם ר' לוי שאמר לו בזעת אפיך תאכל לחם עד שובך . . . אין שובך אלא לשון תשובה . . . (תנחומא, תזריע, יא [B])

[4] Gen. 3:19, עד שובך אל האדמה.

[5] ויצא קין מלפני ה' וישב בארץ נוד (בראשית ד, ט"ז), עד שהוא יוצא פגע בו אדם הראשון א"ל מה נעשה בדינך, אמר אילולי שהודיתי כבר הייתי אבוד מן העולם. באותה שעה אמר אדם הראשון טוב להודות לה' (תהלים צ"ב, ב) (תנחומא, בראשית, כה [B]). Cf. שוחר טוב, פצ"ב, מ.

[6] קין אמר לאדם. עשיתי תשובה ונתפשרתי . . . התחיל אדם הראשון מטפח על פניו אמר כך היא כחה של תשובה, ואני לא הייתי יודע, מיד עמד אדם הראשון ואמר מזמור שיר ליום השבת, טוב להודות לה' (בראשית רבה, פכ"ב, יב). Cf. B. ‘A. Z. 8a; *Lev. Rab.* 10, 5.

but one thousand years hence (God's day), so that he would have ample time to repent.[7]

Ṭabarī and Zamakhsharī[8] relate that Adam pleaded with God: "Didst Thou create me? Didst Thou imbue me with Thy spirit? Didst Thou place mercy before anger?" Such a plea is, to our knowledge, not to be found in rabbinic sources. However, the idea that God placed mercy before anger in His dealing with Adam is explicitly mentioned in rabbinic sources where it is stated that the reason for God's calling to Adam, "Where art thou?", was to place mercy before judgment and thus induce Adam to repent.[9] Teaching Adam to repent has influenced the whole world to learn the art of asking forgiveness.[10]

[7] הקב"ה גזר על אדה"ר כי ביום אכלך ממנו מות תמות ואדם התפלל שלא יהיה זה ממש באותו היום אלא ימתין לו יומו של הקב"ה בכדי שיעשה תשובה וגזר על עצמו תענית כל ימיו (עשרה מאמרות, דף ל"ה, ע"ג' quoted in מדרש תלפיות ענף אדם הראשון).

[8] Ṭabarī, Vol. I, p. 187:

...قال اي رب الم تخلقني بيدك قال بلى قال اي رب الم تنفخ في من روحك قال بلى قال اي رب الم تسكني جنتك قال بلى قال اي رب الم تسبق رحمتك غضبك قال بلى....

Zamakhsharī, Vol. I, p. 70:

...قال يا ربّ الم تخلقني بيدك قال بلى قال يا ربّ الم تنفخ في الروح من روحك قال بلى قال يا ربّ الم تسبق رحمتُك غضبك قال بلى...

[9] ויקרא ה' אל' אל האדם... אין ה' אלא מדת הרחמים... הקדים לו מדת הרחמים למדת הדין... שיעשה תשובה (תנחומא תזריע, יא [B]). ויאמר לו איכה, וכי אין הקב"ה יודע היכן הוא אלא שפתח לו דרך אולי ישוב כו' (מדרש אגדה, T.S., Vol. II, p. 262 n.). Cf. also: ועתה פן ישלח ידו אמר רבי אבא בר כהנא מלמד שפתח לו הקב"ה פתח של תשובה (בראשית רבה, כ"א, ו).

[10] אדם הראשון אחר שחטא ישב בתענית כל ימיו... ומה עשה הקב"ה פשט ימינו שהוא מדת החסד וקבלו כי בחסד יכופר עון והעלהו בתשובה והוריד נשמתו של שת וזהו משה מת בתשובה וממנו למדו כל הדורות לעשות תשובה (ספר הפליאה במדרש תלפיות, ענף אדם הראשון).

VERSES 38 and 44

> O ye children of Israel! remember my favours with which I have favoured you; fulfil my covenant and I will fulfil your covenant.
>
> O ye children of Israel! remember my favours which I have favoured you with, and that I have preferred you above the worlds.

Compare the rabbinic dictum: "You have made me a unique object of your love in the world, and I shall make you a unique object of My love in the world."[1]

Similarly, the Bible states: "And I will establish My covenant[2] between Me and thee and thy seed after thee throughout their generations for an everlasting covenant, to be a God unto thee and to thy seed after thee. And I will give unto thee, and to thy seed after thee, the land of thy sojournings, all the land of Canaan, for an everlasting possession; and I will be their God" (Gen. 17:7–9). The word "covenant" is frequently mentioned in the Scriptures,[3] e. g.: "Now therefore, if ye will hearken unto My voice indeed, and keep My covenant, then ye shall be Mine own treasure[4] from among all peoples; for all the earth is Mine" (Exod. 19:5).

According to *Midrash Tanḥuma* the foundation of the world is the Torah, with which God favored the Israelites, that they should study and obey its precepts day and night, and be blessed by Him.[5] A similar idea is found in Ṭabarī, who also interprets the favors

[1] B. Ḥag. 3a. Cf. ברית הן הן הדברים שנאמרו לו למשה בסיני (פסחים לח, ע״ב) and שבמדה שאדם מודד בה מודדים לו . . . (ספרי בהעלתך, פסקא ק״ו [F]). See 3:111: "What ye do of good surely God will not deny, for God knows those who fear." Also 2:147.

[2] Cf. וזכרתי אני את בריתי . . . והקימותי לך ברית עולם (יחזקאל ט״ז, ס); והקימותי אני את בריתי (יחזקאל ט״ז, ס״ב).

[3] Ps. 105:8, 9, 10, זכר לעולם בריתו . . . אשר כרת את אברהם . . . לחק לישראל ברית עולם. Cf. Exod. 19:5; 34:28; Deut. 5:3; 9:9–11; 26:18; Mishnah Ab. 3:18: חביבים ישראל.

[4] The Hebrew term *'am segullah* is translated by some as "peculiar treasure" or "peculiar people," the Latin translation being *peculium*. The Targumim, both *Onkelos* and *Yerushalmi* give as its meaning "beloved," חביבין מכל עממיא. Cf. also: ומלת סגלה. דבר נכבד ונחמד ולא ימצא אחר כמהו. וטעם כי לי כל הארץ, דבק עם מכל העמים. כמו כי לי כל עמי הארץ. וזהו ואבדיל אתכם מכל העמים להיות לי (אבן עזרא, שמות י״ט, ה).

[5] Gen. 1, 13 [B]; the Torah was given to Adam after he repented as a substitute for the Garden of Eden which he had lost (אדר״נ, פרקים א–ב). Cf.: כי אם שמוע תשמע

as referring to the Scriptures, the prophets and to the miracles in Egypt.[6] The Rashbam offers a similar explanation.[7] But Rabbi Obadia Sforno gives a more specific reason. He says: "Although the entire human species is dear to Me . . . yet you are dearest of all . . . thereby will you be more beloved to Me than all the other peoples for you shall be to Me a kingdom of priests, to understand and to teach the entire human race to call in the name of the Lord and to worship Him."[8]

לקולי ועשית כל אשר אדבר והייתם לי סגולה מכל העמים שתהיו בידי סגולה כדבר נחמד לא ימסרנו המלך ביד אחר. . . ואמר כי לי כל הארץ. כטעם אשר חלק ה' אותם לכל העמים, ואתכם לקח ה' (רמב"ן, שמות י"ט, ה).

[6] Ṭabarī, Vol. I, p. 191:

اصطفاؤه منهم الرسل وانزاله عليهم الكتب واستنقاذه اياهم مما كانوا فيه من البلاء والضراء من فرعون.....

[7] *Ad loc.*; cf. Moshe Greenberg, "Segullā," *JAOS*, 1952, Vol. LXXI (3), pp. 172–74; Boaz Cohen, "Peculium in Jewish and Roman Law," in *PAAJR*, XX (1951), pp. 135–234. The divine communication with Moses was for the sake of Israel. B. B. B. 121b; Rashi to Deut. 2:17: ללמדך שאין השכינה שורה על הנביאים אלא בשביל ישראל.

[8] אף על פי שכל המין האנושי יקר אצלי מכל יתר הנמצאים השפלים כי הוא לבדו המכוון בהם. כאמרם ז"ל (אבות) חביב אדם שנברא בצלם. מכל מקום אתם תהיו לי סגולה מכלם. . . ובזה תהיו סגולה מכלם כי תהיו ממלכת כהנים להבין ולהורות לכל המין האנושי לקרא כלם בשם יי' ולעבדו שכם אחד כמו שיהיה ענין ישראל לעתיד לבא. כאמרו ואתם כהני יי' תקראו, וכאמרו כי מציון תצא תורה (ספורנו, שמות י"ט, ה, ו).

VERSE 46

> When we saved you from Pharaoh's people who sought to wreak you evil and woe, slaughtering your sons and letting your women live; in that was a great trial for you from your Lord.

Muḥammad here combines two stories: the biblical tale about Pharaoh's decree to kill the sons "upon the birthstool"[1] and the midrashic legend that Pharaoh was stricken with leprosy and ordered the slaughter of the Israelite children in order to bathe in their blood.[2]

Zamakhsharī,[3] Baiḍāwī and Ṭabarī[4] quote a tradition that the Egyptian wise men foretold to Pharaoh that a male child would be born that year who would inflict defeat upon him and crush his empire. This caused Pharaoh to decree the death of all male children.

This tradition is well known in the Talmud, where it is related that Pharaoh decreed the slaughter of all male children, because the astrologers had warned him that a boy was soon to be born to the Israelites who would overthrow him.[5]

The Midrash also describes how Pharaoh's people "sought to wreak" the Israelites "evil and woe." "The taskmasters of Pharaoh were beating the Israelites in order that they should make (for them) the tale of bricks, and it is said, 'And the tale of the bricks, which they did make heretofore, ye shall lay upon them' (Ex. 5:8). The

[1] Exod. 1:15–22; Rashi, *ad loc.*

[2] למה נתאנחו לפי שאמרו חרטומי מצרים אין לך רפואה אם לא נשחוט מקטני ישראל מאה וחמשים בערב ומאה וחמשים בבקר ורחץ בדמיהם שתי פעמים ביום (שמות רבה פא, לד). Cf. also: והוה ביומיא סגיאייא האינון ואיתכתש מלכא דמצרים ופקיד לקטלא בוכרייא דבני ישראל בגין למיסחי באדמיהון ואתאנחו בני ישראל... (תרגום ירושלמי, שמות ב', כ"ג).

[3] Zamakhsharī, Vol. I, p. 75:

لان الكهنة انذروا فرعون بانه يُولَد مولود يكون على يده هلاكه.

Cf. Baiḍāwī, *ad loc.*

[4] Ṭabarī, Vol. I, p. 208:

فقالت الكهنة سيولد العام بمصر غلام يكون هلاكك على يديه فبعث في اهل مصر نساء قوابل فاذا ولدت امرأة غلاما اتى به فرعون فقتله...

[5] B. Soṭ. 12a; cf. [B] ילקוט שמעוני שמות, רמז קס"ד; לקח טוב, שמות א', טז.

Israelites were gathering the straw of the wilderness, and they were carrying it on their asses and (also on) their wives, and their sons. The straw of the wilderness pierced their heels, and the blood was mingled with the mortar . . . the Holy One, blessed be He, descended and smote the firstborn of the Egyptians . . ."[6]

Pharaoh's cruel decree brought havoc to the whole community. It is related in the Talmud that "Amram was the greatest man of his generation; when he saw that the wicked Pharaoh had decreed '*Every son that is born ye shall cast into the river*,' he said, In vain do we labour. He rose and divorced his wife. All (the Israelites) thereupon arose and divorced their wives. His daughter said to him, 'Father, thy decree is more severe than Pharaoh's; because Pharaoh decreed only against the males whereas thou hast decreed against the males and females. Pharaoh only decreed concerning this world whereas thou hast decreed concerning this world and the World to Come. In the case of the wicked Pharaoh there is a doubt whether his decree will be fulfilled or not, whereas in thy case, though thou art righteous, it is certain that thy decree will be fulfilled . . . He arose and took his wife back; and they all arose and took their wives back."[7]

The style in Verses 46–95 of this Sura is much like that of the Mosaic admonitions in the Book of Deuteronomy.[8] It also recalls the biblical expressions describing the hardships of the Israelites at the hands of the Egyptian taskmasters.[9]

[6] *P.R.E.*, pp. 385–86; cf. Geiger, *op. cit.*, pp. 153–54.

[7] B. Soṭ. 12a. Cf. Exod. 1:11–21.

[8] Deut. 29:1–5.

[9] Rashi in explaining the Hebrew word בפרך in Exod. 1:13 writes that the Israelites were put to rigorous labor which crushed and shattered their bodies. See also B. B. Soṭ. 12a–b.

VERSE 47

When we divided for you the sea and saved you and drowned Pharaoh's people while ye looked on.

Chapter 14, verses 1–29 in Exodus relates the entire history of the Israelites in Egypt culminating in the events related in the 30th verse: "Thus the Lord saved Israel that day out of the hand of the Egyptians; and Israel saw the Egyptians dead upon the sea-shore." In verse 21, God commands Moses to stretch out "his hand over the sea." According to the Midrash, when Moses "stretched out his hand over the sea" the waters refused to be divided. "What did the Holy One, blessed be He, do? He looked at the sea, and the waters saw the face of the Holy One, blessed be He, and they trembled and quaked, and descended into the depth . . ."[1] The Egyptians then "entered the sea after him (Pharaoh) . . . Forthwith the waters returned, and covered them . . ."[2]

Ṭabarī writes that the Koran in using the word *bikum* implies that the sea was divided[3] into twelve parts, a number equal to the twelve tribes. This is found in the *Mekilta Beshalaḥ*.[4]

According to Zamakhsharī, the Israelites refused to cross the sea unless the tribes, separated by the walls of water, were able to see each other while crossing.[5]

[1] *P.R.E.*, pp. 329–30.

[2] *Ibid.*, p. 331; cf. [W] מכילתא, בשלח, פ"ו.

[3] Ṭabarī, Vol. I, p. 210:

فصلنا بكم البحر لانهم كانوا اثنى عشر سبطا ففرق البحر اثنى عشر طريقا فسلك كل سبط منهم طريقا منها.

Cf. Zamakhsharī, Vol. I, p. 75:

فان قلت ما معنى [بكم] — قلت فيه اوجه — ان يراد انها كانوا يسلكونه ويتفرق الماء عند سلوكهم فكانما فرق بهم كما يفرق بين الشيئين بما يوسط بينهما.

[4] ([W] מכילתא דויסע, בשלח פ"א) . . . ברא שנים עשר מבועין כנגד שנים עשר שבטי יעקב . . .
Cf. Ps. 136:13: לגזר ים סוף לגזרים as well as: (פדר"א, פמ"ב) ונעשו לשנים עשר שבילים.

[5] Zamakhsharī, Vol. I, p. 75:

وروى ان بني اسرائيل قالوا لموسى اين اصحابنا لا نراهم قال سيروا فانهم على طريق مثل طريقكم قالوا لا نرضى حتى نراهم

That the Israelites agreed to cross the sea only provided Moses met their conditions is also told in the Midrash.[6] According to Jewish tradition, making the walls transparent so that the tribes could see one another was one of the ten miracles performed at the Red Sea.[7]

Jewish tradition also relates that Pharaoh sent along some Egyptians to see that Israel returned after three days. When the Egyptians notified Pharaoh that Israel refused to return, Pharaoh mobilized his army and set out in six hundred iron chariots. At the end of the sixth day of the Exodus, the Israelites noticed the Egyptians approaching. Moses ordered his followers to advance all that night. The Egyptian chariots lost their wheels in the heat of the fiery pillar that moved behind Israel and therefore proceeded with great difficulty. Finally Israel reached the Sea. It separated and Israel passed to the other side. The Egyptians followed. When they were all in the midst of the Sea, the waters began pouring back and drowned them all.[8]

Ṭabarī relates that when all the Israelites entered the sea, Pharaoh watched them from the shore while riding on a male horse. Then Gabriel appeared on a female horse and when the male horse saw her, he ran after her. Pharaoh's horse was followed by the other Egyptian horsemen and they all entered the sea.[9] This legend is found in

فقال اللّهم اعنّي على اخلاقهم السّيئة فاوحي اليه ان قُل بعصاك هكذا فقال بها على الحيطان فصارت فيه كوى فتراءوا وتسامعوا كلامهم.

[6] בשעה שעמדו אבותינו על הים אמר משה להם קומו עברו אמרו לא נעבור עד שנרא' הים נקבים נקבים נטל משה מטהו והכה על הים ונעש' הים נקבים נקבים (אדר"נ, פל"ג; מכילתא, בשלח פ"ד [W]).

[7] וקפאו המים ונעשו ככלי זכוכית (תנחומא, בשלח, עט, ע"ב). Cf. Grünbaum, *op. cit.*, p. 167.

[8] [W] מכילתא, בשלח פ"ו; cf. B. Pes. 118b.

[9] Ṭabarī, Vol. I, p. 211:

لما دخلت بنو اسرائيل فلم يبق منهم احد اقبل فرعون وهو على حصان له من الخيل حتى وقف على شفير البحر وهو قائم على حاله فهاب الحصان ان ينفذ فعرض له جبريل على فرس انثى وديق فقربها منه فشمها الفحل فلما شمها تبعها فتقدم معها الحصان عليه فرعون فلما راى خيل فرعون فرعون قد دخل دخلوا معه وجبريل امامه وهم يتبعون فرعون وميكائيل على فرس من

Jewish sources. "The Egyptians desired to follow after Israel, but they turned backwards, fearing lest the waters would return over them. What did the Holy One, blessed be He, do? He appeared before them like a man riding on the back of a mare, as it is said, 'To a steed in Pharaoh's chariots' (Cant. 1:9). The horse on which Pharaoh rode saw the mare (of God), and it neighed and ran and entered the sea after it."[10]

In the Pentateuch there is no statement to the effect that Pharaoh himself was drowned. It tells only about Pharaoh's people. Rabbinic sources,[11] however, tell that Pharaoh was saved in order to relate to the Egyptians the great miracles God had shown His people. Similarly does the Koran (8:56; 11:99) talk about the Egyptians and state that Pharaoh was saved because he began to believe in God and in order that he might be an example for future generations.

According to Zamakhsharī, the Israelites saw how the Egyptians were drowned and all their doubts disappeared.[12] The same idea is

خلف القوم يسوقهم يقول الحقوا بصاحبكم حتى اذا فصل جبريل
من البحر ليس امامه احد ووقف ميكائيل على ناحيته الاخرى
وليس خلفه احد....

Ṭabarī's reference to Michael recalls the following Midrash: התחילו שרי האומות מלמדים סנגוריא על מצרים. כיון שראה מיכאל כך, רמז לגבריאל וטס למצרים טיסה אחת ושמט לבנה עם טיטה... מיד ישב עליהם הקב"ה במדת־הדין וטבעם בים (מדרש אבכיר). Cf. הראה להם הקב"ה דמות נקבה בים, והסוסים היו מזוינים רדפו אחריהם (לקח טוב, בשלח, פי"ד, כג [B]).

[10] *P.R.E.*, p. 331; cf. בשעה שירדו ישראל לים ירד גבריאל עמהם (מדרש אבכיר); מדרש הגדול, בשלח; Grünbaum, *op. cit.* p. 166; 10:90–2; Geiger, *op. cit.*, p. 162; *Aggadath Shir ha-Shirim* (Sch.), p. 17; אדר"נ, פרק כ"ז; and לקח טוב, בשלח, כג [B].

[11] חוץ מפרעה (מכילתא בשלח פ"ו [W]). Cf. also: רבי נחוניא בן הקנה אומר תדע לך כח התשובה. בא וראה מפרעה מלך מצרים, שמרד בצור עליון הרבה מאד, שנאמר מי ה' אשר אשמע בקולו (שמות ה, ב) ובאותו לשון שחטא בו בלשון עשה תשובה שנאמר (שמות ט"ו, י"א) מי כמוכה באלים ה' והצילו הקב"ה מבין המתים. ומניין שלא מת? שנאמר: כי עתה שלחתי את ידי ואך אותך (שמות ט, ט"ו) והעמידו הקב"ה מן המתים, לספר כח גבורתו. ומנין שהעמידו? שנאמר (שם, ט"ז): ואולם בעבור זאת העמדתיך. והלך ומלך בנינוה (פדר"א, פמ"ג); and: פרעה נעשה מלך בנינוה ותיכף ציית לקריאת יונה; פרעה נשאר להגיד ולספר כח וגבורה של מלכו של עולם (מדרש ויושע 154, א) (לקח טוב, בשלח, פי"ד, כח [B]). However, Hirschberg (*op. cit.*, p. 237) and Horovitz (*Kor. Unt.*, pp. 23 f.) see in this story Islāmic influence. See Ps. 136:15; שמו"ר כ, א; שו"ט ק"ו, ה.

[12] Zamakhsharī, Vol. I, p. 75: [وانتم تنظرون] الى ذلك وتشاهدونه ولا تشكّون فيه.

found in the Aggada: The Israelites saw the Egyptians dead in order that they should not say that the Egyptians escaped from the other side of the sea just as the Israelites came out from this side.[13]

The Koranic expression "while you looked on" recalls the following legend: "Rabbi Simon said: On the fourth day the Israelites encamped by the edge of the sea. . . . The Egyptians were floating . . . upon the surface of the waters, and a north wind went forth and cast them opposite the camp of Israel, and the Israelites went and saw them, and they recognized them . . ."[14]

[13] כדי (ואחד מן הדברים הוא) מפני ארבע דברים ראו ישראל את המצרים מתים, שלא יהיו אומרים כשם שעלינו מן הים מצד זה כך המצרים עלו מן הים מצד אחר (מכילתא, בשלח, פ"ו [W]). Cf. also, [B] לקח טוב, בשלח, פי"ד, ל.

[14] *P.R.E.*, p. 332.

VERSES 48–51

> When we treated with Moses forty nights, then ye took the calf after he had gone and ye did wrong. Yet then we forgave you after that; perhaps ye may be grateful. And when we gave Moses the Scriptures and the Discrimination; perhaps ye will be guided. When Moses said to his people, 'O my people! Ye have wronged yourselves in taking this calf; repent unto your Creator and kill each other!'

The Talmud relates: "When Moses ascended on high, he said to Israel, I will return at the end of forty days, at the beginning of the sixth hour (at midday). At the end of forty days Satan came and confounded the world. Said he to them: 'Where is your teacher Moses?' 'He has ascended on high,' they answered him. 'The sixth (hour) has come,' said he to them, but they disregarded him . . . (Thereupon) he showed them a vision of his bier, and this is what they said to Aaron, *for* this *Moses*, *the man*, etc."[1] Thus, upon Moses' seeming disappearance, the people sought a divine substitute to "go before us" (Exod. 32:1).

The Koran speaks here of forty nights only, ignoring the biblical forty days: "And Moses entered into the midst of the cloud, and went up into the mount; and Moses was in the mount forty days and forty nights" (Ex. 24:18). This is perhaps explained by an interpretation found in Rashi[2] in his comment on Exodus 32:1, which most likely is taken from early midrashic sources: "When Moses went up to the mountain he said to them, 'At the end of forty days I shall return within (the first) six hours (of the day).' They thought that the same day that he went up was part of the number (of forty); but he had said to them whole (days), (i. e.) forty days and their nights together with them, but the day of his ascent did not (include) its night together with it." . . .[3] Thus it happened that when Moses did not return at

[1] B. Shab. 89a; cf. notes to 2:52, 53, 54, 57, 80, 86, 87, 102.

[2] כתרגומו לשון איחור . . . כי כשעלה משה להר אמר להם לסוף ארבעים יום אני בא בתוך ו' שעות כסבורים הם שאותו יום שעלה מן המנין הוא והוא אמר שלמים ארבעים יום ולילו עמו ויום עליית ואין לילו שהרי עמו בז' בסיון עלה נמצא יום ארבעים בשבעה עשר בתמוז בי"ו בא השטן וערבב את העולם והראה דמות חשך ואפלה וערבוביא לומר ודאי מת משה לכך בא ערבוביא לעולם אמר להם מת משה שכבר באו שש שעות ולא בא . . . וא"א לומר שלא טעו אלא ביום המעונן בין קודם חצות בין לאחר חצות שהרי לא ירד משה עד יום המחרת . . . (רש"י, שמות, ל"ב, א)

[3] *P.R.C.*, Vol. II, p. 399.

the expected hour, the Israelites made the golden calf. This may be the reason why Muḥammad refers to the forty nights only, since it was the fortieth night that caused Israel's sin.[4]

The Midrash also relates that Moses "burnt the calf with fire, and powdered it, like the dust of the earth, and he cast its dust upon the face of the waters . . . He made Israel drink the water (with the dust of the calf). Everyone who had kissed the calf with all his heart, his upper lip and bones became golden, and the tribe of Levi (which did not associate itself with the affair of the calf) slew him, until there fell of Israel about three thousand men."[5]

Comparably with these details the Koran says: "then ye took the calf after he had gone and ye did wrong." In 2:87, repeating the sin of the calf, the Koran states: "and they were made to drink the calf down into their hearts for their unbelief,"— a detail found in Exodus 32:20: "And he took the calf which they had made, and burnt it with fire, and ground it to powder, and strewed it upon the water, and made the children of Israel drink of it." This would indicate that the Koranic calf, like the biblical, was not a live one.

The Koranic statement: "Yet then we forgave you after that; perhaps ye may be grateful," is also paralleled in the Midrash. "By the merit of the three patriarchs, the three angels, Wrath, Anger, and Temper, were restrained from (doing harm to) Israel. But two (angels) remained. Moses spake before the Holy One, blessed be He: Sovereign of all the Universe! For the sake of the oath which Thou didst swear unto them, keep back (the angel) Destruction from Israel . . . and Destruction was kept back from Israel, as it is said, 'But he, being full of compassion, forgave their iniquity and *destroyed* them not' (Ps. 78:38). Moses spake before the Holy One, blessed be He: Sovereign of all worlds! For the sake of Thy great and holy Name, which Thou didst make known unto me, hold back from Israel (the angel called) Glow of Anger . . . What did Moses do? He dug into the earth in the possession of Gad, as (though for the foundation of) a large dwelling, and he buried 'Fierce Anger' in the earth, like a man who is bound in the prison. Every time Israel sins it arises and opens its mouth to bite with its breath, and to destroy Israel. Moses pronounced against it the (divine) Name, and brought it back beneath the earth. Therefore is its name called Peor (the one who opens)."[6]

[4] Cf. Zamakhsharī and Baiḍāwī *ad loc.*, about the forty nights.

[5] *P.R.E.*, pp. 356–57; cf. *Targum Yerushalmi*, Exod. 32:20.

[6] *Ibid.*, pp. 357–58. Cf. also: . . . והיה מדבר עם משה היאך מאבדן וכיון שאמר משה זכור לאברהם וגו' זכר הקב"ה ואמר אם כן חוזר אני בי מיד וינחם ה' וגו' . . . (אגדת בראשית, ע' ט"ו).

The Koranic reference to the Book points to the verse: "And this is the law which Moses set before the children of Israel" (Deut. 4:44). Scholars and commentators have been puzzled by the meaning of the term *Furqān.*[7] Some have rendered it as the *illumination* (3:2), *deliverance* (8:29), *Mosaic Revelation* (2:50, 21:49, 25:1), *distinction* (between right and wrong) (2:181), or *divine help* (21:49). Professor Margoliouth suggests: "there is some probability that the 'Sayings of the Fathers' called by the Jews *Perākīm* lies hidden in the name of a sacred book which he (Muḥammad) calls Furqān."[8] Baiḍawī suggests that it means the Psalms.[9] Our present study shows a large number of references in the Koran to *Pirḳe Aboth* and to the Psalms,[10] which would lead us to the conclusion that Muḥammad was aware of these books since they were used reverently by the Jews in Arabia. They were read by the latter in their Synagogues, taught by them in their schools and were considered a guide for ethical conduct. According to Horovitz: "it is not quite out of place to call attention to the Aramaic form 'pirḳīn,' which Mohammed may have changed into 'furḳān,' and the word 'pirḳān' would be even still closer to the Ḳoranic form, which form 'pirḳān' is repeatedly mentioned in the Baraita Erubin 54b and which is there employed with reference to the doctrines handed over by Moses to the individual groups and to the people as a whole."[11]

[7] Geiger, *op. cit.*, p. 55; Hirschfeld, *New Researches* . . ., p. 68; Margoliouth, *ERE*, Vol. X, p. 539; Nöldeke, *Neue Beiträge* . . ., pp. 23 f.; J. Wensinck, *Furḳān*, E. I., Vol. II (1927), p. 120; Mark Lidzbarski, "Islām und Salām" in *ZSVG*, Vol. I, p. 92; J. Horovitz, *HUCA*, pp. 216–18; R. Dvorak, "Über die Fremdwörter im Koran," in *Sitzungsberichte der Wiener Akademie*, Philos.-hist. Klasse, Bd. 109 (Wien, 1885), p. 499.

[8] D. S. Margoliouth, *op. cit.*, p. 145.

[9] Baiḍāwī, 3:2 الزبور. However, Baiḍāwī, Vol. I, p. 24, in his comment on this verse, explains the term فرقان as a derivation from the verb فرق, *i. e.* "to separate," which denotes the Torah, since the Torah distinguishes between truth and falsehood and between things permitted and prohibited. Zamakhsharī gives the same explanation, Vol. I, p. 75. Cf. Horovitz, *HUCA*, pp. 205–6; Fränkel, *Fremdwörter*, p. 248; 4:163; Ṭabarī, *Tafsīr*, Vol. 6, p. 18.

[10] Many of the sayings and ideas in Suras two and three appear to be a replica of Psalms 104–8. In another place in the Koran, Muḥammad states, "and already we have written in the Psalms (الزبور) after the reminder that 'the earth shall my righteous servants inherit'" (21:105). The latter phrase repeats Ps. 37:29, "the righteous shall inherit the land, and dwell therein forever." Cf. Schwally, *ZDMG*, LII, p. 133; Is. 60:21.

[11] Horovitz, *HUCA*, pp. 217–18. It is possible that Muḥammad adopted the

As for the clause, "and kill each other," the original reads *faqtulū anfusakum*[12] which may also mean "kill yourselves." In Baiḍāwī and Zamakhsharī we find two explanations: one, that those who did not worship the golden calf should kill those who did;[13] the second, that they should destroy their evil inclinations, for he who never chastises himself never pleases himself, and he who never kills himself never lives.[14] The first explanation has a counterpart in rabbinic literature. The Talmud[15] states that Levi's tribe did not worship the golden calf and therefore was told to kill the sinners.

Regarding the expression "kill each other," Baiḍāwī comments: "Kill yourselves so that you may live."[16] This is a counterpart of the talmudic statement: "What shall a man do to live? They replied: 'Let him mortify himself.' "[17]

As to *thumma 'afaunā 'ankum*[18] (then we forgave you), Zamakhsharī states that it refers to the Israelites making atonement[19] for the sin of the golden calf. A broader concept of the efficacy of repentance, no matter how grievous the sins might be, is constantly stressed by the rabbis: "The Israelites made the (golden) calf only in order to place a good argument in the mouth of the penitents."[20]

term *furqān* from the word לפרקים in the talmudic passage: הלומד תורה לפרקים (סנהדרין צ״ט, ע״ב). Of interest is the phrase *yauma 'l-furqāni* in 8:43 which is identical with the expression in the Targum I Sam. 11:13, פורקנא, meaning "deliverance." See, however, J. Rivlin, "הפרקאן (الفرقان) בקוראן" in *Gotthold Weil Jubilee Volume*, pp. 24–33.

[12] فَاقْتُلُوا أَنْفُسَكُم.

[13] Zamakhsharī, Vol. I, p. 75:

وقيل أُمر من لم يعبد العجل ان يقتلوا العَبَدَةَ.

[14] Baiḍāwī, Vol. I, p. 25:

قطع الشهوات كما قيل من لم يعذب نفسه لم ينعمها ومن لم يقتلها لم يحيها.

[15] B. Yom. 66b.

[16] Baiḍāwī, Vol. I, p. 25.

[17] Literally, " 'kill himself,' with study and hard work," מה יעבד איניש ויחיה אמרו ליה ימות עצמו (תמיד ל״ב, ע״א). Cf. 2:149, note 7.

[18] ثم عفونا عنكم.

[19] Zamakhsharī, Vol. I, p. 75, حين تبتم.

[20] לא עשו ישראל את העגל אלא ליתן פתחון פה לבעלי תשובה (עבודה זרה, ד, ע״ב).

VERSE 52

And when ye said to Moses, 'O Moses! we will not believe in thee until we see God manifestly,' and the thunderbolt caught you while ye yet looked on.[1]

This story is found in the Midrash: "The voice of the second (commandment) went forth, and they (the Israelites) were quickened (after they were alive and had fallen on their faces and died), and they stood upon their feet and said to Moses: Moses, our teacher! We are unable to hear any more the voice of the Holy One, blessed be He, for we shall die even as we died (just now), as it is said, 'And they said unto Moses, Speak thou with us, and we will hear: but let not God speak with us, *lest we die*' (Exod. 20:19). And now, why should we die as we died (just now)?"[2]

Sifre[3] takes the Hebrew word *Bamar'ah* in Num. 12:6 to mean the vision of the word and not of the *Shekinah*. According to Sa'adia Gaon and others, the various allusions in the Bible to "seeing God" refer to a special light created for the vision of the prophets.[4] The phrase "They saw the God of Israel" (Ex. 24:10) is explained by Abraham Ibn Ezra to mean "They saw in a vision."[5] In like manner, Isaiah and Ezekiel "saw" the throne of God. The Talmud states that at "every word which went forth from the mouth of the Holy One, blessed be He, the souls of Israel departed, for it is said, *My soul went forth when he spake* (Cant. 5:6) . . . . He brought down the dew with which He will resurrect the dead and revive them, as it is said: *Thou, O God, didst send a plentiful rain, Thou didst confirm thine inheritance, when it was weary*" (Ps. 68:10).[6]

[1] Cf. notes to 2:26, 60; and 4:152.

[2] *P.R.E.*, p. 325. According to Reckendorf, "Muḥammad invented this story about the Israelites' desire to 'see God manifestly,' but they were unable to see his vision and died. Then Moses interceded for them and God revived them," זאת בדה מחמד מלבו כי בני ישראל בקשו לראות ה׳ עין בעין ויראה להם, אך לא יכלו לישא את מראהו וימותו כלם; ובהתפלל משה בעדם החיים ה׳. (אלקורן או המקרא מאת צבי חיים הרמן רקנדארף, לפסיא [לייפציג], תרי״ז, דף ה).

[3] [F] ספרי, בהעלותך, פיסקא קג; B. Shab. 88b–89a.

[4] V. Aptowitzer, בית המדרש של מעלה על פי האגדה, *Tarbiẓ*, Vol. II, # 3, 1931, pp. 278 f.

[5] במראה נבואה.

[6] B. Shab. 88b; cf. Geiger, *op. cit.*, pp. 161–62, quoting the following rabbinical story: שני דברים שאלו ישראל מלפני הקב״ה שיראו כבודו וישמעו קולו והיו רואין את כבודו

According to Baiḍāwī and Zamakhsharī, seventy[7] leaders requested of Moses to see God, otherwise they would not believe in Him. This probably is based on the story in the Bible that seventy of the elders of Israel saw the God of Israel: "Then went up Moses, and Aaron, Nadab, and Abihu, and seventy of the elders of Israel; and they saw the God of Israel . . ." (Exod. 24:9–10).

ושומעין את קולו שנ' הן הראנו ה' אלהינו את כבודו ואת גדלו וכתיב ואת קולו שמענו מתוך האש ולא היה בהם כח לעמוד כיון שבאו לסיני ונגלה להם פרחה נשמתם על שדבר עמהם שנ' נפשי יצאה בדברו אבל התורה בקשה עליהם רחמים מלפני הקב"ה יש מלך משיא בתו והרג אנשי ביתו כל העולם כלו שמחים ובניך מתים מיד חזרה נשמתן שנאמר תורת ה' תמימה משיבת נפש. However, Hirschfeld in *New Researches . . .*, p. 107 n., claims that Geiger misunderstood verse 52. For, says he, in the Koran "it is the people who desire to see God, whilst Muhammed confounded Ex. 20:19 with 33:18 and Num. 16:22–35." Cf. also [W] מכילתא יתרו, פ"ט; [B] לקח טוב, יתרו פי"ט יד, כ; and A. S. Yahuda, "A Contribution to Qur'ān and Ḥadīth Interpretation" in *Goldziher Memorial Volume*, Budapest, 1948, Part I, pp. 286 f.

[7] Zamakhsharī, Vol. I, p. 76: سبعون. Cf. Baiḍāwī, *ad loc.*

VERSE 53

Then we raised you up after your death; perhaps ye may be grateful.

According to Moslem commentators, when Moses saw his seventy companions stricken dead he immediately "interceded for their restoration to life, on the ground that the people might suspect him of their murder." God then restored them to life.[1] This Koranic verse seems to refer to the legend in the Talmud[2] that the Israelites, upon hearing the divine voice, died and were later restored to life. Another version in the Talmud states that the Israelites were restored by the intercession of the Torah itself.[3]

Ṭabarī comments: After the seventy were restored to life, they gazed at each other with amazement and said (to Moses): All your requests from God are fulfilled; pray that we too may become prophets. Moses implored God, whereupon they were inspired with prophecy. This is the meaning of the Koranic sentence: "Then we raised you up after your death."[4] This tradition about the seventy people who became prophets probably has its origin in the biblical story (Num. 11:25): "and the Lord came down in the cloud, . . . and took of the spirit that was upon him, and put it upon the seventy elders . . ."

According to Baiḍāwī,[5] they were punished because of their insistence on seeing God or comprehending Him in corporeal form, imagin-

[1] *Tafsīr-i-Raufi*, quoted by Wherry, *op. cit.*, Vol. I, p. 309.

[2] B. Shab. 88b; cf. notes to 2:52; B. Ḥag. 12b.

[3] 2:52 note 3; cf. Ps. 106:8; "Nevertheless He saved them for His name's sake . . ." Ps. 106:23: "Had not Moses His chosen stood before Him in the breach, to turn back His wrath, lest He should destroy them." Also שני דברים שאלו ישראל מלפני הקב"ה שיראו כבודו וישמעו קולו והיו רואין את כבודו ושומעין את קולו . . . ולא היה בהם כח לעמוד שכיון שבאו לסיני ונגלה להם פרחה נשמתם על שדבר עמהם שנאמר נפשי יצאה בדברו, אבל התורה בקשה עליהם רחמים מלפני הקב"ה . . . מיד חזרה נשמתן . . . (שמות רבה, פכ"ט, ג) see also (במדבר רבה, פ"י, ג) באותה שעה חזר הקב"ה והמתיק להם את הדבור; and Jellinek, *op. cit.*, Part I, p. 69

[4] Ṭabarī, Vol. I, p. 224:

فقاموا وعاشوا رجلا رجلا ينظر بعضهم الى بعض كيف يحيون
فقالوا انت تدعو الله فلا تسأله شيئا الا اعطاك فادعه يجعلنا
انبياء فدعا الله ... فجعلهم انبياء ....

[5] Referring to 2:52.

ing that God possesses dimensions and is comprehensible to the human senses. He adds that some Moslem traditionalists maintain that a fire descended from heaven and killed them.[6] This very same idea is found in Maimonides' *Guide*: "But the 'nobles of the Children of Israel' were impetuous, and allowed their thoughts to go unrestrained: what they perceived was but imperfect"... "They are blamed for the nature of their perception, which was to a certain extent corporeal — a result which necessarily followed, from the fact that they ventured too far before being perfectly prepared. They deserved to perish, but at the intercession of Moses this fate was averted by God for the time. They were afterwards burnt at Taberah, except Nadab and Abihu, who were burnt in the Tabernacle of the congregation, according to what is stated by authentic tradition."[7]

[6] Baiḍāwī, Vol. I, p. 25:
لفرط العناد والتعنت وطلب المستحيل فانهم ظنوا انه تعالى يشبه الاجسام فطلبوا رؤيته رؤية الاجسام في الجهات والاحياز المقابلة للرائى وهى محال بل الممكن ان يرى رؤية منزهة عن الكيفية وذلك للمؤمنين في الآخرة... قيل جاءت نار من السماء فاحرقتهم...
Cf. נשרפו באש שיצאה מן השמים (ספרא, שמיני, עמ"ה [W]).

[7] Moses Maimonides, *The Guide for the Perplexed*, tr. by M. Friedländer, London, 2nd ed. 1942, pp. 18–19. Cf. א"ר לוי וכי לא היה גלוי לפני המקום שאם הוא מראה כבודו לישראל ומשמיען קולו שאינן יכולין לעמוד. אלא צפה הקב"ה שהן עתידין לעשות ע"ז שלא יהו אומרין אילו הראנו את כבודו ואת גדלו והשמיענו את קולו לא היינו עושים ע"ז לכך נאמר שמעה עמי ואדברה (שמות רבה, כט, ג).

VERSE 54

And we overshadowed you with the cloud, and sent down the manna and the quails; 'Eat of the good things we have given you.' They did not wrong us, but it was themselves they were wronging.

In this verse,[1] the Koran mentions the great events in the life of the Israelites in the desert, the pillars of cloud, the manna and the quails. The former served as a protection and the latter provided them with sustenance.

The Talmud declares that the pillar of cloud completed[2] the pillar of fire, and the pillar of fire completed the pillar of cloud. According to a Jewish tradition, when Israel was almost overtaken by the Egyptians before they reached the Sea of Reeds, the pillars changed direction. "And the angel of God, who went before the camp of Israel, removed and went behind them" (Exod. 14:19).[3] This, the Midrash explains, was due to the approach of the Egyptians who had been throwing arrows and stones at the Israelites. The pillar of cloud served as a protection by intercepting the missiles.[4]

The pillar of cloud (one of seven) that moved in front of Israel also served to level hills[5] and to fill valleys so that Israel might have an easy road on which to travel.[6]

[1] Compare Ps. 105:39–40, "He spread a cloud for a screen; And fire to give light in the night. They asked, and He brought quails, And gave them in plenty the bread of heaven."

[2] *I. e.* overlapped (משלים). B. Shab. 23b. Cf. also: לא ימוש הענן מגיד הכתוב שעדיין עמוד הענן קיים היה עמוד האש צומח (מכילתא בשלח, פ"א).

[3] Cf.: ויהי הענן והחשך. הענן לישראל, והחשך למצריים: ויאר את הלילה. ישראל באורה ומצרים באפילה, רואין את ישראל שהיו באורה ואוכלין ושותין ושמחים והיו המצרים מזרקין בהם חצים ואבני בליסטראות, והמלאך והענן מקבלים אותם (לקח טוב, שמות, בשלח פי"ד, כ [B]); also: והיה הענן והמלאך מגין עליהם (מכילתא בשלח, פ"ד).

[4] ונטל מלאכא דיי דמדבר קדם משרייתא דישראל ואתא מן בתריהון ונטל עמודא דעננא מן קדמיהון ושרא מן בתריהון מן בגלל מצראי דבתקין גירין ואבנין לישראל והוה עננא מקביל יתהון (תרגום ירושלמי, שמות, י"ד, י"ט). Also: "... If one of the Israelites dropped out from under the wings of the cloud, the pillar of cloud gathered him from behind until he joined the main body." M.S.N., p. 61.

[5] ואחד שהיה מהלך לפניהם כל הנמוך מגביהו וכל הגבוה מנמיכו . . . (ילקוט שמעוני, בשלח, רמז רכ"ח).

[6] M.S.N., p. 61: "Every hilly place it (the cloud) levelled, and every depression it raised, and it killed the serpents and the scorpions . . ."

Regarding the second part of the Koranic[7] verse, we find a comparable idea in the Talmud: "The flesh for which they asked improperly was given to them at an improper time; whereas the bread for which they asked properly was given to them in its proper time."[8]

The Moslem commentators who discuss this Koranic verse about the miracles in the desert reveal a thorough acquaintance with rabbinic lore. Zamakhsharī writes that the clouds came down to Israel as a protection and followed the Israelites in all their vicissitudes in order to protect them against the sun. Likewise, a pillar of fire descended in the night to illuminate their way. Also their apparel was protected from mud or from being worn out.[9] Each one of these remarks is traceable to rabbinic sources. The rabbis tell us that the clouds formed a canopy,[10] that is, a protection against the sun,[11] and also served to protect the clothing of the Israelites.[12] "The clouds encased them, preventing their apparel from wrinkling and protecting them from dust, thus avoiding the need for laundering."[13]

According to Ṭabarī, the clothing also expanded in proportion with the growth of the people.[14] This tradition, too, has its origin in Jewish sources, which claim that "the Divine clouds of glory rubbed the dirt from their garments and bleached them so that they looked like new; and as the children grew, their garments grew with them."[15]

[7] The Koranic terms for "manna" and "quails" (*Mann* and *Salwā*) are similar to the Hebrew *man* and *selaw* and always occur together. The Aramaic is *Salwe* or *Salwai* (*Targum Jonathan* Num. 11:32). Cf. Horovitz, *HUCA*, pp. 210, 222.

[8] B. Yoma 75a–75b.

[9] Zamakhsharī, Vol. I, p. 77:

وجعلنا الغمام يظلّكم وذلك في التيه سخّر الله لهم السحابَ يسير بسيرهم يظلّهم من الشمس وينزل بالليل عمود من نار يسيرون في ضوءه وثيابهم لا تتّسخ ولا تبلى.

[10] בסכות ענני כבוד היו (ספרא, ויקרא אמור, ע' קג [W]); cf. אין סוכות אלא ענני כבוד (מכילתא, בשלח, פ"א [W]).

[11] וסכה תהיה לצל־יומם מחרב (ישעיה ד, ו). Cf. B. Suk. 2a.

[12] שמלתך לא בלתה מעליך (דברים ח, ד).

[13] ולא היו צריכין תכבוסת . . . ענני כבוד היו מגהצין אותן (ילקוט שמעוני, עקב, רמז תת"נ).

[14] Ṭabarī, Vol. I, p. 227:

وكانت ثيابهم تطول معهم كما تطول الصبيان ولا ينخرق لهم ثوب.

[15] S. Ch., p. 1035 n.; cf.: רבי אלעזר ברבי שמעון שאל את ר"ש בן לקוניא . . . מהו דין

In discussing the manna, Zamakhsharī and Ṭabarī quote a tradition to the effect that it was the kind of food called *Taranjabīn* in Persian.[16] In Jewish literature, the heretic Ḥiwī al-Balkhī, who lived in the 9th century, expresses the same opinion.[17]

Zamakhsharī also adds that the south wind gathered the manna daily for the Israelites.[18] Since there is no mention of a wind in the Bible in connection with the manna, it would appear that Zamakhsharī confuses this with the quails, about which it is stated in the Bible: "And there went forth a wind from the Lord, and brought across quails from the sea, and let them fall by the camp . . ." (Num. 11:31) This is also in line with Ṭabarī's comment that the south wind gathered the quails.[19]

דכתיב שמלתך לא בלתה מעליך . . . ולא היו גדלין? א"ל חלזון הזה כל מה שהוא גדל נרתיקו גדל עמו (ילקוט שמעוני, עקב, רמז תת"נ).

[16] Zamakhsharī, Vol. I, p. 77:
وينزل عليهم [المن] وهو الترنجبين مثل الثلج من طلوع الفجر الى طلوع الشمس لكل انسان صاع. Ṭabarī, Vol. I, p. 225:
المن الترنجبين...

[17] J. Rosenthal, "Ḥiwī al-Balkhī," in *JQR* (New Series), XXXVIII #3, p. 18; cf. Ibn Ezra to Exod. 16:13.

[18] Zamakhsharī, Vol. I, p. 77: ويبعث الله الجنوب فتحشر عليهم.

[19] Ṭabarī, Vol. I, p. 226:
....السلوى طائر كانت تحشرها عليهم الريح الجنوب...

VERSE 57

> When Moses, too, asked drink for his people and we said, 'Strike with thy staff the rock,' and from it burst forth twelve springs; each man among them knew his drinking place. 'Eat and drink of what God has provided, and transgress not on the earth as evildoers.'

In one place in the Bible, Moses was directed to strike the rock: "And the people thirsted there for water; and the people murmured against Moses, and said: 'Wherefore hast thou brought us up out of Egypt, to kill us and our children and our cattle with thirst?' And Moses cried unto the Lord, saying: 'What shall I do unto this people? they are almost ready to stone me.' And the Lord said unto Moses: 'Pass on before the people, and take with thee of the elders of Israel; and thy rod, wherewith thou smotest the river, take in thy hand, and go. Behold, I will stand before thee there upon the rock in Horeb; and thou shalt smite the rock, and there shall come water out of it, that the people may drink' " (Exod. 17:3–6). In another passage, however, Moses was told to speak to the rock: "And the Lord spoke unto Moses, saying: 'Take the rod, and assemble the congregation, thou, and Aaron thy brother, and speak ye unto the rock before their eyes, that it give forth water; and thou shalt bring forth to them water out of the rock; so thou shalt give the congregation and their cattle drink' " (Num. 20:7–8). In this Koranic verse Muḥammad uses the first version.[1]

Zamakhsharī seems to be aware of both references in the Bible and comments that first Moses struck the rock and water emerged, but then the Israelites said, 'Should the rod be lost, we too will be lost.' Therefore, God said to Moses, 'Speak to the rock but do not use the rod to strike it; perhaps they will be instructed.'[2]

The references in the Bible about "striking" or "speaking" to the rock are also discussed by the rabbis. According to them, just as punishment and coercion are required in the training of a child,

[1] Cf. Ps. 105:41: "He opened the rock, and waters gushed out; They ran, a river in the dry places."

[2] Zamakhsharī, Vol. I, p. 78:

وقيل كان يضربه بعصاه فينفجر ويضربه بها فَيَيْبَسُ فقالوا ان
فَقَدَ موسى عصاه مُتنا عطشًا فاوحى اليه لا تقرع الحجارة وكَلِّمَها
تُطِعْك لعلّهم يعتبرون.

and whereas words are used when he is mature, so here, too, Moses was directed to "strike" the rock when it was a *small* stone, but to "speak" to it when it developed into a rock.[3] A less naive explanation is found in Midrash *Leḳaḥ Ṭob*. There we find that God's miracles assumed differing meanings. At the beginning, God told Moses "to strike the rock," and later on "to speak to it," in order to prove the might of God as it reveals itself in different forms.[4]

Another interesting tradition is found in Zamakhsharī, viz. that Adam brought the rock down from Paradise. From him it passed through many hands and finally fell into the hands of Jethro,[5] who gave it to Moses, his son-in-law, together with the rod.[6] There is no mention of the rock[7] in rabbinic literature, but we do find reference to

[3] ודברתם אל הסלע, והכיתם לא נאמר, א"ל כשהנער קטן רבו מכהו ומלמדו כיון שהגדיל בדבור הוא מיסרו, כך אמר הקב"ה למשה כשהיה סלע זה קטן הכית אותו שנא' והכית בצור, אבל עכשו ודברתם אל הסלע (ילקוט שמעוני, חקת, רמז תשסג).

[4] [B] לקח טוב, בשלח, יז; cf. ... לפי שאותותיו של הקב"ה אינן דומין זה לזה, בתחלה אמר להם והכית בצור ויצאו ממנו מים ובשניה אמר להם ודברתם, להודיע כח גבורתו של הקב"ה ... למדנו שאין אותות ומופתים של מי שאמר והיה העולם דומין זה לזה, אלא חדשים לבקרים לכך נאמר לא האמנתם בי להקדישני כדי שיאמרו בדבר יי יצאו המים אלא עשיתם האחרון דומה לראשון (פסיקתא זוטרתא, במדבר, חקת, כב, ז).

[5] Shu'aib شعيب; cf. Nöldeke-Schwally, *op. cit.*, Vol. I, p. 151 note 9; Horovitz, *HUCA*, p. 172.

[6] Zamakhsharī, Vol. I, p. 78:

وقيل اهبطه آدم من الجنّة فتوارثوه حتى وقع الى شعيب فدفعه اليه مع العصا.

[7] The rock could, however, be identified, and it was so pointed out to Moses by God (*Pesiḳta Num.* 20). According to the *Yalḳuṭ* (763), mentioned in footnote 3 of this verse, it was the same rock that Moses used in Ḥoreb and in the Wilderness of Zion. Thus, the Moslem idea of the rock having passed through many hands may have some relation to the rock carried around by Moses. Zamakhsharī (*ibid.*) also relates that the rock had four corners (square), and out of each corner there flowed three springs, one for each tribe. The Israelites, he says, were 600,000 in number, and camped on a plain twelve miles long.

وكان حجرًا مربّعا له اربعة اوجه كانت تنبع من كل وجه ثلث آعيْن لكل سبط عين تسيل في جدول الى السبط الذي اُمر ان يسقيهم وكانوا ست مائة الف وسَعَة المعسكر اثنا عشر ميلا.

That the camp of Israel occupied a space of twelve miles is found in Talmud Yerushalmi where it is stated that a disciple should not give an Halakic decision in the place where his teacher resides, unless there is a distance of twelve miles

the rod.[8] The rod was one of the ten things created by God at twilight on the eve of the Sabbath.[9]

The reference here to "twelve springs" is probably based on the story in the Aggada about the travels of the Israelites in the desert when rivers were said to have formed around each tribe.[10]

between them, comparable to the space occupied by the camp of Israel. שאסור לתלמיד להורות הלכה לפני רבו עד שיהא רחוק ממנו י"ב מיל כמחנה ישראל (תלמוד ירושלמי, שביעית פ"ו, ה"א). Cf. B. Sanh. 5b; B. ʻErub. 55b, and Maimonides, *Hilkot Talmud Torah*, V, Halakah 3.

8 ספרי וזאת הברכה, פיסקא שנ"ה [F]; תרגום יונתן שמות ד, כ; cf. ילקוט שמעוני, שמות, רמז קס"ח; פסחים נד, ע"א; משנה אבות ה, ח.

9 ר' לוי אומר המטה שנברא בין השמשות נמסר לאדם הראשון בגן עדן ואדם מסרו לחנוך וחנוך מסרו . . . לשם ושם מסרו לאברהם ואברהם מסרו ליצחק ויצחק מסרו ליעקב ויעקב הורידו למצרים ומסרו ליוסף בנו. וכשמת יוסף נשלל כל ביתו ונתן בפלטרין של פרעה והיה יתרו אחד מחרטומי מצרים וראה את המטה ואת האותות אשר עליו וחמד אותם בלבו ולקחו והביאו ונטעו בתוך גן ביתו . . . (פדר"א, פ"מ). Cf. Grünbaum, *op. cit.*, p. 163.

10 . . . כיון שעמדו קלעי החצר היו י"ב נשיאים עומדים על הבאר ואומרים שירה והיו מימי הבאר יוצאים ונעשים נהרים נהרים: נהר אחד יוצא ומקיף את מחנה שכינה, ומאותו נהר יוצאים ונעשים נהרים . . . לבסוף מתערבים ומקיפים את כל מחנה הלוים ומהלכים בין משפחה למשפחה ונראים טבליות טבליות מקיפין מחנה שכינה ונהר גדול מקיף את כל מחנה ישראל מבחוץ ונעשים נהרים נהרים בין כל שבט ושבט (ילקוט שמעוני, פקודי, רמז תכו). וכל אחד ואחד מושך במקלו איש לשבטו . . . (תוספתא, סוכה, ג, יא [Z]). Cf. Exod. 15:27 and Rashi *ad loc.*

VERSE 58

> And when they said, 'O Moses, we cannot always bear one kind of food; pray then thy Lord to bring forth for us of what the earth grows, its green herbs, its cucumbers, its garlic, its lentils, and its onions.' Said he, 'Do ye ask what is meaner instead of what is best? Go down to Egypt, — there is what ye ask.' Then they were smitten with abasement and poverty, and met with wrath from God. That was because they had misbelieved in God's signs and killed the prophets undeservedly;[1] that was for that they were rebellious and had transgressed.

In the *Yalkuṭ* it is stated that the Israelites were afraid that the manna would cause their intestines to burst, and kill them.[2] Commenting on the first part of the Koranic sentence Ṭabarī writes: "Moses said to the Israelites: 'Would you prefer a thing of importance though small and limited in its nutritious value to a thing of greater importance and of higher nutritious value?' "[3] This tale parallels the story found in *Sifre*,[4] which reads as follows: "R. Shimeon says: 'The manna tasted according to their fancy, except for those five kinds of food (viz. melons, cucumber, leeks, onions and garlic) . . . The sages say: 'The manna tasted according to their fancy, but they saw only manna, as it is said: Our soul is dried away, there is nothing at all save this manna *to look upon*.' "[5]

The Koranic expression, "Go down to Egypt,"[6] is reminiscent of

[1] Cf. 3:20, 108, 177.

[2] ועתה נפשינו יבשה . . . אמרו עתיד המן לתפח בתוך כרסנו להרגנו (ילקוט שמעוני, בהעלותך, רמז תשלד).

[3] Ṭabarī, Vol. I, p. 237:

قال أتستبدلون الذي هو ادنى بالذي هو خير قال لهم موسى أتاخذون الذي هو اخسّ خطرا وقيمة وقدرا من العيش بدلا بالذي هو خير منه خطرا وقيمة وقدرا.

[4] Cf. וחכמים אומרים מן היה משתנה להם לישראל לכל דבר שרוצים אלא שלא היו רואים בעיניהם שנאמר אין כל בלתי אל המן עינינו אין לנו אלא מן בשחר ומן בערב (ספרי, בהעלותך, פיסקא פז [F]).

[5] M.S.N., p. 68; cf. B. Yom. 75a.

[6] Ali, *op. cit.*, p. 36 n., considers the translation "Go down to Egypt" as erroneous and renders the phrase as "Enter a City," since the word *miṣr* is used here as a common noun. This *city* would probably refer to Hazeroth (Num. 11:35).

Moses' admonitions, where the great leader rebukes the Israelites for their disobedience, and threatens: "And the Lord shall bring thee back into Egypt in ships, by the way whereof I said unto thee: 'Thou shalt see it no more again . . .' " (Deut. 28:68).

As for the last part of this Koranic verse, telling of the unjust slaying of the prophets, Geiger thinks that it is probably a reference to Jesus.[7] However, there is in the Aggada a comparable story that the Israelites, during Moses' first stay on Mount Sinai, called upon their Elders to make a god for them. When the Elders refused, Israel killed them outright; they also killed Ḥur, the prophet, son of Miriam, for the same reason.[8]

The Talmud comments on the biblical verse, "And when Aaron saw this, he built an altar before it" (Exod. 32:5), as follows: "What did he (Aaron) actually see? . . . He saw Hur lying slain before him and said (to himself): if I do not obey them, they will now do unto me as they did unto Hur, and so will be fulfilled (the fear of) the prophet, *Shall the priest and the prophet be slain in the sanctuary of God?*" (Lam. 2:20).[9]

[7] Geiger, *op. cit.*, p. 196, "Was sich wohl auf Jesus bezieht."

[8] נכנסו כל ישראל אצל הזקנים ואמרו להן . . . קום עשה לנו אלהים . . . כיון ששמעו כך אמרו להם מה אתם מכעיסין למי שעשה לכם כל אותן הנסים והנפלאות ולא שמעו להם והרגום ולפי שעמד חור כנגדן בדברים קשים עמדו עליו עוד והרגוהו . . . כיון שראה אהרן מה שעשו לזקנים ולחור נתיירא מהן (במדבר רבה, פט"ו, יז).

[9] B. Sanh. 7a; cf. Rashi to Exod. 32:5.

VERSE 60

> And when we took a covenant with you and held the mountain over you; 'Accept what we have brought you with strong will, and bear in mind what is therein, haply ye yet may fear.'

According to Zamakhsharī, Moses brought the tablets to the Israelites and when they became aware of the burdening and taxing precepts contained therein, they refused to accept them. Whereupon, God commanded Gabriel to uproot the mountain and hold it over their heads, saying, "Accept them (the precepts) lest I shall drop it (the mountain) on you."[1]

A counterpart to this interpretation is found in the Talmud: "R. Abdimi b. Ḥama b. Ḥasa said: This teaches that the Holy One, blessed be He, overturned the mountain upon them like an (inverted) cask, and said to them, 'If ye accept the Torah, 'tis well; if not, there shall be your burial.' "[2]

Ṭabarī calls attention to the fact that the word *Ṭūr*, used here for mountain, is of foreign (Syriac) origin. He states that some maintain that this is the mountain Moses spoke from.[3] This is merely a further illustration of the linguistic influence of Judaism on the Koran which is evidenced by the Koranic usage of many biblical terms and names such as: *Ṣaum* (*Ẓom*—fast); *Ṣadaqah* (*Ẓedaḳah*—righteousness, charity); *Malak* (*Mal'ak*—Angel); *Shaiṭān* (*Saṭan*—leader of the devils); *Kitāb* (*Ketab*—Scriptures); *Taurat* (*Torah*—Torah); *Ḥai* (*Ḥay*—Liv-

[1] Zamakhsharī, Vol. I, p. 80:

وذلك ان موسى عليه السلام جاءهم بالالواح فرآوا ما فيها
من الاصار والتكاليف الشاقة فكبرت عليهم وابوا قبولها فأُمِر
جبرئيل فقلع الطور من اصله ورفعه فظلّله فوقهم وقال لهم
موسى ان قبلتم والا القي عليكم حتى قبلوا.

[2] B. Shab. 88a; cf. כפה . . . ואע"פ שכבר הקדימו נעשה לנשמע שמא יהיו חוזרים כשיראו האש הגדולה (תוספות, שבת פ"ח ע"א). As for the people who refused to accept the Torah because of the many precepts they would have to fulfill, see *Mekilta*, *Yithro*, ch. 5 [W].

[3] Ṭabarī, Vol. I, p. 247:

والطور بالسريانية الجبل....
قال ابو جعفر واما الطور فانه الجبل في كلام العرب . . .
وقيل انه اسم جبل بعينه وذكر انه الجبل الذي ناجى الله عليه موسى.

ing); *Qayyūm* (*Ḳayyam*—Abiding); *Al-Wāḥid* (*'Eḥad*—the one); *Sabt* (*Shabbat*—Sabbath); *Khaṭīah* (*Ḥeṭ*—sin); *Jahannam* (*Gehinnom*—hell); *Dīn* (*Din*—judgment); *Jannah* (*Gan 'Eden*—Paradise); *Ādam* (*Adam*—Adam); *Nūḥ* (*Noaḥ*—Noah); *Ibrāhīm* (*Abraham*—Abraham); *Lūṭ* (*Loṭ*—Lot); *Ismā'īl* (*Yishma'el*—Ishmael); *Isḥāq* (*Yiẓḥaḳ*—Isaac); *Ya'qūb* (*Ya'aḳob*—Jacob); *Yūsuf* (*Yosef*—Joseph); *Mūsā* (*Moshe*—Moses); *Hārūn* (*'Aharon*—Aaron); *Aiyūb* (*'Iyob*—Job); *Dā'ūd* (*David*—David); *Sulaimān* (*Shelomoh*—Solomon); *Ilyās* (*'Eliahu*—Elijah); *Alyasa'* (*'Elisha'*—Elisha); *Yūnus* (*Yonah*—Jonah); *'Uzair* (*'Ezra*—Ezra).[4]

Here Muḥammad uses the term *Ṭūr* for mountain because it is called *Ṭūrā* in the Targumim.[5]

[4] Horovitz, *HUCA*, pp. 145–87; cf. David Kuenstlinger, " 'Kitāb' und 'ahlu l-kitāb' im Ḳurān," in *Rocznik Orientalistyczny*, Lwów, 1928, Vol. IV, pp. 238–47; 2:1–2; 2:20; 2:28–30; 179–81.

[5] Exod. 19:18. See, however, A. Mingana, *Syriac Influence on the Style of the Ḳur'ān*, reprint, 1927, pp. 11–17; A. S. Yahuda, *Goldziher Memorial Volume*, Part I, p. 282 f.; A. Geiger, *ZDMG*, Vol. XXI, p. 688; Nöldeke-Schwally, *op. cit.*, Vol. I, pp. 112 f.; Hirschfeld, *Beiträge . . .*, p. 38; Lidzbarski, "Neue Götter," *Nachrichten von der Königlichen Gesellschaft der Wissenschaften zu Göttingen*, Philologisch-*historische Klasse*, 1916, Berlin, p. 90; David Kuenstlinger, "Ṭūr und Gabal im Ḳurān," *ibid.*, pp. 58–67.

VERSE 61

> Then did ye turn aside after this, and were it not for God's grace towards you and His mercy, ye would have been of those who lose. Ye know too of those among you who transgressed upon the Sabbath,[1] and we said, 'Become ye apes, despised and spurned.'

Torrey states that there is no Aggadic source for "the incident of the Breakers of the Sabbath, who changed into apes."[2] However, it is possible that Muḥammad derived this bit of legend from the story in the Talmud about the transformation of a class of sinners into apes, wild beasts and other wild animals.[3] "R. Jeremiah b. Eleazar said: They split up into three parties. One said, 'Let us ascend and dwell there;' the second, 'Let us ascend and serve idols;' and the third said, 'Let us ascend, and wage war (with God).' The party which proposed, 'Let us ascend, and dwell there' — *the Lord scattered them*: the one that said 'Let us ascend and wage war' were turned to apes, spirits, devils and night-demons . . ."[4]

The word *Sabt*[5] (used in Arabic for the seventh day) is the equiv-

[1] Cf. 4:153; 7:163–166; 16:125. Cf. Hirschberg, *op. cit.*, p. 316 note 41.

[2] *Op. cit.*, p. 68; Torrey's statement is based on Geiger's remark (p. 181) that no trace is to be found of such a transformation in Jewish writings.

[3] Hirschfeld, *op. cit.*, p. 108, doubts whether Muḥammad knew of this legend. He claims that "The matter seems to me to rest on a misunderstanding on the part of the compilers, or those who copied the revelations from the original notes. The word in question, *qiradatan*, [قِرَدَةً], is recorded in the dictionaries as plural of *qird*, meaning an ape. If we read *qirdân* [قِرْدَان], vermin (and in the archetype of that passage the difference between these two readings was probably difficult to distinguish), the verse would be a mistaken rendition of Exod. 16:20, 24. The mistake was probably caused by the circumstance that the transformation of living human beings into apes seemed much more fitting than into worms. Now the reason of the transformation is, in the *Qorân*, disobedience in connection with the Sabbath, which is the same cause as mentioned in the Pentateuch. Instead of the food left over night, Muhammed has the disobedient persons transformed. The words, 'those who go too far', are perhaps a rendering of Exod. 16:29, and refer to a given space of ground in the sense of the Rabbinical interpretation (Mishnah Erûbin, 2:3)."

[4] Cf. B. Sanh. 109a; Hirschfeld, *Jüdische Elemente* . . . p. 65.

[5] سبت.

alent of the Hebrew *Shabbat*[6] and the Aramaic *Shabtā*[7] (Exod. 20:8).[8] Muḥammad, perhaps relying upon Ex. 16:4,[9] considered only the Jews to be obligated to observe the Sabbath as stated in Ex. 30:13, 17[10] and in the Midrash.[11] Though Muḥammad chose Friday to take the place of the Jewish Saturday and the Christian Sunday, yet this day on which Moslems are allowed to work, unlike the Jewish Sabbath, is not called the day of rest, but the "day of assembly,"[12] being the holy day of the week.[13] In the time of Muḥammad, Jews in Arabia observed the Sabbath early on Friday.[14] It is quite possible that Muḥammad took this pattern as a model for his "day of assembly."[15] For he

[6] שבת.

[7] שבתא. Cf. Horovitz, *Koranische . . .*, p. 96.

[8] Dozy (p. 177) claims that the Arabs adopted the names of the week-days from the Jews. The seventh day they call *Sabt* only. Cf. J. J. Rivlin, *Gesetz im Koran*, p. 20 n.: "Es verdient immerhin Beachtung, dass der feierlichste Sabbatgottesdienst, die קבלת שבת, schon am Freitag, und zwar bei den jemenitischen Juden am frühen Nachmittag, stattfindet. Vielleicht ist diese קבלת שבת in der von Becker Islam III 379, zitierten Tradition gemeint, in der M. sagt 'wähle den Tag aus, an dem die Juden ihren Sabbat vorbereiten.'" See, however, I. Goldziher, "Die Sabbatinstitution im Islam" in *Sefer Hazikaron D. Kaufmann*, Breslau, 1900, p. 6.

[9] למען אנסנו הילך בתורתי אם לא. Cf. Goldziher, *ibid.*, pp. 86 f.

[10] Cf. בתורה ובנביאים ובכתובים מצינו שהשבת שקולה כנגד כל המצוות שבתורה (תלמוד ירושלמי נדרים, פ"ג ה"ט).

[11] אות היא לעולם מגיד שאין שבת בטלה מישראל (מכילתא מסכתא דשבתא, כי תשא פ"א [W]). Cf. also: עכו"ם ששבת חייב מיתה שנאמר ויום ולילה לא ישבתו (סנהדרין נ"ח ע"ב); and the Sabbath Prayer Book: ולא נתתו יי אלהינו לגויי הארצות ולא הנחלתו מלכנו לעובדי פסילים, וגם במנוחתו לא ישכנו ערלים, כי לישראל עמך נתתו באהבה לזרע יעקב, אשר בם בחרת.

[12] يوم الجمعة. Cf. ... ובלשון ערבי קראו חמשה ימים על דרך המספר. ויום ששי אלג'ומע על שם חבורם. כי הוא להם היום הנכבד בשבוע. ויום שבת קראו אותו סב"ת כי השי"ן והסמ"ך מתחלפים בכתיבתם ואלה מישראל למדו (פירוש אבן עזרא, שמות ט"ז, א).

[13] Even in the *Jāhilīyah* period the term عروبة was used for Friday, which is derived, according to Rivlin, from the Hebrew ערב. يوم الجمعة was probably influenced by the Hebrew and Aramaic כנסת, כנשתא. Cf. J. J. Rivlin, *Gesetz im Koran*, p. 20 n.

[14] רב צלי של שבת בערב שבת (ברכות כ"ז, ע"ב); also: יש לו לאדם לקדש על הכוס ערב שבת מבעוד יום אעפ"י שלא נכנסה השבת (רמב"ם, יד החזקה, הלכות שבת פכ"ט, הלכה י"א).

[15] جمعة (congregation) is the term used for the sixth day of the week and every Moslem is commanded by Muḥammad to observe it (62:9). Muḥammad

accepted the Jewish idea of making Friday a day of special prayers and also followed the Jewish practice of including a sermon in the service and making his followers bathe their bodies and wear special attire for the "day of assembly. "[16]Yet the spirit of a complete day of rest as practised by the Jews was alien to Muḥammad.[17]

As for the Koranic statement about the Jews having transgressed the Sabbath, Baiḍāwī says that this happened in the reign of King David, when a Jewish community dwelt in the city of Elath on the Red Sea. The Jews of Elath dug pits on the eve of the Sabbath so that on the day of rest the fish flowed abundantly into them. (God did this in order to tempt the people). And on Sunday the Israelites drew them out.[18]

It is possible that this legend came into Moslem tradition through Karaite literature. For, according to talmudic and post-talmudic Halakah, it is permissible to spread "snares for wild beasts, fowls and fish" on the eve of the Sabbath.[19] Nets for wild animals may not

also ordered his followers not to fast on Fridays, which follows the Jewish practice in connection with the Sabbath. Hirschberg, *op. cit.*, p. 196, cites a Moslem tradition that Muḥammad told his followers that the commandment not to engage in war on the Sabbath was given to the Jews alone. Cf. Geiger, *op. cit.*, p. 53.

[16] According to Moslem tradition each service must be preceded by a sermon which is considered part of it. Cf. Bu., Vol. I, p. 233:

كان النبيّ .... يخطب قائما ... بينما النبي ... يخطب يوم الجمعة ...

[17] Wellhausen, *Reste* . . ., Vol. I, p. 142; Pollack, *op. cit.*, p. 133; I. Goldziher, "Die Sabbatinstitution im Islam," in *Gedenkbuch . . . D. Kaufmann*, pp. 86–91; M. Steinschneider, *Polemische und Apologetische Literatur in Arabischer Sprache*, Leipzig, 1877, pp. 320 f.; A. Strauss, "דרכי הפולמוס האסלאמי" in ספר הזכרון לבית מדרש לרבנים בוינה, Jerusalem, 1950, pp. 46 f.; Mittwoch, *op. cit.*, pp. 27 f.

[18] Baiḍāwī, Vol. I, p. 26:

فاعتدى فيه ناس منهم في زمن داود عليه السلام واشتغلوا بالصيد
وذلك انهم كانوا يسكنون قرية على ساحل يقال لها ايلة واذا
كان يوم السبت لم يبق حوت في البحر الاخضر هناك واخرج
خرطومه فاذا مضى تفرقت فحفروا حياضا وشرعوا اليها الجداول
وكانت الحيتان تدخلها يوم السبت فيصطادونها يوم الاحد.

[19] שבת י"ז, ע"ב.

be spread, however, unless they may be caught the same day. But the school of Hillel permit it,[20] so that they could be caught naturally in the net on the day of rest.[21] It is only according to the Karaite Halakah that the spreading of nets for fish on the eve of the Sabbath was prohibited unless they could be caught while it is yet day.[22]

[20] *Ibid.*, ב"ש אומרים אין פורסין מצודות חיה ועופות ודגים אלא כדי שיצודו מבעוד יום וב"ה מתירין.

[21] לתתה מבעוד יום והיא קולטת כל הלילה (רש"י, שבת י"ז, ע"ב). It seems unlikely that the Moslems were aware of the non-accepted opinion of the school of Shammai.

[22] אדרת אליהו, ענין שבת, פ"ז; גן עדן, ענין שבת, פ"ז.

VERSES 63–66

And when Moses said to his people, 'God bids you slaughter a cow,' they said, 'Art thou making a jest of us?' Said he, 'I seek refuge with God from being one of the unwise.' They said, 'Then pray thy Lord for us to show us what she is to be.' He answered, 'He saith it is a cow, nor old, nor young, of middle age between the two; so do as ye are bid.' They said, 'Pray now thy Lord to show us what her colour is to be.' He answered, 'He saith it is a dun cow, intensely dun, her colour delighting those who look upon her.' Again they said, 'Pray thy Lord to show us what she is to be; for cows appear the same to us; then we, if God will, shall be guided.' He answered, 'He saith, it is a cow, not broken in to plough the earth or irrigate the tilth, a sound one with no blemish on her.' They said, 'Now hast thou brought the truth.' And they slaughtered her, though they came near leaving it undone.

It is apparent that we have here a mixture of the story of the heifer in Num. 19 with the story of the calf mentioned in Deut. 21:1–9. In Jewish sources the red cow appears to be insensitive.[1] The expression "not broken in to plough the earth or irrigate the tilth" recalls the words in Num. 19:2, "faultless, wherein is no blemish, and upon which never came yoke," as well as the discussion in the Talmud[2] about the prohibition of doing other work. *Sifre* compares the red cow with the heifer "which hath not been wrought with (Deut. 21:3)" and whose neck was broken in the valley.[3]

As for the age of the cow, there are two opinions in the Talmud. Rabbi Jose says she must be two years old, but the sages maintain that she may be three years old, and the prevailing law is that of the sages.[4] It seems likely that the frequent talmudic comparisons between the red cow and the heifer caused Muḥammad this confusion.

[1] גוי אחד שאל את ר' יוחנן בן זכאי, וא"ל אלין מלייא דאתון עבדין נראין כמין כשפים, מביאים פרה ושוחטין אותה ושורפין אותה, וכותשין אותה, ונוטלין את אפרה, וכי הוה אחד מכם מטמא למת, מזין עליו שתים ושלשה פעמים (פסיקתא דרב כהנא, פ' פרה, פסקא ד, ע"מ [B]).

[2] B. Soṭ. 46a; cf. Rashi, *ad loc.*; פסיקתא רבתי, פי"ד עס"ה [F]; תנחומא, חקת, ג [B]; במדבר רבה, פי"ט, ד.

[3] ומה עגלה שאין המום פוסל בה עשה בה שאר מלאכה כעול פרה: ספרי, חקת, פיסקא קכג [F] שהמום פוסל בה דין הוא שנעשה בה שאר מלאכה כעול; cf. also: והורדו זקני העיר ההיא את העגלה אל נחל איתן אשר לא יעבד בו ולא יזרע וערפו שם את העגלה בנחל (דברים כ"א, ד).

[4] Mishnah, Par. 1:2. Cf. *Sifre*, *ibid.*

Zamakhsharī says that the cow had to be "dun" completely, even to its horns and hooves,[5] and a similar statement is found in the Mishnah.[6]

Ṭabarī relates: "There was a man in Israel who proudly honored his father. Once a man passed by him and offered to sell him precious stones. The father was then asleep and had the key to the money under his head. The man said, 'I will sell you the pearls for 70,000 worth of currency if you pay it immediately.' But the devoted son answered, 'Wait until my revered father will awaken, and then I'll pay you 80,000.' The man said, 'Wake him up right now and I'll sell them to you for 60,000,' and so he went on until he offered them to the son for 30,000. The son refused, however, to awaken his father and increased the price to 100,000 if the man would wait. Finally the son said, 'For no price will I disturb the sleep of my father.' The reward of the pious son was that a red cow was born among his herd for which Moses gave him a very high price."[7]

This story with slight variations recalls the legend in Ḳiddushin: "It was propounded of R. 'Ulla: How far does the honour of parents (extend)? — He replied, Go forth and see what a certain heathen,

[5] Zamakhsharī, Vol. I, pp. 82–83:
لا لمعة فى نقبتها من لون اخر سوى الصفرة فهي صفراء كلها حتى قرنها وظلفها.

[6] Mishnah, Par. 2:2: פרה שקרניה וטלפיה שחורים יגוד.

[7] Ṭabarī, Vol. I, p. 258:
وكان رجل من بنى اسرائيل من ابرّ الناس بابيه وان رجلا مرّ به معه لؤلؤ يبيعه فكان ابوه نائما تحت راسه المفتاح فقال له الرجل تشترى مني هذا اللؤلؤ بسبعين الفا فقال له الفتى كما انت حتى يستيقظ ابي فاخذه بثمانين الفا فقال له الآخر ايقظ اباك وهو لك بستين الفاً فجعل التاجر يحط له حتى بلغ ثلاثين الفا وزاد الآخر على ان ينتظر حتى يستيقظ ابوه حتى بلغ مائة الف فلما اكثر عليه قال لا والله لا اشتريه منك بشئ ابداً وابى ان يوقظ اباه .... فمرت به بنو اسرائيل يطلبون البقرة .... فسالوه ان يبيعهم اياها فابى .... فانطلقوا به الى موسى .... وقال للقوم ارضوا صاحبكم فاعطوه وزنها ذهبا فابى .... حتى اعطوه وزنها عشر مرات فباعهم اياها ....

Dama son of Nethinah by name, did in Askelon. The Sages once desired merchandise from him, in which there was 600,000 (gold denarii) profit, but the key was lying under his father, and so he did not trouble him. Rab Judah said in Samuel's name: R. Eliezer was asked, How far does the honour of parents (extend)? — Said he, Go forth and see what a certain heathen, Dama son of Nethinah by name, did in Askelon. The Sages sought jewels for the ephod, at a profit of 600,000 (gold denarii) — R. Kahana taught: at a profit of 800,000 — but as the key was lying under his father's pillow, he did not trouble him. The following year the Holy One, blessed be He, gave him his reward. A red heifer was born to him in his herd."[8]

[8] B. Ḳid., 31a.

VERSE 69

> Yet were your hearts hardened even after that, till they were as stones or harder still, for verily of stones are some from which streams burst forth, and of them there are some that burst asunder and the water issues out, and of them there are some that fall down for fear of God; but God is never careless of what ye do.

Compare: "Behold, I will stand before thee there upon the rock in Horeb; and thou shalt smite the rock, and there shall come water out of it, that the people may drink . . ." (Exod. 17:6); "And Moses and Aaron gathered the assembly together before the rock, and he said unto them: 'Hear now, ye rebels; are we to bring you forth water out of this rock?'" (Num. 20:10). The Koranic phrase "your hearts hardened"[1] recalls the Biblical words in Deut. 10:16.[2] Similarly the idea that the heart hardens as stone recalls Ezekiel: "And I will give them one heart, and I will put a new spirit within you; and I will remove the stony heart out of their flesh, and will give them a heart of flesh" (Ezek. 11:19).[3]

A parallel to the Koranic idea that man's heart is harder than stone is found in Rashi's commentary on Num. 20:12: "For if you had spoken to the rock and it had brought forth (water), I would have been sanctified in the eyes of the congregation, and they would have said; If this rock, which does not speak and does not hear, and does not require sustenance, fulfills the word of the Omnipresent, then certainly we (should do so)."[4]

According to Rashi's interpretation, which is undoubtedly based on midrashic lore, man can learn a lesson from the stone. Though a stone does not depend much on God's support, yet it readily fulfills His will, *a fortiori* a human being, who is sustained by God.

[1] قست قلوبكم. Cf. 2:82, قلوبنا غلف.

[2] ערלי לב . . . and כבד לב פרעה; cf. Zech. 7:12 ולבם שמו שמיר and Jer. 5:3.

[3] Cf. Ezek. 36:26: "A new heart also will I give you, and a new spirit will I put within you; and I will take away the stony heart out of your flesh, and I will give you a heart of flesh." Also, *Targum, ad loc.*: ואתבר ית לבא דרשיעא דהוא תקיף . . . כאבנא . . .

[4] *P. R. C.*, Vol. IV, pp. 204–5.

VERSE 73

And some of them there are, illiterate folk, that know not the Book,[1] but only idle tales; for they do but fancy. But woe to those who write out the Book with their hands and say 'this is from God'; to buy therewith a little price! and woe to them for what their hands have written, and woe to them for what they gain!

Zamakhsharī commenting on "illiterate folk," states that they are unable to write well, hence they consult the Torah to verify its contents.[2]

Rodwell and Lane hold that the word "illiterate"[3] (*ummiyūn*, plural of *ummī*) refers to a non-Jew, who is unaware of or does not possess the Scriptures. Torrey, upholding this view, suggests that this is "simply the transfer into Arabic of the Hebrew *gōi*, *gōyīm*. It was not coined by Mohammed, but was taken over by him from the speech which he heard. It designated any and all *who were not of the Israelite race* (as has already been said, and as is well known, Mohammed does not distinguish Christians from Israelites). The passage 2:73, which has made trouble for previous explanations of the problematic term, expresses the indignation and scorn with which the prophet replies to certain *proselytes* in one of the Medinese tribes, who had tried to trick or ridicule him by means of some 'scripture' of their own composition — a most natural proceeding for would-be Israelites. He has just been speaking of the Jews, and now continues: 'And among them there are certain *gōyīm*, who do not know the scriptures, but only hope to appear to, and who think vain things. Woe to those who write out scriptures with their hands and then, say, This is from God!' Here, the adjective is plainly used in reproach and contempt; elsewhere, it means precisely 'Gentile,' most obviously in 3:69![4] The Koran, then, gives no ground whatever for supposing Mohammed unlettered."[5]

[1] Cf. the expressions: עד מתי אתה מעוות עלינו את הכתובים (ילקוט שמעוני זכריה, רמז תקע"ה); עד מתי אתה עוקם עלינו את המקרא (שוחר טוב, פי"ב, כה).

[2] Zamakhsharī, Vol. I, p. 86:

لا يحسنون الكتب فيطالعوا التوراة ويتحققوا ما فيها.

[3] أميّون, *i. e.* "gentile, non-Jew or heathen."

[4] Cf. Geiger, *op. cit.*, p. 49; Gastfreund, *op. cit.*, Part I, p. 12.

[5] Torrey, *op. cit.*, p. 38. Torrey also quotes Nöldeke-Schwally, *op. cit.*, p. 14, who maintain that the term *ummī* refers to those "who do not have ('or know') the ancient holy scriptures." Cf. Bu., Vol. IV, p. 400.

Horovitz thinks that in this verse "it is possible that the word might have been confused with the 'ammē hā-'āreṣ,' those among the Jews who do not know the law."[6] . . . However, in 62:2 "Allah is praised for having raised up among the 'ummiyūn' a prophet who was one of their midst, and for this reason Mohammed calls himself 'an-nabī al ummi' in 7:156, 158, because he came from the ranks of the Arabs, i. e., from one of the 'ummōt hā-'ōlām,' and not from Israel. . ."[7] Muḥammad "learned of the 'ummōt hā-'ōlām' through the Jews in Medina and formed the word 'ummi' in accordance with this term."[8]

Thus it is possible that the term *ummīyūn* here and in 7:156[9] is derived from the Hebrew "*Ummot ha'Olam.*" Muḥammad in announcing himself "the seal of the prophets" wished to indicate that he is the "prophet unto all the nations."[10]

[6] Horovitz, *HUCA*, p. 191.

[7] *Ibid.*, p. 190.

[8] *Ibid.*, pp. 190–91. As to the term Nabī, see Horovitz, *HUCA*, p. 223 and Nöldeke-Schwally, *op. cit.*, Vol. I, pp. 159 f., and notes to 2:254; 3:4,75.

[9] الرسول النبي الاميّ.

[10] Jer. 1:5, נביא לגוים; cf. 7:156, 158, "Whom they find written down with them in the law (في التوراة) . . . Say, 'O ye folk! Verily, I am the apostle of God unto you all,' — of Him whose is the kingdom of the heavens and the earth . . ."

VERSE 74

> And then they say, 'Hell fire shall not touch us save for a number of days.'[1] Say, 'Have ye taken a covenant with God?' but God breaks not His covenant. Or do ye say of God that which ye do not know?

The Koranic reference to "a number of days" recalls the talmudic statement that the trial of the transgressors in hell lasts twelve[2] months.[3] In 2:161 Muḥammad states: "When those who are followed clear themselves of those who followed them, and see the torment, and the cords are cut asunder." This idea brings to mind the rabbinic statement that on the Day of Judgment God will separate (untie) the (bad) followers from their leaders who will not be able to be helped by the latter.[4]

[1] Cf. 3:23.

[2] According to R. Johanan b. Nuri the judgment of certain sinners will last "(only) from Passover to Pentecost," *i. e.* seven weeks. Mishnah 'Eduy. 2:10 [D].

[3] משפט רשעים בגיהנם י"ב חדש (משנה, עדיות, פרק ב'); cf. 2:160.

[4] The Talmud distinguishes incidental sinners from heretics and consigns to never extinguished fire those who misled others and caused them to sin, and those who isolated themselves from the community (B. R. H. 17a).

VERSE 77

> And when we took[1] from the children of Israel a covenant, saying, 'Serve ye none but God, and to your two parents show kindness, and to your kindred and the orphans and the poor, and speak to men kindly, and be steadfast in prayer, and give alms'; and then ye turned back, save a few of you, and swerved aside.

Chapter nineteen in Leviticus, which, as the rabbis rightly note, contains the major principles of Judaism,[2] embraces almost every precept enumerated in this Koranic verse, i. e., monotheism, covenant, honorable dealing, no talebearing or malice, reverence for parents, consideration for the poor, for the needy and for the stranger.[3] Though prayer is not explicitly mentioned in Leviticus 19, the precept has been deduced from the biblical command, "Ye shall be holy; for I the Lord your God am holy" (Lev. 19:2).[4] As to "speak to men kindly," we may find a parallel in the rabbis' interpretation of the words "not (to) bear sin" (Lev. 19:17). According to them even an admonition to improve one's deeds should be uttered in a friendly way.[5] Other parallels are found in *Aboth*: "and judge all men in the scale of merit,"[6] and in the Talmud, where it is stated that "addressing words of comfort" is even higher than charity.[7]

[1] Ali, *Holy Qur-ān*, p. 44, translates "we made a covenant with."

[2] Rashi to Lev. 19:2: דבר אל כל עדת בני ישראל . . . מלמד שנאמרה פרשה זו בהקהל מפני שרוב גופי תורה תלויין בה.

[3] *Ibid.*; the Midrash, too, equates the precepts enumerated here to the ten commandments (לפי שכל הדברות כלולין בתוכה (תנחומא, קדושים ג [B].

[4] Ḳedushah (holiness) is attained "by doing justly, loving mercy, and walking humbly with our God," P. H., p. 498 n. קדושים תהיו . . . כך אמר הקב"ה לישראל, שמרו מצותי, מצות קריאת שמע שחרית וערבית, ואני משמר אתכם . . . (תנחומא, קדושים, ו [B]).

[5] והוכח תוכיח . . . יכול אפילו את מוכיחו ופניו משתנות ת"ל ולא תשא עליו חטא (ספרא, קדושים, עפ"ט [W]); א"ר יצחק כל הנותן פרוטה לעני מתברך בו' ברכות והמפייסו בדברים מתברך בי"א ברכות (ב"ב, ט, ע"ב).

[6] Mishnah Ab., 1:6.

[7] B. Shab. 127a; cf. also the following: והוי מקבל את כל האדם בסבר פנים יפות כיצד מלמד שאם אדם נתן לחבירו כל מתנות טובות שבעולם ופניו כבושים בארץ מעלה עליו הכתוב כאילו לא נתן לו כלום אבל המקבל את חבירו בסבר פנים יפות אפי' לא נתן לו כלום מעלה עליו הכתוב כאילו נתן לו כל מתנות טובות שבעולם (אבדר"נ סוף פי"ג); תלמוד ירושלמי תענית פ"ב, ה"א and "Good manners are preferred for you," Bu., Vol. IV, p. 167, قال سلّم الصغير على الكبير انّ خيركم أحسنكم خلقاً.

Other relevant biblical passages are: "And He declared unto you His covenant, which He commanded you to perform . . ." (Deut. 4:13). "Thou shalt have no other gods before Me" (Ex. 20:3). "And ye shall serve the Lord your God" (Exod. 23:25). "Honor thy father and thy mother" (Ex. 20:12 and Deut. 5:16) . . . . "Thou shalt surely open thy hand unto thy poor and needy brother, in thy land" (Deut. 15:11). "When thou hast made an end of tithing all the tithe of thine increase in the third year, which is the year of tithing, and hast given it unto the Levite, to the stranger, to the fatherless, and to the widow, that they may eat within thy gates, and be satisfied, then thou shalt say before the Lord thy God: I have put away the hallowed things out of my house, and also have given them unto the Levite and unto the stranger, to the fatherless and to the widow, according to all Thy commandments which Thou hast commanded me . . ." (Deut. 26:12–14). "At the end of every three years, even in the same year, thou shalt bring forth all the tithe of thine increase, and shalt lay it up within thy gates. And the Levite, because he hath no portion nor inheritance with thee, and the stranger, and the fatherless, and the widow, that are within thy gates, shall come, and shall eat and be satisfied; that the Lord thy God may bless thee in all the work of thy hand which thou doest" (Deut. 14:28–29).[8]

[8] Cf. Is. 1:17, "Learn to do well; Seek justice, relieve the oppressed, Judge the fatherless, plead for the widow." For an elaborate discussion on prayers and charity in Islām see notes to 2:1–2, 172, 211, 239, 240, 246, 272, 273, 280: 3:128.

VERSE 80

> Those who have bought this worldly life with the Future, the torment shall not be lightened from them nor shall they be helped.[1]

Baiḍāwī interprets the words, "have bought this worldly life," to mean that they give preference to the values of this world.[2] A striking parallel to this Koranic verse as well as to Baiḍāwī is found in the Talmud: "They forsake life eternal and engage in life temporal!"[3] Other parallels are also found in Jeremiah 12:1: "Wherefore doth the way of the wicked prosper?" and in the Talmud: ". . . why is it that (righteous men) . . . . are in adversity, (and) . . . . wicked men prosper? . . ."[4] According to *Targum Yerushalmi*, God pays to those who dislike him the reward for the minor good deeds they have done in this world so as to destroy them in the world to come.[5]

The Talmud interprets the biblical phrase: "which I command thee this day, to do them" (Deut. 7:11) as " '*This day* (you are) *to do them*' but you cannot postpone doing them to tomorrow (after death); *this day* (you are in a position) *to do them* and tomorrow (after death is reserved) for receiving reward for (doing) them."[6] A closer parallel is found in the Mishnah: "For in the hour of the departure of a man (from the world), there accompany him neither gold nor silver, nor precious stones nor pearls, but Torah and good deeds alone . . ."[7] The Midrash also states that wealth is of no avail on the day of judgment and only deeds of merit "shall come to meet thee there even before thou hast arrived, for it is said, thy righteousness shall go before thee."[8]

[1] Cf. 3:14.

[2] Baiḍāwī, Vol. I, p. 30: آثروا الحياة الدنيا على الآخرة.

[3] B. Shab. 33b.

[4] B. Ber. 7a.

[5] ומשלם לשנאוי אגר מצוון קלילן דאית בידיהון בעלמא הדין מן בגלל למשיצייא יתהון לעלמא דאתי ולא משהי למשלמא לשנאוי אגר מצוון קלילן דאית בידיהון בעלמא הדין (תרגום ירושלמי, דברים, ז, י).

[6] B. 'Erub. 22a.

[7] Mishnah Ab. 6:9.

[8] פדר"א, פל"ד. Cf. [F] פסיקתא רבתי, בחדש השביעי, פ"מ, קס"ז, ע"ב and "R. Joshua b. Levi also said: 'All the good deeds which Israel does in this world will bear testimony unto them in the world to come.' " B. 'A. Z. 4b.

VERSE 86

Moses came to you with manifest signs, then ye took up with the calf when he had gone and did so wrong.[1]

The Bible records that when God told Moses to bring forth the children of Israel, the latter said: " 'But, behold, they will not believe me, nor hearken unto my voice; for they will say: The Lord hath not appeared unto thee' " (Exod. 4:1). It was then that God gave several signs into the hands of Moses with the promise that: ". . . if they will not believe thee, neither hearken to the voice of the first sign, that they will believe the voice of the latter sign" (*ibid.*, verse 8).

The Midrash argues that Moses was wrong in assuming that Israel will not believe him, after God has said: "And they shall hearken to thy voice" (Exod. 3:18). God, however, responded to Moses' thinking and gave the signs to him.[2]

The Koranic verse also recalls the biblical statements: "And the people believed" (Exod. 4:31) . . . "And they believed in the Lord, and in His servant Moses" (Exod. 14:31) . . . "and made it a molten calf" (Exod. 32:4).[3]

According to the Moslem commentaries,[4] the signs mentioned here refer to the miracles in connection with the Exodus which Moses performed before Pharaoh and the Israelites.[5] Among these miracles, according to Ṭabarī,[6] are: the rod turning into a serpent, the hand of Moses turning again "as his other flesh," and the crossing of the Red Sea. The miracles were performed to testify to the truth of Moses' prophecy.

[1] Cf. 3:184.

[2] ויען משה ויאמר והן לא יאמינו לי. אותה שעה דבר משה שלא כהוגן, הקב"ה אמר לו ושמעו לקולך והוא אמר והן לא יאמינו לי. מיד השיבו הקב"ה בשיטתו נתן לו אותות לפי דבריו (שמות רבה, ג, טו).

[3] Cf. 2:48–51.

[4] Cf. Baiḍāwī, *ad loc.*, Vol. I, p. 31:

الايات التسع المذكورة في قوله تعالى ولقد آتينا موسى تسع آيات بينات.

[5] These miracles, according to Baiḍāwī and Zamakhsharī, are: Moses casting the rod, stretching forth his hand, bringing up the frogs, the dust of the earth becoming gnats, bringing up the locusts, the waters in Egypt becoming blood, the smiting of the rock, the crossing of the sea and the raising of the mountain over the Israelites.

[6] Ṭabarī, Vol. I, p. 317:

جائكم بالبينات الدالة على صدقه وحقية نبوته كالعصا التى تحولت ثعبانا مبينا ويده التى اخرجها بيضاء للناظرين وفلق البحر...

VERSE 87

> And when we took a covenant with you and raised the mountain over you, 'Take what we have given you with resolution and hear;' they said, 'We hear but disobey'; and they were made to drink the calf down into their hearts for their unbelief. Say, 'An evil thing is it which your belief bids you do, if ye be true believers.'

Muḥammad here[1] connects the acceptance of the Torah with the making of the molten calf, whereas in 2:285 he refers to the acceptance of the Torah only.[2]

According to the Aggada, when Moses told the Israelites that God would give them the Torah, they said: "We will do, and obey."[3] The rendition in 285, "We will hear and obey," reverses the biblical statement, "We will do, and obey."[4] In Shabbath 88b the biblical expression is given special emphasis.[5] However, some noted Hebrew gram-

[1] Cf. 2:60, 285 and Ali's commentary, p. 48 n.: "*We hear the words and disobey the command*." See also Rashbam's commentary to Exod. 24:7: "We will do what He has said and obey what He will command us in the future."

[2] There the statement, "We hear and obey" (2:285), is like the Hebrew ושמענו ועשינו (Deut. 5:24), "And we will hear it, and do it."

[3] Exod. 24:7, נעשה ונשמע, "we will do, and obey."

[4] According to Hirschfeld, *New Researches* . . . , p. 109, Muḥammad identified 'asīnu (עשינו) (we do it) with Arabic 'aṣainâ (عصينا), which has an opposite meaning. Sometime later he became aware of the error. "To correct it was, however, impossible, since the true version did not suit his purposes at all. He therefore replaced the faulty word by 'we obey,' placing this avowal into the mouth of the Believers who believe in Allâh, His angels, His Books, and His Messengers (we make no difference between any of His messengers) and they say: We hear and obey" (2:285). However, in view of note 1, there is no need to attribute a different meaning to the Koranic text. Cf. Horovitz, *HUCA*, p. 214.

[5] דרש ר' סימאי בשעה שהקדימו ישראל נעשה לנשמע באו ששים ריבוא של מלאכי השר' לכל אחד ואחד מישראל קשרו לו שני כתרים אחד כנגד נעשה ואחד כנגד נשמע וכיון שחטאו ישראל ירדו מאה ועשרים ריבוא מלאכי חבלה ופרקום שנאמר (שמות, ל"ג) ויתנצלו בני ישראל את עדים מהר חורב אמר רב חמא בר חנינא בחורב טענו בחורב פרקו בחורב טענו כדאמרן בחורב פרקו דכתיב ויתנצלו בני ישראל וגו' א"ר יוחנן וכלן זכה משה ונטלן דסמיך ליה ומשה יקח את האהל אמר ר"ל ועתיד הקב"ה להחזירן לנו שנאמר (ישעי', ל"ה) ופדויי ה' ישובון ובאו ציון ברנה ושמחת עולם על ראשם שמחה שמעולם על ראשם אמר רבי אלעזר בשעה שהקדימו ישראל נעשה לנשמע יצתה בת קול ואמרה להן מי גילה לבני רז זה שמלאכי השרת משתמשין בו . . . למה נמשלו ישראל לתפוח לומר לך מה תפוח זה פריו קודם לעליו אף ישראל הקדימו נעשה לנשמע . . . (שבת פ"ח, ע"א).

marians and commentators do not see any difference between "we will do, and obey" and "we will obey, and we will do." Sa'adia in his *Tafsīr* (commentary) renders the phrase *na'aseh wenishma'* as *neḳablah veniẓna'ah.*[6]

The Koranic expression, "And they were made to drink the calf down . . .," recalls the verse in Exod. 32:20: "And he took the calf which they had made, and burnt it with fire, and ground it to powder, and strewed it upon the water, and made the children of Israel drink of it."

Ṭabarī comments that they drank the water in which the ashes of the burnt calf were mixed. In a more detailed explanation, Ṭabarī writes, that when Moses came and saw the Israelites assembled around the calf, he burnt it, put the ashes into the water and commanded them to drink it.[7] Those who participated in the making of the calf received a sign of gold on their lips and in this way Moses was able to recognize them.[8] The Talmud, too, states that they were tested by the drinking of the water as was the Soṭah.[9]

[6] נקבלה ונצנעה (Exod. 24:7), J. Dérenbourg (ed.), *Les Œuvres complètes de Saadia*, Paris, 1893. Jonah Ibn Janāḥ in his *Sefer Hariqma*, ed. M. Wilensky, Berlin, 1924, p. 360, writes: נעשה ונשמע משפטו נשמע ונעשה.

[7] This is also in line with the *Targum* commentary on Song of Songs, 1:14, . . . אזל משה ושף ית עגלא ובדר ית עפריה לנחלא ואשקי ית בני ישראל וקטיל ית כל מן דאתחיב קטול וסליק זמנא תניתא לרקיעא וצלי קדם דיי וכפר על בני ישראל.

[8] Ṭabarī, Vol. I, p. 318:

سقوا الماء الذي ذرى فيه مُحالة العجل.... لما رجع موسى الى قومه اخذ العجل الذى وجدهم عاكفين عليه فذبحه ثم خرقه بالمبرد ثم ذراه في اليم.... ثم قال لهم موسى اشربوا ... فمن كان يحبّه خرج على شاربه الذهب....

Cf. Exod. 32:20: "And he (Moses) took the calf which they had made, and burnt it with fire, and ground it to powder, and strewed it upon the water, and made the children of Israel drink of it." According to Ibn Ezra, *ad loc.*, "the water had a visible effect upon the guilty which the Levites were able to detect." S. Ch. p. 552n.

[9] לא נתכוין אלא לבודקן כסוטות (עבודה זרה מ"ד, ע"א). Cf. Rashi to Exod. 32:20: נתכוין לבודקן כסוטור. See also רשב"ם, *ad loc.*, בדקן כסוטות.

VERSES 88–89

> Say, 'If the abode of the future with God is yours alone and not mankind's: long for death then if ye speak the truth.' But they will never long for it because of what their hands have sent on before; but God is knowing as to the wrong doers.

Muḥammad seems to reject the idea that all Israel have a portion in the world to come.[1] Nor is he aware of the liberal talmudic concept, as found in early rabbinic literature, that if "a gentile occupies himself with the study of the Torah he equals (in status) the High Priest," for it is said: "Ye shall therefore keep My statutes, and Mine ordinances, which if a man do, he shall live by them: I am the Lord" (Lev. 18:5). This is based on the fact that the Bible does not say " 'priests, Levites and Israelites,' but '*a man*.' "[2] Here Muḥammad accuses the Jews and the Christians of maintaining that they alone are entitled to Paradise and of considering themselves specially favored by God.[3]

[1] כל ישראל יש להם חלק לעולם הבא שנאמר ועמך כלם צדיקים לעולם ירשו ארץ (סנהדרין צ, ע״א).

[2] B. B. K. 38a; cf. B. Sanh. 59a.

[3] Cf. 3:59; 5:72.

VERSE 91

Say[1] "Who is an enemy to Gabriel?" for he hath revealed[2] to thy heart, with God's permission, confirmation of what had been before, and a guidance and glad tidings to believers.

According to Moslem tradition, the Jews objected to Muḥammad's assertion that Gabriel revealed the Koran to him, because they considered Gabriel an enemy and a messenger of wrath who announced the destruction of the first Temple, whereas the angel Michael was their friend, who brought them prosperity and plenty.[3]

Moslem commentators and exegetes also maintain that Gabriel "was charged to convey the gift of prophecy to the Israelites, and he conveyed it to another people, i. e. the Ishmaelites."[4]

Zamakhsharī relates that Omar owned a piece of land in Medina and in order to approach it he had to pass synagogues. From time to time he would visit a synagogue and listen to the discussions there. Once the Jews remarked to him, "We love you and desire you," to which Omar replied that he had some doubts pertaining to religious

[1] قل recalls the biblical דבר אל בני ישראל which appears often in the Bible, or אמר in כה אמר יהוה.

[2] *I. e.*, the Koran.

[3] Baiḍāwī, Vol. I, p. 32:

نزل في عبد الله بن صوريا سأل.... عمن ينزل عليه بالوحى فقال جبريل فقال ذاك عدونا عادانا مرارًا واشدها انه انزل على نبينا ان بيت المقدس سيخربه بختنصر.

Zamakhsharī, *ad loc.* and Margoliouth, *Mohammed* . . ., p. 91, "the angel (Gabriel) who in the New Testament conveys messages." In Luke 1:11–38 Gabriel appears as the angel of Annunciation, informing of the births of John the Baptist and of Jesus. Cf. H. L. Strack, and P. Billerbeck, *Kommentar zum Neuen Testament aus Talmud und Midrasch*, Munich, 1922, Vol. I, pp. 59–60. Although one rabbinic source claims that Gabriel set fire to the Temple at Jerusalem (L. Ginzberg, *The Legends of the Jews*, Philadelphia, 1925, Vol. V, p. 71), and another source maintains that Michael and Gabriel "carried out the work of the destruction" (*ibid.*, Vol. VI, 1928, p. 392), the authorities are unanimous in their opinion that both Michael and Gabriel were the keepers of the Temple, which was indestructible as long as they watched over it (*ibid.*).

[4] Ali, *op. cit.*, p. 50 n. 40. Cf. Ṭabarī, Vol. I, pp. 324 f.

matters and came to seek more knowledge and information. He also inquired about angel Gabriel and was told that Gabriel was the enemy of the Jews because he disclosed their secrets to Muḥammad. They further told him that Gabriel to the Jews, is the messenger of affliction and punishment, whereas, Michael is their bearer of prosperity and peace. Omar then inquired: "How are they (the angels) placed with God?" They replied: "Gabriel is on the right hand of God and Michael on the left."[5]

Geiger,[6] relying on a Responsum[7] of Rabbi Solomon ben Adret of Barcelona (1225–1310), sees some justification for Moslem tradition about Gabriel, but attributes it to the fact that the Moslem exegetes perverted the truth and failed to realize that to the Jews Gabriel is the messenger of God for the punishment of sinners only. In fact, Geiger argues that the Talmud presents Gabriel as one who "hides the sins of Israel,"[8] i. e. wipes them away.

Although at times Gabriel's mission is that of destruction as is the case when he came to Abraham to inform him that he would overturn

[5] Zamakhsharī, Vol. I, p. 92:
وروي انه كان لعمر رضي الله عنه ارض باعلى المدينة وكان ممرّه على مدارس اليهود وكان يجلس اليهم ويسمع كلامهم فقالوا يا عمر قد احببناك وانا لنطمع فيك فقال والله ما اجيئكم لحبكم ولا اسالكم لانّى شاك في ديني وانما ادخل عليكم لازداد بصيرة في امر محمد... وارى آثاره في كتابكم ثم سالهم عن جبرئيل فقالوا ذاك عدوّنا يُطلع محمداً على اسرارنا وهو صاحب كل خسف وعذاب وان ميكائيل يجيئ بالخصب والسلام فقال لهم وما منزلتهما من الله تعالى قالوا اقرب منزلة جبرئيل عن يمينه وميكائيل عن يساره. Cf. Ṭabarī, Vol. I, p. 327.

[6] Geiger, *op. cit.*, pp. 13–14.

[7] On B. B. B. 74b: חכמינו זכרונם לברכה כנו בכל מקום מדת הדין לגבריאל כאמרם בא גבריאל וחבטן בקרקע גבריאל בא להפוך את סדום.

[8] "Und allerdings demnach manches Wahre in dieser Geschichte enthalten ist, so ist doch selbst der angeführte Ausspruch verdreht, indem Gabriel als Boten Gottes bloss die Bestrafung der Sünder obliegt und von ihm sogar an einer andern Stelle des Talmud Sanh. 44 gesagt wird, er heisse אטמון 'Verstopfer' שאוטם עונתיהם של ישראל 'weil er verstopft die Sünden Israels', sie verwischt, also den Israeliten durchaus nicht als Feind dargestellt wird," *ibid.*, p. 14.

Sodom,[9] there is no source found in the Talmud and subsequent rabbinic literature that would indicate in any way that Gabriel was an enemy of the Jews.[10] On the contrary, Gabriel is known in the Talmud as the "intercessory spirit" who always intercedes on behalf of Israel.[11] He is also known in rabbinic literature as the angel who pleads for mitigation of punishment and as the bearer of good tidings.[12] He is one of the four angels surrounding the throne of the Almighty and is the recorder of all human deeds and thoughts.[13] All angels, states the Talmud, are created for specific missions; but Michael and Gabriel are eternal.[14] Even though, in Jewish tradition, Michael is placed on the right side and Gabriel on the left side of the Almighty,[15] both share equally in importance and in function,[16] and very often Gabriel's position is featured. Thus, Gabriel was the first to be sent by God to fetch the dust collected from the corners of the earth for the creation of man,[17] a legend quoted by Ṭabarī.[18]

The Midrash relates that Abraham "was still communing with himself when the angel Gabriel approached him and met him with the greeting, 'Peace be with thee,' and Abraham returned, 'With thee be peace,' and asked, 'Who art thou?' And Gabriel answered, and said, 'I am the angel Gabriel, the messenger of God,' and he led Abraham to a spring of water near by, and Abraham washed his face

[9] והנה שלשה אנשים נצבים עליו; . . . גבריאל אזל למיהפכיה לסדום (בבא מציעא פו, ע"ב; cf. תרגום ירושלמי, בראשית יח, ב; בראשית רבה, פ"נ, ב').

[10] מיכאל וגבריאל שרי ישראל הם (ילקוט ראובני בראשית כ"ו, ע"ג). Cf. שמות רבה, פי"ח, ה.

[11] B. Sanh. 44b; cf. "'Iṭmon" in *Aruch Completum*, ed. A. Kohut, Vienna, 1878 and דקדוקי סופרים, יומא, קכ"א.

[12] Louis Ginzberg, *The Legends of the Jews*, Vol. VI, p. 434. Cf. שמות רבה, פי"ח, ה; B. Yom. 77a.

[13] כשם שברא הקב"ה ד' רוחות וכנגדן ד' דגלים כך סיבב לכסאו ד' מלאכים מיכאל וגבריאל ואוריאל ורפאל . . . גבריאל מלפניו כנגד מלכות יהודה (במדבר רבה פ"ב, י; מדרש תלפיות אות ד' ענף דגים).

[14] מיכאל וגבריאל שהן שרים של מעלה דכולא מתחלפין ואינון לא מתחלפין (בראשית רבה פע"ח א; בכל יום בורא הקב"ה כת חדשה של מלאכים ואומרים שירה חוץ ממיכאל וגבריאל (מקדש מלך לזהר שמיני פ"י רמז ל"ט סע"ב); cf. also איכה רבתי פ"ב ג.)

[15] מיכאל מימינא גבריאל משמאלא . . . (זהר במדבר קי"ח ב'); cf. סדור, קריאת שמע על המטה and *Maḥzor Yom Kippur*.

[16] שיר השירים רבה פ"ג, ו; מדרש תלפיות אות דלת, ענף דגים; cf. S. A. Horodetzky, "Michael und Gabriel," *MGWJ* (1928), pp. 449–50; Ginzberg, *op. cit.*, Vol. V, p. 71.

[17] M. Gaster, *The Chronicles of Yeraḥmeel*, London, 1899, p. 15.

[18] Ṭabarī, *Annals*, Vol. I, p. 87:

فبعث الله جبرئيل عم الى الارض ليأتيه بطين منها...

and his hands and feet, and he prayed to God, bowing down and prostrating himself."[19] It was Gabriel who bade Abraham "to proclaim the true faith to his father and his mother."[20] Gabriel also dwelt with Abraham in prison and provided him with food and water.[21] Similarly when Abraham proclaimed God when still a babe it was Gabriel, according to Jewish tradition, who was sent to assist and care for him.[22] The Midrash abounds in legends designating Gabriel as the protector of Abraham during the vicissitudes of his life.[23]

Similarly we observe the importance of Gabriel's position in the life of Moses.[24] Gabriel was a witness when God proclaimed the New Moon before Moses and Aaron,[25] and was appointed by God to take charge of it.[26] It was through Gabriel that Pharaoh's daughter had

[19] Ginzberg, *op. cit.*, Vol. I, 1913, pp. 189–90.

[20] *Ibid.*, p. 193.

[21] *Ibid.*, p. 198.

[22] *Ibid.*, Vol. V, pp. 210 f.; cf. R. Margaliyuth, מלאכי עליון, Jerusalem, 1935, p. 32. Gabriel also acted as a guide to Ishmael in his ascension to heaven (J. D. Eisenstein, *'Oẓar Midrashim*, New York, 1918, p. 400). He was also the protector of Isaac (זהר בא, מ"א, ב).

[23] Cf. "(For) when the wicked Nimrod cast our father Abraham into the fiery furnace, Gabriel said to the Holy One, blessed be He: 'Sovereign of the Universe! Let me go down, cool (it), and deliver that righteous man from the fiery furnace.' Said the Holy One, blessed be He, to him: 'I am unique (יחיד) in My world, and he is unique (יחיד) in his world: it is fitting for Him who is unique (ליחיד) to deliver him who is unique (יחיד)'. But because the Holy One, blessed be He, does not withhold the (merited) reward of any creature, he said to him, 'Thou shalt be privileged to deliver three of his descendants' " (B. Pes. 118a).

Simon the Shilonite remarked: "When the wicked Nebuchadnezzar cast Hananiah, Mishael, and Azariah into the fiery furnace, Yurḳami, Prince of hail, rose before the Holy One, blessed be He, and said to Him: 'Sovereign of the Universe! Let me go down and cool the furnace and save these righteous men from the fiery furnace.' Said Gabriel to him, 'The might of the Holy One, blessed be He, is not thus (manifested), for thou art the Prince of hail, and all know that water extinguishes fire. But I, the Prince of fire, will go down and cool it within and heat it without (to burn those who threw them into it), and will thus perform a double miracle (נס בתוך נס).' Said the Holy One, blessed be He, to him, 'Go down.' It was then that Gabriel commenced (with praise) and said, '*And the truth of the Lord endureth for ever*' " (B. Pes. 118a–118b); see also [B] תנחומא, תצוה ח.

[24] Ginzberg, *op. cit.*, Vol. II, p. 331; Vol. III, pp. 440, 472; Vol. V, p. 415; cf. R. Margaliyuth, *op. cit.*, p. 35.

[25] *Ibid.*, Vol. II, p. 362.

[26] *Ibid.*, Vol. V, p. 164.

compassion on Moses when she found him, since he caused Moses to cry.[27] Later on as a child, in Pharaoh's home, when seated in the lap of the king, Moses chanced to remove the crown from the head of the Egyptian ruler and placed it on his own head. Pharaoh then became alarmed and sought advice from his counsellors,[28] who interpreted this act as a threat to Pharaoh's crown. He was therefore urged to test Moses' intelligence by placing before him two bowls; one full of gold coins and the other full of live coal. Should the infant reach for the gold it would prove his superior intelligence and he would be put to death. In order to save Moses' life Gabriel directed the infant's little fingers to the live coal. The child threw the hot coal into his mouth, burnt his tongue, and remained tongue-tied for life.[29]

According to Jewish tradition, the angel of the Lord who appeared before Moses in the flame of fire from the midst of the bush was the angel Gabriel,[30] and in crossing the Red Sea it was Gabriel who kept the waters from drowning the Israelites.[31] At the revelation on Sinai, Michael and Gabriel took hold of the two hands of Moses,[32] and it was Gabriel who taught him how to fashion the candlestick.[33]

As for Gabriel's mission in the future, the Talmud relates that both Michael and Gabriel will appear before God to plead for the restoration of the Jewish people.[34] Similarly in the world to come when God will bring the righteous to Paradise, Gabriel will be instructed by God to greet them in His name. "Soon Gabriel together with Michael, as the angels of Israel, will proceed to the entrance and welcome them."[35]

It appears, in view of the above, that the real reason for choosing Gabriel as the angel of Muḥammad's revelation was Gabriel's unique position in the lives of Abraham and Moses, the expounder of Monotheism and the author of the Mosaic Law, respectively.

As in Jewish tradition, Muḥammad, too, treats Moses and

[27] ... בא גבריאל והכה למשה כדי שיבכה ותתמלא עליו רחמים (שמות רבה פ"א, כ"ח)

[28] Ginzberg, *op. cit.*, Vol. II, p. 274.

[29] ובא גבריאל ודחה את ידו ותפש את הגחלת והכניס ידו עם הגחלת לתוך פיו ונכוה לשונו וממנו נעשה כבד פה וכבד לשון (שמות רבה פ"א לא; ילקוט שמעוני שמות, רמז קס"ו).

[30] שמות רבה, פב, ח.

[31] בשעה שירדו ישראל לים ירד גבריאל עמהם והקיפם ושמרם כחומה, והיה מכריז... הזהרו בישראל שעתידין לקבל התורה... (ילקוט שמעוני, בשלח, רמז רל"ד).

[32] פדר"א, פמ"א.

[33] אמר ר' יוחנן גבריאל חגור כמין פסקיא היה והראה לו למשה מעשה מנורה (מנחות, כ"ט, ע"א).

[34] B. Pes. 118b; cf. שמות רבה פי"ח, ה.

[35] R. Margaliyuth, *op. cit.*, p. 44.

Abraham as well as Joseph[36] as teachers and great leaders. It is interesting that in the Mecca Suras, when Islām is still in the embryonic stage, Gabriel is not mentioned at all. Only later in the Medina period, when Muḥammad crystallized his theory on Islām, does Gabriel appear.[37] In Judaism Moses is considered superior to all the prophets. Similarly in the Koran, Muḥammad is considered "the Seal of the Prophets,"[39] and like Moses, a shepherd[40] chosen in the desert,[41] a messenger of God to lead his people,[42] Muḥammad, too, calls himself Rasūl,[43] the messenger of God.

[36] Gabriel taught Joseph seventy languages (B. Soṭ. 36b). Similarly to Jewish tradition, Muḥammad emphasizes Gabriel's important role in the life of Joseph. In the Koran he devotes a whole Sura (XII) to Joseph. Islāmic tradition, too, knows of Joseph's knowledge of *seventy* languages. Zamakhsharī, (Vol. I, p. 663) states: وكان الملك يتكلم بسبعين لسانا فكلمه بها فاجابه بجميعها فتعجب منه.

Muḥammad was thus much impressed by Joseph and no wonder that he refers to the story of Joseph in the Koran as "the most beautiful." Cf. Schapiro, I., *Die haggadischen Elemente* . . . , Leipzig, 1907, p. 51.

[37] Hirschfeld, *Neue Beitr.* . . ., p. 19; Horovitz, *HUCA*, p. 158 and *Koranische* . . ., p. 107. Abraham and Moses are the most frequently mentioned biblical personages in the Koran. Abraham is mentioned about seventy times, and Moses over one hundred and thirty times.

[38] אבי הנביאים, ויקרא רבה, פ"א, טו; Maimonides, הלכות יסודי התורה פ"ז, ה"ו; cf. "And there hath not arisen a prophet since in Israel like unto Moses, whom the Lord knew face to face" (Deut. 34:10); notes to 2:254. See also מכילתא, מסכתא דשירה, בשלח, פ"ט [W]; B. Yeb. 49b and וכל מי שהיה מתנבא מעין נבואתו של משה היה (שמות רבה, פמ"ב, ח).

[39] خاتم النبيين, 33:40. Cf. Ḥag. 2:23: ושמתיך כחותם; Hirschfeld, *op. cit.*, p. 22, re the discovery of the Seal of Prophecy by the Christian monk Baḥīra.

[40] Exod. 3:1–2 ". . . and he led the flock to the farthest end of the wilderness, and came to the mountain of God, unto Horeb. And the angel of the Lord appeared unto him in a flame of fire out of the midst of a bush . . ." Cf. Reynold A. Nicholson, *A Literary History of the Arabs*, p. 147, and 16:121; 20:13.

[41] Exod. 3:1 רעה את צאן יתרו; cf. Nicholson, *op. cit.*, pp. 147–62. A tradition from the prophet states that " 'God has never chosen a man to be a prophet, who has not herded sheep'," Bu., 26:2; 60:29; 70:50, quoted by W. Thomson, *op. cit.*, p. 99.

[42] Muḥammad considered himself closer to Moses than the Jews (Bu., Vol. I, p. 498): ... فانا احق بموسى منكم ....

Cf. Ps. 106:23: ". . . Had not Moses His chosen stood before Him in the

To establish that he was the first and true monotheist, Muḥammad claimed that Abraham was neither a Jew nor a Christian,[44] but the true expounder of monotheism and that the Koran as revealed to him by Allah through the angel Gabriel[45] embodied the true monotheistic teachings which the Jews and the Christians had failed to follow.[46] Tracing his genealogy to Abraham[47] through his son Ishmael, Muḥammad seemed to have selected Gabriel as the angel of Revelation because to him Gabriel was the only one closely associated with the exalted of all the prophets and with the "father of monotheism,"[48] the law giver[49] and expounder of the "true" revelation, respectively.[50]

---

breach . . ." Cf. Exod. 7:16: ... אל' העברים שלחני אליך and Deut. 34:11: אשר שלחו יהוה; 2:125, 179–181; 7:141 and compare with رسول. See also A. Sprenger, *Das Leben* . . ., Vol. II, p. 251 f.; Horovitz, *Kor. Unt.* . . ., p. 44; Wensinck, "Rasul," *Acta Orientalia*, Vol. II, 1922, p. 168; S. D. Goitein, "Who Were Muhammed's Chief Teachers?" in *Weil Jubilee Volume*, Jerusalem, 1953, p. 20 n. 37.

[43] 2:101 (Ali ed.): ولما جاءهم رسول من عند الله. Cf. A. Jeffery, *The Qur'ān* . . ., p. 19.

[44] 3:60, 89. Cf. 2:118, 125.

[45] Bu., Vol. I, p. 6:

وكان رسول الله.... بعد ذلك اذا اتاه جبرئيل استمع فاذا انطلق جبرئيل قرأه النبي.... كما قرأ.

[46] Jalālain 2:141:

ومن اظلم ممن الخ اى لا احدا اظلم منه وهم اليهود كتموا شهادة في التوراة لابراهيم بالحنيفة.

[47] Cf. 2:129, 134; 3:60; 6:79; 16:121, 124; *Gen. Rab.* 14,6.

[48] According to Baidawī, Vol. I, p. 80, the sect of Islām is essentially the sect of Abraham": ملة الاسلام التي هي في الاصل ابراهيم.

[49] Cf. Maimonides, מורה נבוכים, ח"ב, פל"ה; הלכות יסודי התורה פ"ח, ה"ב.

[50] See notes to 2:118–19, 125, 260, 262. Cf. קיים אברהם אבינו כל התורה כולה (יומא כח, ע"ב); Mishnah Ḳid. 4:14 and B. Ber. 13a: אברם הוא אברהם בתחלה נעשה אברהם אבינו ... היה ראש לכל הצדיקים; אב לארם ולבסוף נעשה אב לכל העולם (שיר השירים רבה פג, יג); and B. Ber. 7b: מיום שברא הקב"ה את העולם לא היה אדם שקראו להקב"ה אדון עד שבא אברהם וקראו אדון. Also Maimonides הלכות עבודת כוכבים, פ"א, ה"ג; וכן אתה מוצא שלא ירש אברהם אבינו העולם הזה והעולם הבא אלא בזכות אמונה שהאמין ביי שנאמר והאמין בה' ויחשבה לו צדקה (מכילתא, מסכתא דויה, בשלח, פ"ו [W]); and מלמד שקיים אברהם אבינו את כל המצוות ואת כל התורות (אגדת בראשית, עכ"ה).

VERSE 96

> And they follow that which the devils recited[1] against Solomon's kingdom;[2] — it was not Solomon who misbelieved, but the devils who misbelieved, teaching men sorcery, — and what has been revealed to the two angels at Babylon, Hârût and Mârût; yet these taught no one until they said, 'We are but a temptation,[3] so do not misbelieve.' Men learn from them only that by which they may part man and wife; but they can harm no one therewith, unless with the permission of God, and they learn what hurts them and profits them not. And yet they knew that he who purchased it would have no portion in the future; but sad is the price at which they have sold their souls, had they but known.

The story of the two angels Hārūt and Mārūt teaching men sorcery by which they might cause division between man and wife is ascribed by Geiger[4] to the Jewish legend about the two angels Shamḥazai and 'Azael[5] who in the time of Noah lived in immorality with the daughters of men, for these were beautiful and they could not tame their lust.[6]

[1] Ali, *op. cit.*, p. 51, translates "the devils fabricated," تتلوا.

[2] *Ibid.*, p. 52, "prophethood," ملك.

[3] *Ibid.*, "a trial," فتنة.

[4] Geiger, *op. cit.*, pp. 105–6. Cf. Horovitz, *Koranische Untersuchungen*, p. 146. For an elaborate discussion on angels in Jewish and Christian traditions who rebelled against God and were cast down as Satan, see B. J. Bamberger, *Fallen Angels*, Philadelphia, 1952, pp. 113–17. Also B. Heller, "La Chute des Anges: Schmhazai, Ouzza, et Azaël," *R.E.J.*, Vol. 60 (1910), pp. 201–3; L. Jung, "Fallen Angels," *JQR* N. S. (1926), 295–310; E. Littman, "Hārūt und Mārūt" in *Festschrift Friedrich Carl Andreas zur Vollendung des Siebzigsten Lebensjahres*, Leipzig, 1916, pp. 70 ff.; H. A. Wolfson, *Philo*, Vol. I, pp. 384–85; Wensinck, "Hārūt," *E. I.* (1927), Vol. II, pp. 272–73.

[5] According to the Talmud: " 'Sihon and Og were the sons of Ahijah the son of Shamhazai' (one of the fallen angels referred to in Gen. 6:2, 4 as '*sons of God*' or '*Nephilim*')" (B. Nid. 61a). Cf. *Gen. Rab.* 26,7.

[6] Geiger, *op. cit.*, p. 105: שאלו תלמידיו את רב יוסף מהו עזאל אמר להם כון שעמדו דור המבול ועבדו עבודה זרה היה הקב"ה מתעצב מיד עמדו שני המלאכים שמחזי ועזאל ואמרו לפניו רבונו של עולם הלא אמרנו לפניך כשבראת את עולמך מה אנוש כי תזכרנו אמר להם ועולם מה יהא עליו אמרו לו רבש"ע היינו מסתפקין בו, א' ל', גלוי וידוע לפני אם אתם שרוין בארץ היה שלט בכם יצר הרע והייתם קשים מבני אדם א' ל' תן לנו

The angel Shamḥazai later repented and hung himself up between heaven and earth.[7]

Zamakhsharī and Baiḍāwī assign this story to the era of Solomon's kingdom. According to these commentators the devils eavesdropped and told their exaggerated lies to the priests who in turn wrote them down in books to be taught to the people. The dissemination of lies by the devils and the priests was so widespread that it was claimed that the reign of Solomon became perfect only because of his contact with the devils and his dominion over them.[8]

רשות ונדור עם הבריות ותראה איך אנו מקדשין שמך א׳ ל׳ רדו ותדורו עמהם מיד ראה שמחזי ריבה אחת ושמה איסטהר נתן עיניו בה אמר השמעי לי אמרה לו איני שמעת לך עד שתלמדני שם המפרש שאתה עלה בו לרקיע בשעה שאתה זכרהו למדה אותו שם הזכירה אותו ועלתה לרקיע ולא קלקלה אמר הקב״ה הואיל ופרשה עצמה מן העברה לכו וקבעוה בין שבעה כוכבים הללו כדי שתזכרו בה לעולם ונקבעה בכימה מיד . . . עמדו ונשאו נשים והולידו בנים היווא והיא ועזאל היה על מיני צבעונים ועל מיני תכשיטין של נשים שמפתין את בני אדם להרהור עברה.

Geiger, *ibid.*, p. 107, claims that the similarity between the Koranic statement and the midrashic story receives full corroboration from later Moslem authors, who, quite in harmony with the midrashic legend, speak in similar vein about these angels. He quotes the following statement from Maracci, Prodromi IV, 82:

وقال مجاهد عجبت الملايكة من ظلم بنى آدم وقد جاءتهم الرسل فقال لهم ربهم اختاروا منكم اثنين انزلهما يحكمان فى الارض فكانا هاروت وماروت فحكما فعدلا حتى نزلت عليهما الزهرة احسن فى صورة امراة تخاصم زوجها فافتتنا بها وارادا على نفسها فطارت الزهرة فرجعت حيث كانت... قال محمد وقد ذكر يحيى من غير مجاهد ان المراة التى افتتنا فيها كانت من اهل الدنيا.

[7] Cf. Horovitz, *Koranische Untersuchungen*, pp. 147 f., and *HUCA*, pp. 164–65.

[8] Zamakhsharī, Vol. I, p. 94:

اي على عهد ملكه وفي زمانه ـــ وذلك ان الشياطين كانوا يسترقون السمع ثم يضمّون الى ما سمعوا اكاذيب يلفّقونها ويُلقونها الى الكَهَنَة وقد دوّنوها فى كتب يقرءونها ويعلّمونها الناس وفشا ذلك في زمن سليمان عليه السلام حتى قالوا ان الجن تَعلَم الغيب وكانوا يقولون هذا علم سليمان وما تمّ لسليمان ملكه الا بهذا العلم وبه تسخّر الانس والجن والريحَ التي تجري بامره.

Cf. Baiḍāwī, *ad loc.*

Arabic tradition also relates that: "The devils, having, by God's permission, tempted Solomon without success, they made use of a trick to blast his character. They wrote several books of magic, and hid them under that prince's throne, and after his death told the chief men that if they wanted to know by what means Solomon had obtained his absolute power over men, genii, and the winds, they should dig under his throne; which having done, they found the aforesaid books, which contained impious superstitions. The better sort refused to learn the evil arts therein delivered, but the common people did; and the priests published this scandalous story of Solomon, which obtained credit among the Jews, till God, say the Muhammadans, cleared that king by the mouth of their prophet, declaring that Solomon was no idolater."[9]

This recalls a Jewish legend about King Solomon whose pride, when he was on his throne, swelled because of his wealth and he overstepped the command of God (Deut. 17:16–17), and collected many horses and horsemen, amassed much silver and gold, and took many wives of foreign nationalities. Soon the wrath of God came upon him. He sent Ashmedai, king of the evil spirits, who drove Solomon off the throne, robbed him of his signet ring, and left Solomon wandering about in punishment for his folly. Solomon thus went from town to town in Judah and Israel crying: "I, Solomon, have been king over Israel and Jerusalem."[10]

Another Jewish legend relates that Ashmedai was chained by Benaiahu son of Jehoiada' at the request of King Solomon. Ashmedai then demanded to be brought before the king and later challenged Solomon to free him. When Solomon complied with his request, Ashmedai hurled the king to a distance of four hundred parasangs. Ashmedai meanwhile took possession of the king's throne, his household and also his wives. Finally he was detected and reported to the religious authorities. Following the rumors about a wandering beggar who claimed that he was the king of Israel, Solomon was finally restored to his throne.[11]

[9] Wherry, *op. cit.*, p. 326, quoting Yahya and Jaláluddín.

[10] כד הוה שלמה מלכא יתיב על כורסי מלכותיה אתגבה לביה לחדא על עתריה ועבר על גזירת מימרא דיי וכנש סוסין ורתיכין ופרשין סגיאין וצבר כספא ודהבא לחדא ואתחתן בעממין נוכראין מן יד תקיף רוגזא דיי עלוהי ושדר לותיה אשמדאי מלכא דשידי וטרד יתיה מן כורסיה מלכותיה ונטל גושפנקיה בגין דיהך מטלטל וגלי בעלמא לאוכיחותיה והוה מחזר על כרכי פילכי וכרכי ארעא דישראל בכא ופגן ואמר אנא קהלת דהוי שמיה שלמה מתקרי מן קדמת דנא הויתי מלכא על ישראל בירושלם (תרגום קהלת א, יב).

[11] B. Giṭ. 68a–68b: אמר מר הכא תרגימו שידה ושידתין . . . אמרו ליה איכא שמירא דאייתי

The Koranic notion of magic power ascribed to Solomon is variously found in early Jewish traditions.[12] Flavius Josephus alludes to it in the legend that God endowed Solomon with the ability to turn the vicious power of the demons into a power working to the advantage of man; that he mastered incantations by which diseases were cured and by which demons were exorcised.[13]

משה לאבני אפוד אמר להו היכא אישתכח אמרי ליה אייתי שידה ושידתן כבשינהו אהדדי איפשר דידעי ומגלו לך אייתי שידה ושידתי כבשינהו אהדדי אמרי אנן לא ידעינן דילמא אשמדאי מלכא דשידי ידע . . . שדריה לבנייהו בן יהוידע יהב ליה שושילתא דחקיק עלה שם ועזקתא דחקיק עלה שם וגבבי דעמרא וזיקי דחמרא אזל כרה בירא מתתאי ושפינהו למיא וסתמינהו בגבבי דעמרא וכרה בירא מעילאי ושפכינהו לחמרא וטמינהו סליק ויתיב באילנא כי אתא סייריה לגושפנקא גלייה אשכחיה חמרא . . . כי צחי לא סגיא ליה אישתי רוה וגנא נחית אתא שדא ביה שושילתא סתמיה כי אתער הוה קא מיפרזל . . . כי מטא להתם לא עיילוה לגביה דשלמה עד תלתא יומי . . . תלתא יומי עייל לקמיה שקל קניא ומשח ארבעה גרמידי ושדא קמיה א״ל מכדי כי מיית ההוא גברא לית ליה בהדין עלמא אלא ארבע׳ גרמידי השתא כבשתיה לכולי עלמא ולא שבעת עד דכבשת נמי לדידי אמר ליה לא קא בעינא מינך מידי בעינא דאיבנייה לבית המקדש וקא מיבעי לי שמירא . . . שקליה לשושילתא מיניה ויהיב ליה עיזקתיה בלעיה אותביה לחד גפיה ברקיעא ולחד גפיה בארעא פתקיה ארבע מאה פרסי על ההיא שעתא אמר שלמה מה יתרון לאדם בכל עמלו שיעמול תחת השמש . . . רב ושמואל חד אמר מלך והדיוט וחד אמר מלך והדיוט ומלך, cf. B. Sanh. 20b; *Yalkuṭ Shime'oni Ecc.* I, § 967.

[12] ומן בתר דוד קם שלמה בריה ואמליך יתיה קודשא בריך הוא על חיות ברא ועל עופי שמיא ועל ריחשא דארעא ועל שידין ועל רוחין ועל לילין והוה ידע ממלל כולהון ואינון ידעין בממליה (תרגום שני על מגלת אסתר, א, ג [M]).

[13] Josephus, *Antiquities of the Jews*, Vol. VIII, 2, 5.

VERSE 101

> Dost thou not know that God's is the kingdom of the heavens and the earth? nor have ye besides God a patron or a help.

The main idea here that only God, the king of the universe, can be of real help to man, abounds in the Bible and in the Aggada. The Psalmist exclaims: "I will lift up mine eyes unto the mountains: From whence shall my help come? My help cometh from the Lord, Who made heaven and earth" (Ps. 121:1–2). The Midrash commenting on this verse states that Israel well knows that help can come from the Creator only.[1] Numerous references are found in the Bible and the Midrash which portray God as the ruler of the heavens and earth. Thus, in Deut. 10:14, "Behold, unto the Lord thy God belongeth the heaven, and the heaven of heavens, the earth, with all that therein is." Also, Ps. 89:12: "Thine are the heavens, Thine also the earth; The world and the fulness thereof, Thou hast founded them."[2] That besides God there is no "patron or help," is also expressed in the Bible: "... And beside Me there is no saviour" (Is. 43:11).[3]

[1] אמר הקב"ה אתם יודעים מי עוזר אתכם עושה שמים וארץ (שוחר טוב קכ"א, ו). Cf. notes to 2:1–2, 109, 256.

[2] Cf. Ps. 24:1; 50:12.

[3] Cf. Jer. 17:7, "Blessed is the man that trusteth in the Lord, And whose trust the Lord is."

VERSE 102

> Do ye wish to question your apostle as Moses was questioned aforetime? but whoso takes misbelief in exchange for faith has erred from the level road.

Muḥammad, who, as already indicated in this study, compared himself to Moses, seems to allude here to Moses' dispute with Korah whom the earth swallowed up.[1] Like Moses,[2] Muḥammad was challenged by his opponents.[3]

Korah was not the only one to speak to Moses in a rebellious spirit. There were others who revolted against the authority of Moses, as is indicated in the biblical verses: "And they met Moses and Aaron, who stood in the way, as they came forth from Pharaoh; and they said unto them: 'The Lord look upon you, and judge; because ye have made our savour to be abhorred in the eyes of Pharaoh, and in the eyes of his servants, to put a sword in their hand to slay us' " (Exod. 5:20–21) or as in Numbers 14:2–3: "And all the children of Israel murmured against Moses and against Aaron; and the whole congregation said unto them: 'Would that we had died in the land of Egypt! or would we had died in this wilderness! and wherefore doth the Lord bring us into this land, to fall by the sword? Our wives and our little ones will be a prey; were it not better for us to return into Egypt?' "

According to rabbinic lore the Israelites in the desert accused Moses of exploiting them and waxing fat on the food and drink he took away from them.[4] The Talmud also tells of the Korahites who questioned Moses' morality, suspecting him of adultery with their wives.[5] There is thus a similarity between the Koranic verse and the challenge of Moses as described in the Bible.

[1] Num. 16.

[2] B. Sanh. 11a.

[3] Gastfreund, *op. cit.*, p. 19.

[4] חזי שקיה חזי כרעין אכיל מן יהודאי שתי מן יהודאי כל מדלי מן יהודאי (תלמוד ירושלמי, בכורים פ"ג, ה"ג).

[5] א"ר שמואל בר יצחק מלמד שכל אחד ואחד קינא את אשתו ממשה (סנהדרין ק"י, ע"א).

VERSE 109

> God's is the east and the west, and wherever ye turn there is God's face; verily, God comprehends and knows.

The Psalmist, too, talks in identical words about God's omnipresence: "Whither shall I go from Thy spirit? Or whither shall I flee from Thy presence? If I ascend up into heaven, Thou are there; If I make my bed in the netherworld, behold, Thou art there. If I take the wings of the morning, and dwell in the uttermost parts of the sea; Even there would Thy hand lead me, And Thy right hand would hold me" (Ps. 139:7–10).[1] Commenting on these verses the Midrash states that David addressed God as follows: "Thou knowest my sitting down and my rising up. Even the step I intend to make is not hidden from you.[2]

[1] Cf. Amos 9:2–3,6: אם יחתרו בשאול משם ידי תקחם ואם יעלו השמים משם אורידם, ואם יחבאו בראש הכרמל משם אחפש ולקחתים ואם יסתרו מנגד עיני בקרקע הים משם אצוה את הנחש ונשכם . . . . . הבונה בשמים מעלותו ואגדתו על ארץ יסדה הקורא למי הים וישפכם על פני הארץ יהוה שמו. See also 2:256.

[2] כך אמר דוד לפני הקב"ה אתה ידעת שבתי וקומי ולא עוד אלא על כל פסיעה ופסיעה שאני עתיד לפסוע כבר גלויה לפניך (שוחר טוב, קל"ט, יד). Cf. Deut. 29:28 הנסתרת ליהוה אלהינו and שאין מקום בארץ פנוי מן השכינה (במדבר רבה, פי"ב, ד).

VERSE 111

> The Originator of the heavens and the earth, when He decrees a matter He doth but say unto it, 'Be,' and it is.

Close parallels to this verse are: "By the word of the Lord were the heavens made; And all the host of them by the breath of His mouth" (Ps. 33:6) . . . . "For He spoke, and it was; He commanded, and it stood" (Ps. 33:9). According to the Talmud, the world was created by ten sayings.[1] The Midrash relates that: "The Holy One, blessed be He, spake one word and the heavens were created[2] as the residence of the Throne of His Glory . . . . He blew with His mouth the wind of the breath of life and all the host of heaven were created (simultaneously)."[3]

In 50:38 Muḥammad states: "We did create the heavens and the earth and what is between the two in six days and no weariness touched us." This idea that "no weariness touched" God in the creation of the universe and that everything was achieved by the Word is also found in the Midrash.[4]

It is interesting to note that Jewish philosophers of the middle ages were disinclined to ascribe to God even the act of speaking,[5] and therefore translated the word *wayy'omer*,[6] in connection with creation, by *wayirẓeh*,[7] meaning willed.[8]

[1] ראש השנה ל"ב, ע"א; מגילה כ"א, ע"ב; בעשרה מאמרות נברא העולם (פרקי אבות ה, א); ברוך שאמר והיה העולם . . . (סדור תפלה שלמה). Cf. אבדר"נ פל"א.

[2] Cf. Is. 45:12: "I, even I, have made the earth, and created man upon it; I, even My hands, have stretched out the heavens, And all their host have I commanded." See also John 1:3 about the Word or the Logos being the Creator.

[3] *P.R.E.*, p. 41. Cf. also, *Mekilta de-Rabbi Ishmael* (ed. J. Z. Lauterbach), Philadelphia, 1933, Vol. II, p. 62: ". . . He by whose word the world came into being spoke the ten commandments in one utterance."

[4] *Gen. Rab.* 3,2, רבי ברכיה בשם רבי יהודה בר סימון פתח בדבר ה' שמים נעשו וברוח פיו וגו'. Cf. שכשברא הקב"ה את עולמו אלא בדבר ה' לא בעמל ולא ביגיעה ברא הקב"ה את העולם לא בראו אלא במאמר (מכילתא, מסכתא דשירה, בשלח, פ"י [W]).

[5] Ibn Ezra's Commentary to Gen. 1:3: אמר הגאון כי פי' ויאמ' כמו וירצה ואילו היה כן היה ראוי להיות אור. רק הוא כמשמעו וכן בדבר יי שמים נעשו, כי הוא צוה ונבראו, והטעם כנוי על המעשה שלא היה ביגעה. Cf. Ramban *ad loc.*: . . . מלת אמירה בכאן להורות על החפץ.

[6] ויאמר.

[7] וירצה.

[8] Arabic شاء (willed). As to the terms *bara'* and *ḥalak*, see A. Jeffery, *The Foreign Vocabulary . . .*, p. 76.

VERSE 118

> And when his Lord tried Abraham with words, and he fulfilled them, He said, 'Verily I will set thee as a high priest[1] for man.' Said he, 'And of my seed?' God said, 'My covenant touches not the evil-doers.'

The story about Abraham's righteousness is found in the Bible and in rabbinic sources: "because that Abraham hearkened to My voice, and kept My charge, My commandments, My statutes, and My laws" (Gen. 26:5). The Mishnah states that: "With ten trials was Abraham, our father, proved, and he stood (firm) in them all; to make known how great was the love of Abraham, our father (peace be upon him)."[2]

The story that Abraham became a priest stems also from the Talmud: "R. Zachariah said on R. Ishmael's authority: The Holy One, blessed be He, intended to bring forth the priesthood from Shem, as it is written, *and he* (Melchizedek) *was the priest of the most high God* (Gen. 14:18). But because he gave precedence in his blessing to Abraham over God (Gen. 14:19), He brought it forth from Abraham . . . ."[3]

[1] *I. e.* اماما. "The primary sense [of *Imām*] is that of being foremost; hence it may mean: (1) leader in religion; (2) leader in congregational prayer; (3) model, pattern, example; (4) a book of guidance and instruction," A. Yusuf Ali, *The Holy Qur-an*, New York, 1934, Vol. I, p. 52 n. According to Palmer it is "the name given to the priest who leads the prayer," p. 15 n. In his lifetime Muḥammad also acted as *Imām* (Bu., Vol. I, p. 175).

[2] Mishnah Ab. 5:3. In *Abot de R. Nathan* the ten trials with which Abraham was tempted and stood steadfast in them all are enumerated: ב' בלך לך ב' בשני בניו ב' בשתי נשיו אחד עם המלכים ואחד בין הבתרים אחד באור כשדים ואחד בברית מילה (בין הבתרים) (אדר"נ פ"לג). Cf. 11:73; 15:53; 37:99–113, etc. See also Isa. 41:8, II Chron. 20:7; 2:91, and אברהם אבינו היה ראש לכל הצדיקים (שיר השירים רבה, פ"ג, ה).

[3] B. Ned. 32b; cf. אברהם כהן גדול היה (בראשית רבה, פמ"ו, ד). See also ילקוט שמעוני, לך לך, רמז עד and: אדם הראשון היה בכורו של עולם וכיון שקירב קרבנו . . . לבש בגדי כהונה גדולה . . . כיון שמת אדם מסרן לשת . . . מת נח ומסרן לשם . . . והלא יפת היה בכור . . . מפני שצפה נח שלשלת האבות עומדת ממנו . . . מת שם ומסרה לאברהם. וכי אברהם היה בכור אלא מפני שהיה צדיק נמסרה לו . . . יעקב מבקש להקריב ולא היה יכול מפני שלא היה בכור (במדבר רבה, פ"ד, ו); ומלכי צדק מלך שלם . . . נח מסר לשם . . . ונקרא כהן . . . ושם מסר לאברהם . . . ונקרא כהן שנאמר נשבע ה' ולא ינחם אתה כהן לעולם (פדר"א, פ"ח).

VERSE 119

> And when we made the House a place of resort unto men, and a sanctuary,[1] and (said) take the station of Abraham[2] for a place of prayer; and covenanted with Abraham and Ishmael, saying, 'Do ye two cleanse my house[3] for those who make the circuit, for those who pay devotions there, for those who bow down, and for those too who adore!"

According to Baiḍāwī and Zamakhsharī, Abraham ascended the mountain Abū Kobeis (near Mecca), and exclaimed: "Oh, people, go up to the sanctuary of your Lord."[4] Similarly, the Talmud relates that Abraham "caused the name of the Holy One, blessed be He, to be uttered by the mouth of every passer-by.[5] How was this? After (travellers) had eaten and drunk, they stood up to bless him; but, said he to them, 'Did you eat of mine? You ate of that which belongs to the God of the Universe. Thank, praise and bless Him who spake and the world came into being.' "[6]

[1] As to the relationship between the Hebrew מקום and the Koranic *Maḳām* consult Horovitz, *HUCA*, pp. 219–20 and Grimme, *Mohammed*, Münster, 1892, Vol. II, p. 46.

[2] Cf. notes to 2:91, 118. Abraham and Isaac are, according to Jewish tradition, the two originators of the sanctuary: למהוי אמרין בטור בית מקדשיה דיי קריב אברהם ית יצחק בריה ובטורא הדין הוא בית מקדשא איתגלית עלוי יקר שכינתא דיי (תרגום ירושלמי, בראשית כ"ב, י"ד). Muḥammad here replaces Isaac by Ishmael.

[3] Palmer (p. 15 n.) states that "the Kaabah or square temple at Mecca is spoken of as Bâit Allâh = Bethel, 'the house of God.' " Cf. Mishna Ber. 11:5, הבית הגדול והקדוש and Ps. 30:1 הבית. Compare, also, the biblical expression, והלכת אל המקום (Deut. 26:2).

[4] M. Grünbaum, *Neue Beiträge . . .*, p. 104: The expression 'thy God' in Deut. 26:3, 4 is used because the priest is "conceived as standing in a special relationship to God; cf. 'the God of Abraham' in the Liturgy." Cf. P. H., p. 859 n.; *Targum Onkelos*, Gen. 22:14: ופלח וצלי אברהם תמן באתרא ההוא ואמר קדם יי הכא יהון פלחן דריא בכן יתאמר ביומא הדין בטורא הדין אברהם קדם יי פלח (ברכות, סב, ע"ב).

[5] Based on the biblical sentence in Gen. 21:33; "And Abraham planted a tamarisk-tree in Beer-sheba, and called there on the name of the Lord, the Everlasting God."

[6] B. Soṭ. 10b; cf. *Targum Jonathan*, Gen. 21:33: ונציב אברהם פרדס בבאר שבע ואתקין בגויה מאכל ומשקה ולתחומיא והוו אכלין ושתיין והוו בעיין למתן ליה טימי די אכלו ושתו ולא

The Talmud also states: "Whosoever has a fixed place for his prayer has the God of Abraham as his helper."[7] According to the rabbis, "there was no man that called the Holy One, blessed be He, *Lord*,[8] until Abraham came and called Him *Lord*."[9]

An Arabic tradition concerning the "station of Abraham" runs as follows: "Abraham visited the house of Ismaīl in his absence, but not liking the treatment he received from his wife, left with her a message for his son, which was understood by Ismaīl to express a desire that he should divorce his wife. This he did, when he married another. Abraham came again in the absence of his son, and being urged by his daughter-in-law to descend from his camel and to permit her to wash his head, he declared that, owing to a vow not to leave his camel till he had completed his journey, he could not get down. Being pressed, however, he so far consented, that with one foot on his camel and the other on a stone he had his head washed! This is 'the place of Abraham.' "[10]

The above story undoubtedly stems from Jewish tradition. A counterpart is found in Jewish lore about the time when Abraham, against his own will, exiled his servant-wife, Hagar, and their son Ishmael. At first, Sarah did not allow Abraham to visit either his wife or his son. After many years of pleading Sarah permitted Abraham such a visit on condition that he remain atop his camel. When Abraham thus came to Ishmael's house, he was not in. Abraham called to his daughter-in-law for a drink of water. She refused to give it to him or even to look at him. She was beating the children and cursing them as well as her husband, Ishmael. Abraham became angry and left a message for his son saying: "An old man from the land of Canaan was here, and asked you to remove the main pillar of your tent and to replace it by a good one." When Ishmael came home and received the message he understood that his father had been to see him and that he was mistreated by his wife. He, therefore, divorced his wife, and married another one. Three years later, Abraham again, under identical circumstances, set out to visit his son, and did not find him home. Ishmael's wife came forth insisting that Abraham partake of food and drink. He refused to get off the camel; the good woman brought forth some food and Abraham ate and drank. Upon leaving,

צבי למקבלה מנהון והוה אמר להון אבונן אברהם מן מה דאמר והוה עלמא במימריה צלון קדם אבוכון דבשמיא דמן דיריה אכלתון ושתיתתון ולא הוו זעין מן אתריהון עד זמן דהוה מנייר יתהון ומליף יתהון אורחא דעלמא ואודי וצלי תמן אברהם בשם מימרא דיי אלהא דעלמא.

[7] B. Ber. 6 b. [8] אדון.

[9] B. Ber. 7 b.

[10] *Tafsīr-i-Raufi*, quoted in Wherry, *op. cit.*, p. 335 n.

he left a message for his son. "The pillar of your tent is very good, keep it." Ishmael now knew that his wife treated her father-in-law respectfully. He then took his whole family and returned to Abraham and remained with him many days.[11]

It is not unlikely that the Koranic verse has its antecedent in the famous prayer of Solomon at the dedication of the Temple at Jerusalem (I Kings 8:22–53). Processions are not strange to either Judaism or Christianity. In the latter there is the practice of street processions. A procession is also staged by Jews in the synagogue during the holiday of Tabernacles.[12]

The phrase, "cleanse my house," is comparable to Exod. 19:10: "and sanctify them to-day and tomorrow, and let them wash their garments." Similarly, the phrase, "a place of worship," is comparable to 1 Kings 8:42–3 where it is stated that the Temple too was supposed to be a place of worship, "when he shall come and pray toward this house" . . . . "and that they may know that Thy name is called upon this house which I have built."[13]

[11] ותקח לו אמו אשה מארץ מצרים ושמה מריבה ותהר ותלד לו ארבעה בנים ובת אחת ויתן לו אלהים בעבור אברהם אביו צאן ובקר ויפרוץ מאד ופני אביו לא ראה. ויהי מימים ויאמר אברהם אל שרה אלך ואראה את ישמעאל בני כי התאויתי לראותו וילך המדברה ויבא אל אהל ישמעאל בחצות היום וימצא אשתו ובניו, וישמעאל ואמו אין עמהם וישאל אברהם אנה ישמעאל ותאמר הלך השדה לצוד ציד ואברהם עודנו יושב על הגמל כי כן נשבע לשרה שלא ירד מעל הגמל ארצה ויאמר לה בתי תנה לי מעט מים כי עיף ויגע אני מהדרך ותאמר אין לנו לא מים ולא לחם ותשב לאהלה ולא הביטה אל אברהם ולא שאלה אותו מי הוא אך מכה את בניה ותקללם אותם ואת ישמעאל בעלה ותחרפם ויחר לאברהם מאד וירע בעיניו ויקרא אברהם אותה לצאת אליו ותצא ויאמר לה אברהם בבא אישך ישמעאל תאמר לו בא הנה איש זקן מארץ פלשתים לבקש אותך וכזה מראהו ותארו וכה אמר האיש בבואך תסיר את יתד האהל ושמת תחתיה יתד אחר וישב לדרכו ובבוא ישמעאל מצידו הוא ואמו ותדבר אשתו כדברים האלה והבין ישמעאל כי היה אביו אשר לא כבדה אותו וישמע בקול אביו ויגרשה ותלך לה. וילך אחר כך ישמעאל ארצה כנען ויקח אשה אחרת מבית אביה ופטימה שמה ויביאה האהלה במקום אשר היה שם. ויהי מקץ ג׳ שנים ויאמר אברהם אלך עוד ואראה את ישמעאל בני וירכב על גמלו ויגיע במדבר לאהל ישמעאל בחצי היום ותצא אשתו מן האהל וישאל על ישמעאל ותאמר איננו פה אדוני כי הלך לצוד השדה ולרעות הגמלים. ותאמר סורה אדוני אל האהל ואכלת פת לחם כי עיפה נפשך מן הדרך ויאמר לא אשב כי ממהר אנכי ללכת לדרכי אך תנה לי מעט מים כי צמאתי ותמהר ותרץ האהלה ותוציא מים ולחם ותתן לפניו ותפצר בו מאד לאכול ויאכל וישת ויטב לבו ויברך את ישמעאל בנו ויכל לאכול ויברך את ה׳ ויאמר לה בבוא ישמעאל תגיד לו בא הנה איש זקן מארץ פלשתים וכה אמר היתד ששמת באהל פה טובה מאד אל תסירנה ויבא ישמעאל ותגד לו אשתו בשמחה את אשר דבר הזקן וידע ישמעאל כי אביו היה ויברך ישמעאל את ה׳ ויקח ישמעאל אשתו ובניו ומקנהו וילך ארץ פלשתים אל אביו וישב עם אביו ימים רבים. (ספר ילקוט ספורים ומדרשים, וירא פי"ט, ט) Cf. also: פדר"א, פ"ל.

[12] הקפות. Cf. Mishnah Suk. 4:5.

[13] Cf. E. Landau, *Synonyma für Gott in der neu-hebräischen Litteratur*, Zürich, 1888, pp. 30–45.

VERSE 125

When his Lord said to him, 'Be resigned' he said, 'I am resigned unto the Lord of the worlds.'

Ali translates Islām as a term denoting "submission."[1] Some scholars suggest that Muḥammad's use of this verb-stem conveys the idea of "coming into the condition of security," which would render Islām as "safety."[2] Torrey claims that the term Islām was adopted by Muḥammad because his two noted ancestors, Abraham and Ishmael, yielded and surrendered themselves to the divine will.[3] Grimme renders its meaning, "man's salvation as a result of his purification."[4] Bravmann interprets Islām to mean "readiness for defiance of death" or "self-sacrifice (for the sake of God and his prophet)," which would be related semantically to *jihād* (warlike efforts for Allah and his Prophet).[5] The latter interpretation of the term Islām seems most plausible and is similar to the concept in Judaism of *Ḳiddush ha-Shem*, i. e. the sublime duty of every Israelite to hallow the Name of God by his life and if necessary by his death.[6]

In view of verses 118 and 119 it is possible that we may have here an allusion to Deut. 26:3, "I profess this day unto the Lord thy God (the God of Abraham)," and to Deut. 27:6, *'Abanim Shelemot* (unhewn stones), i. e. "whole or peaceful stones."[7] The adjective *shelemot* is of the same root as "*shalom*" (peace, salvation) or of the cognate Arabic *salām* meaning "peace."

[1] *Op. cit.*, p. 55; cf. T. W. Arnold, "Islam," *EI*, pp. 539 f.; Ch. Lyall, *JRAS* (1903), p. 784; Horovitz, *Koranische Untersuchungen . . .*, p. 54.

[2] M. Lidzbarski, "Islām und Salām," *Zeitschrift für Semitistik und verwandete Gebiete*, I (1922), pp. 85 f.

[3] *Ibid.*, pp. 101 f.; cf. Nöldeke-Schwally, *Geschichte des Qôrans*, Vol. II, p. 206, and Martin Hartmann, *Der Islam: Geschichte — Glaube — Recht*, Leipzig, 1909, pp. 26 f.

[4] Grimme, *op. cit.*, I, p. 16; Tor Andrae, *Mohammed*, pp. 55 f.

[5] M. Bravmann, "On the Spiritual Background of Early Islam and the History of its Principal Concepts" in *Muséon*, LXIV, Louvain (1951), pp. 325 f. Cf. *Tarbiẓ*, XVIII (1946–47), pp. 69–79.

[6] B. Sanh. 74a. Abraham's readiness to sacrifice his life in order to hallow the name of God is also expressed in the Midrash, [B] תנחומא, לך לך, ב.

[7] אבנים שלמות.. As to the Hebrew *Shalom*, see M. Jastrow, *Dictionary of the Talmud . . .*, Ḥoreb ed. (1926), Vol. II, p. 1579 and Eliezer Ben Yehuda, *A Complete Dictionary of Ancient and Modern Hebrew*, edited by Prof. N. H. Tur-Sinai, Jerusalem, 1952, Vol. 14, pp. 7130–35.

Moslem tradition maintains that Abraham was the first to employ the term Islām in connection with monotheism.[8] The Bible as well as the rabbis also stressed the idea that Abraham was the first true monotheist: "The Lord appeared to Abraham and said unto him: 'I am God Almighty; walk before Me, and be thou wholehearted'" (Gen. 17:1).[9] The Talmud, commenting on Psalm 15, writes: "He who walks uprightly" refers to Abraham,[10] who by virtue of his circumcision, became upright according to God's command.[11] This idea is found in the Koranic expression, "Resign thyself (to God)."

Abraham in the Bible uses the expression *Yir'at 'Elohim*[12] (the fear of God), which connotes "submission"[13] or unquestioning obedience to God.[14] To Muḥammad this expression would have meant a great deal in formulating his new religion.[15] It is interesting that the Koran refers to God as the "Peace-Giver"[16] which is identical with the biblical and talmudic concept that God is Shalom.[17]

[8] Baiḍāwī, 3:89: "(the sect of) Islām is essentially the sect of Abraham." Cf. Jalālein, 2:141: "Abraham being of the supreme faith."

[9] Cf. Thomson's statement that Abraham is considered "the pattern of all true believers in the New Testament, and that for Philo he is the type of the man who abandons home for the sake of God," *op. cit.*, p. 132. See also M. Friedländer, *Geschichte der jüdischen Apologetik*, Zürich, 1903, pp. 306 f.; and H. A. Wolfson, *Philo*, Vol. I, pp. 876 f.

[10] ...הולך תמים זה אברהם דכתיב התהלך לפני והיה תמים (מכות כ"ד, ע"א) cf. Maimonides, הלכות עבודת כוכבים פ"א, ה"ג.

[11] Cf. אמר לו הקב"ה מה את סבור שאתה תמים שלם אתה חסר מחמשה אברים, א"ל הקב"ה עד שלא תמול היה שמך אברם, ... מאתים וארבעים ושלשה ומנין אברים שבאדם מאתים וארבעים ושמונה מול והיה תמים כשמל א"ל הקב"ה לא יקרא עוד שמך אברם והיה שמך אברהם הוסיף לו ה' חמשה מנין רמ"ח אברים לפי' והיה תמים (תנחומא, לך־לך כ, ע"א).

[12] יראת אלהים.

[13] اسلام.

[14] Gen. 20:11: ויאמר אברהם כי אמרתי רק אין יראת אלהים במקום הזה; cf. Gen. 15:6: והאמן ביהוה ויחשבה לו צדקה. Cf. שהיה אברהם מגייר את האנשים (במדבר רבה, פי"ד, כג).

[15] Cf. 2:106; 3:17, 78; and Gen. 22:12, כי עתה ידעתי כי ירא אלהים אתה.

[16] 59:23, وهو الله ... السلام. Cf. Is. 42:19 מי עור כמשלם, which is explained by Rashi *ad loc.*, thus: והרי הוא כמשלם כל תגמוליו ויוצא נקי. The interpretation of the commentators on כמשלם corresponds to the Koranic idea of Islām. See מצדת דוד, *ad loc.*, כמשלם — השלם במדות.

[17] B. Shab. 10b: אסור לאדם שיתן שלום לחבירו בבית המרחץ משום שנא' ויקרא לו ה' שלום. Cf. Judg. 6:24, יהוה שלום and Rashi, *ad loc.*

The Koran states: "Lord! and send them an apostle from amongst themselves."[18] This, too, is reminiscent of a biblical sentence: "A prophet will the Lord thy God raise up unto thee, from the midst of thee, of thy brethren, like unto me . . ."[19]

[18] 2:123.

[19] Exod. 3:13, אלהי אבותיכם שלחני אליכם and Exod. 3:14, אהיה שלחני אליכם; compare שלחני with رسل; also ולא על ידי שליח אני ולא השליח or ולא על ידי שליח in הגדה של פסח; cf. notes to 2:91, 254.

VERSE 127

> Were ye then witnesses when Jacob was facing death, when he said to his son, 'What will ye serve when I am gone?' They said, 'We will serve thy God, and the God of thy fathers Abraham, and Ishmael, and Isaac, one God; and we are unto Him resigned.'

A similar story about Jacob is found in the Talmud: "R. Simeon b. Laḳish said: *And Jacob called unto his sons, and said: Gather yourselves together, that I may tell you* (*that which shall befall you in the end of the days*) (Gen. 49:1). Jacob wished to reveal to his sons the 'end of the days' (Dan. 12:13), whereupon the *Shechinah* departed from him. Said he, 'Perhaps, Heaven forfend! there is one unfit among my children, like Abraham, from whom there issued Ishmael, or like my father Isaac, from whom there issued Esau.' (But) his sons answered him, 'Hear O Israel (Jacob), the Lord our God the Lord is One: just as there is only One in thy heart, so is there in our heart only One.' In that moment our father Jacob opened (his mouth) and exclaimed, 'Blessed be the name of His glorious kingdom for ever and ever . . . .' "[1]

The *Targum Yerushalmi* is more descriptive of Jacob's position at the time. It repeats the story almost exactly with one exception. It adds to Abraham's unworthy seed all the children of Ḳeṭurah, Abraham's second wife, who were born to him after the death of Sarah.[2] It is understandable that the many legends originally related in rabbinic lore to Isaac, should later be attributed by Muḥammad to Ishmael.

Baiḍāwī writes that here Jacob designates Ishmael as one of the Patriarchs. The reason given is that Muḥammad considers an uncle (i. e. Ishmael) to be "a part of the father."[3]

[1] B. Pes. 56a. Cf. בראשית רבה, פצ״ח, ד.

[2] וקרא אבונן יעקב לבנוי ואמר להון אתכנישו ואתני לכון קיצא גניזא רזיא טמיריא ומיתין אגריא דצדיקיא ופורענותהון דרשיעיא וטליותיה דעדן מה הוא כחדא אתכנשו תרי עשרתי שבטיא דיעקב ומקפין לדרגשה דדהבה דהוה אבונן יעקב רביע בגוה בעיין די יתני להון קץ ברכתא ונחמתא מן די אתגלי ליה רזא איתכסי מניה מן די אפתח לה תרעא איטרד מניה חזר אבונן יעקב ובריך לבנוי גבר כעובדוי טביא בריך יתהון: מן דאתכנשו תרי עשרתי שבטוי דיעקב ואקיפו דרגשא דדהבא דהוה אבונן יעקב רביע בגוה סברין דהוא גלי להון סדרי ברכתא ונחמתא ואיתכסי מניה: ענה אבונן יעקב ואמר להון אברהם אבוי דאבא קם מניה פיסול ישמעאל וכל בני קטורה ויצחק אבא קם מניה פיסול עשו אחי ואנא דחיל דלא יהי ביניכון גבר לביה פליג על אחוי למיזל למפלח קדם טעוון אוחרניין עניין תרי עשרתי שבטוי דיעקב כולהון כחדא ואמרין שמע מנן ישראל אבונן יי אלהנא יי חד עני יעקב אבונן ואמר יהא שמיה רבא מברך לעלמי עלמין (תרגום ירושלמי, בראשית מ״ט, א).

[3] Baiḍāwī, Vol. I, p. 39: وعد اسمعيل من آبائه تغليبا للاب والجد او لانه كالاب لقوله عليه الصلاة والسلام عم الرجل صنو ابيه كما قال عليه الصلاة والسلام في العباس رضى الله عنه هذا بقية آبائى.

VERSE 129

> . . . But the faith of Abraham the 'Hanîf, he was not of the idolators.'

In this verse as well as in 3:89; 4:124; 6:162; 16:121, 124, Muḥammad refers to Abraham as *ḥanīf* (pl. *ḥunafa'*), whereas in 6:79; 10:105; 30:29, he claims himself to be one of the *ḥunafa'* and requests his followers to join him in their ways and customs, since the *ḥunafa'* possessed the real and true religion. Scholars are puzzled by the origin and meaning of the term *ḥanīf*. According to Torrey, the word "came originally from the Hebrew חנף, *ḥānēf*; and probably its employment by him (Muḥammad) as a term of praise, rather than of reproach, indicates that in his mind it designated one who '*turned away*' from the surrounding paganism."[1] Nicholson suggests that it is "connected with the Hebrew *ḥánef*" (profane).[2] However, Wellhausen thinks that *ḥanīf* originally meant a Christian ascetic and regards it as a native Arab development.[3]

In describing his condition when the angel appeared to him, Muḥammad used the word *Taḥannuth*.[4] Hirschfeld states: "The term has caused the traditionalists some embarrassment. I. Ish. explains it by *taḥannuf* (to profess to be a *Ḥanîf*), and adds a remark which is interesting from a linguistic point of view, *viz.*, that *th* and *f* interchange in Arabic. This remark is welcomed with satisfaction by Sprenger, who finds it a support of his *Hanyferei*. I believe, however, that *taḥannuth* is nothing but the Hebrew pluralis *t'eḥinnôth*, 'prayers,' a word very common among Jews to express voluntary devotions apart from the official liturgy. There is little doubt, that Muhammed heard this word often in Medina before he framed his report of the affair, and employed it readily on account of its strange and sacred character."[5]

[1] Torrey, *op. cit.*, p. 87.

[2] Nicholson, *op. cit.*, p. 149.

[3] *Reste* . . . , II, pp. 238 f.; cf. J. A. Montgomery, "Ascetic Strains in Early Judaism," *JBL*, Vol. LI (1932), pp. 183 f.

[4] Numerous articles have appeared on this word. Cf. Faris-Glidden, *JAOS*, Vol. 19 (1939), pp. 1 f., who consider the term to stem from Greek; A. J. Wensinck, *Acta Orientalia*, Vol. II, p. 191; Ahrens, *op. cit.*, p. 14; D. S. Margoliouth, *JRAS*, 1903, pp. 467–93; J. Horovitz, *Koranische Untersuchungen*, p. 56; A. Jeffery, *Foreign Vocabulary* . . ., pp. 112–15.

[5] Hirschfeld, *New Researches* . . ., p. 19 n.; cf. Tor Andrae, *Der Ursprung des*

Nöldeke defines the root *ḥannath*[6] as "leading a solitary life," which the *Ḥanīfs* must have followed. According to the Talmud,[7] the devotee who spends the night studying the Torah is commended. Similarly, Muḥammad states: "Of the people of the Book there is a nation upright reciting God's signs through the night, as they adore the while" (3:109).

Islam und das Christentum, Uppsala, 1926, p. 40; Charles Lyall, "The Words 'Ḥanif' and 'Muslim'," *JRAS* (1903), p. 772; Sprenger, *Das Leben . . .*, Vol. I, pp. 45–134; Bravmann, *op. cit.*, p. 342.

[6] حنث. *Geschichte des Qorâns*, p. 67; cf. Hirschberg, *op. cit.*, pp. 211 f.

[7] B. Tam. 32b.

VERSE 136

> The fools among men will say, 'What has turned them from their quiblah,[1] on which they were agreed?' Say, 'God's is the east and the west, He guides whom He will unto the right path.'

Muḥammad never intended to make Islām a new religion.[2] At the beginning he considered himself "a guardian over it,"[3] to preserve the truth and "confirming what was before it."[4] It is for this reason that at first he saw no difference between Christianity and Judaism[5] and, according to scholars, was almost converted to Judaism.[6] He believed that both Jews and Christians would welcome him as the "Seal of the Prophets."[7] It was only later, when he realized that he could gain support from neither camp, that he presented Islām as a new faith,[8] and changed the *qiblah* from Jerusalem to Mecca.[9]

Jalāluddīn[10] writes that after the *hijrah*, Muḥammad, in order to

[1] *Qiblah* is the place towards which prayer is to be made. Cf. Wensinck, "Ka'ba," *E. I.*, pp. 583 f.; Grimme, *Mohammed*, p. 45; Wellhausen, *Reste arabischen Heidentums*, p. 73; J. L. Burckhardt, *Travels in Arabia*, London, 1829, Vol. I, pp. 87 f.

[2] Cf. 51:50; 74:2; 88:21–22; J. A. Montgomery, *Arabia and the Bible*, Philadelphia, 1934, pp. 31 f.

[3] 5:48, مهيمنا عليه. Cf. Baiḍāwī, Vol. I, p. 131:
ورقيبا على سائر الكتب يحفظه عن التغيير ويشهد له بالصحة والثبات.

[4] 3:2; Muḥammad is quoted to have said: "Transmit (what you hear) from me, be it only a verse; relate also (what you hear) from the children of Israel; thereby is no sin incurred." Bu., 60:589, cited by W. R. Taylor, *op. cit.*, p. 196.

[5] Cf. 2:285; 3:2, 78; cf. Baiḍāwī, Vol. I, p. 70: "He has sent down to thee the Book in truth . . . to Moses and Jesus respectively."

[6] Margoliouth, *Relations* . . ., p. 67.

[7] 33:40, خاتم النبيين. Cf. 2:91.

[8] 3:61 f.

[9] J. Rivlin, "Muḥammad Hameḥoḳeḳ," in *Kenesset* (1933), p. 295 n.: במשך ימי נבואתו הוא מדמה להיות שליח לכל העולם. בענין זה בא שינוי בהשקפתו על שליחותו שלכתחילה ראה את עצמו כשליח לערבים. . . . נבואתו כנבואתם העתקה היא מספר אלהים אשר אתו בשמים.

[10] Quoted by Geiger, *op. cit.*, p. 19:
لما هاجر امر باستقبال بيت المقدس تالفا لليهود ستة او سبعة شهرا.

please the Jews, instructed his followers to turn the *qiblah* to Jerusalem[11] rather than to Mecca, the place which the ancient Arabs had always regarded as holy. Only later on, when he was convinced of his failure to conciliate the Jews did Muḥammad change back to the original direction.[12]

According to Moslem tradition, "the whole earth is a mosque and if there is no house of worship, prayers may be offered anywhere."[13] This follows the Jewish tradition that Divine presence is everywhere.[14] As to the last phrase in the Koranic verse, "God's is the east and the west . . .," Jewish tradition abounds in references praising the universality of God.[15]

[11] Dan. 6:11; cf. Ben-Zeeb, *op. cit.*, p. 29, quoting Ibn Hishām, Vol. I, pp. 217, 314.

[12] The Jews of Arabia were never pleased with Muḥammad's order to turn to Jerusalem. Cf. Ṭabarī, Vol. II, p. 12; Wensinck, *op. cit.*, pp. 105, 133; Nöldeke-Schwally, p. 74; Hirschberg, *op. cit.*, p. 317 note 47, and Pollack, *op. cit.*, p. 68: שינוי זה של הַקִּבְלָה (כיוון־התפילה) חל בשעת תפילת הצבור, באמצע חדש רג׳ב או שעבאן.

[13] Bu., Vol. I, p. 93:

وجُعلت لي الارض مسجدًا وطهورا فايما رجل من امتي ادركته الصلوة فليصل.

[14] Cf. שאין מקום בארץ פנוי מן השכינה (במדבר רבה, פי״ב, ד); and: תנא בשם ר׳ אחא בר יעקב . . . מקוה ישראל ה׳ מה המקוה הזה מטהר את הטמאים אף הקב״ה מטהר את ישראל. ומי ראוי לילך אצל מי הוי אומר הטמא צריך לילך אצל המקוה ולטבול בו. כך אמר הקב״ה אני אמרתי כשאתה מתפלל התפלל בבית הכנסת שבעירך. ואם אתה אינך יכול לילך בבית הכנסת שבעירך. התפלל בתוך ביתך ואם אין אתה יכול לילך להתפלל תתפלל על מטתך. ואם אין את יכול לדבר הרהר בלבך. הה״ד אמרו בלבבכם על משכבכם ודומו סלה (שוחר טוב, ד, מה).

[15] לה׳ הארץ ומלואה . . . מלא כל הארץ כבודו. And cf.: אבל הקב״ה מלא עליונים ותחתונים שנאמר . . . הודו על ארץ ושמים, ואומר . . . הלא את השמים ואת הארץ אני מלא (שוחר טוב, כ״ד, יא).

VERSE 137

> Thus have we made you a middle nation,[1] to be witnesses against men, and that the Apostle may be a witness against you.[2]

Translators vary as to the meaning of the phrase, "a middle nation." Some take it to mean an "intermediate people" between the Jews and the Christians. Others translate it "exalted" or "a chosen people" or a most good and just nation.[3] The last explanations seem plausible. The Arabs, no less than other nations, boasted of being a chosen people, in direct imitation of the biblical statements: "then ye shall be Mine own treasure from among all peoples" (Exod. 19:5) and "and ye shall be unto Me a kingdom of priests" (*ibid.* 19:6).[4]

Some Moslem commentators also explain the meaning of the above words as "a well balanced nation." That is, the midst is equally distant from all extremities.[5] A similar explanation is found in Judah Hallevi's *Kitab Al-Khazari*,[6] in connection with the high qualities of Israel and the Holy Land. Being situated in the midst of the world,[7] the Holy Land enjoys the most well-balanced climate.[8]

[1] امة وسطا.

[2] Cf. 3:106.

[3] Ali, *op. cit.*, p. 66, note 182.

[4] Compare Deut. 14:2 and notes to verse 44.

[5] Zamakhsharī, Vol. II, p. 110:
لان الوسط عدل بين الاطراف ليس الى بعضها اقرب من بعض.

[6] Translated by Hartwig Hirschfeld, London 1931 (rev. edition); cf. A. Zifroni ed., (Hebrew), Tel-Aviv, 1948.

[7] *Ibid.*, p. 85: "All roads lead up to Palestine." Cf. Ez. 5:5 ... זאת ירושלם בתוך הגוים שמתיה וסביבותיה ארצות, and Mishnah Ket. 13:11; *Yalkuṭ Ezekiel*, § 336.

[8] *Ibid.*, p. 78: "Priority belongs, in the first instance, to the people which ... is the essence and kernel (of the nations) ... No other place (than Palestine) would share the distinction of the divine influence ..." Cf.: ארץ ישראל יושבת באמציתו של עולם, וירושלים באמצע ארץ ישראל, ובית המקדש באמצע ירושלים ... (תנחומא, קדושים, י [B]). See also B. Sanh. 38a; B. Yom. 56b and Rashi to Ezek. 5:5 בתוך הגוים שמתיה. באמצע העולם.

VERSE 144

> From whencesoever thou comest forth, there turn thy face towards the Sacred Mosque, for it is surely truth from thy Lord; God is not careless about what ye do.

Compare the Mishnaic dictum: "If he is riding on an ass he dismounts and prays. If he is unable to dismount he should turn his face (toward Jerusalem); and if he cannot turn his face he should concentrate his thoughts on the Holy of Holies."[1]

Similarly the rabbis teach that: "If one is standing outside Palestine, he should turn mentally toward Eretz Israel ... If he stands in Eretz Israel he should turn mentally towards Jerusalem .... If he is standing in Jerusalem he should turn mentally towards the Sanctuary .... If he is standing in the Sanctuary, he should turn mentally towards the Holy of Holies .... R. Abin ... said: What text confirms this? — *Thy neck is like the tower of David builded with turrets* (talpioth) (Cant. 4:4), the elevation (*tel*) towards which all mouths (*piyyoth*) turn."[2]

[1] Mishnah Ber. 28 b.

[2] B. Ber. 30a.

VERSE 147

> Remember me, then, and I will remember you; thank me, and do not misbelieve.[1]

Moslem commentators interpret this Koranic verse as follows: "Remember me with gifts, that I may remember you with favours; or remember me with worship, that I may remember you with benefits; or remember me with prayer, that I may remember you with blessings; or remember me among the people, that I may remember you among the angels."[2]

To remember God's favors is also a biblical command. The Psalmist urges: "Remember His marvellous works that He hath done, His wonders, and the judgments of His mouth" (Ps. 105:5). Similarly, David, giving thanks to the Lord, says: "Remember His marvellous works that He hath done, His wonders, and the judgments of His mouth" (1 Chron. 16:12). At Mount Sinai God speaks to Moses to tell the children of Israel, "in every place where I cause My name to be mentioned[3] I will come unto thee and bless thee" (Exod. 20:21).

The Talmud Yerushalmi[4] interprets the words, "I cause to be mentioned,"[5] as if they were written in the second person,[6] i. e. remembering God in the sense of prayer.

[1] *I. e.* "be not ungrateful," Palmer, p. 19 n.; cf. notes to 2:38, 44; 3:11.

[2] *Tafsīr-i-Raufi*, quoted by Wherry, *op. cit.*, p. 345 n.

[3] בכל המקום אשר אזכיר את שמי. Cf. Rashi, *ad loc.*: וזהו בית הבחירה שם נתן רשות לכהנים להזכיר שם המפורש בנשיאת כפים לברך את העם.

[4] בכל המקום אשר אזכיר את שמי אשר תזכיר את שמי. תלמוד ירושלמי, ברכות פ"ד, ה"ד.

[5] אזכיר.

[6] תזכיר.

VERSE 149

> And say not of those who are slain in God's way[1] (that they are) dead, but rather living; but ye do not perceive.

A similar statement is found in 3:163: "Count not those who are killed in the way of God as dead, but living with their Lord." Baiḍāwī, commenting on the verse in Sura 3, writes that they are "alive"[2] rather than "dead."[3]

The Talmud, too, emphasizes the greatness of those who die in order to sanctify God's name.[4] Similar to the Koranic expression, is the rabbinic one: "The righteous in their death are called living,"[5] and "The righteous, whom the Holy One, blessed be He, will resurrect, will not revert to dust . . . just as the Holy One endures for ever, so shall they endure for ever."[6] In 3:151 Muḥammad states: "And if, indeed, ye be killed in God's way or die, surely forgiveness from God and mercy is better than what ye gather; and if ye die or be killed it is to God ye shall be assembled." To this Baiḍāwī comments, "kill yourselves so that you may live,"[7] which recalls the talmudic statement: "What shall a man do to live? They replied: Let him mortify himself."[8]

[1] *I. e.* "in the cause of religion," Palmer, p. 19 n. في سبيل الله.

[2] Baiḍāwī, Vol. I, p. 90: على معنى بل احسبهم احياء .... تاكيد لكونهم احياء.

[3] اموات.

[4] הרוגי מלכות אין אדם יכל לעמוד במחיצתן (פסחים נ, ע"א).

[5] B. Ber. 18a.

[6] B. Sanh. 92a; cf. כל ת"ח שעוסק ;גדולים צדיקים במיתתן יותר מבחייהן (חולין ז, ע"ב) בתורה מקטנותו ועד זקנותו ומת באמת לא מת אלא הוא עדין בחיים לעולם ולעולמי עולמים (אליהו רבא, פ"ד, ז).

[7] Cf. notes 16–17 to 2:48–51.

[8] B. Tam. 32a; cf. 2:48–51 n. 14. To "mortify himself" means to " 'kill himself,' with study and hard work."

VERSES 154–55

> Verily, those who hide what we have revealed of manifest signs and of guidance after we have manifested it to men in the Book, them God shall curse, and those who curse shall curse them too. Save those who turn and do right and make (the signs) manifest; these will I turn to again, for I am easy to be turned and merciful.

A similar pronouncement against those who do not obey God's precepts is found in the following passages of the Pentateuch: "But if ye will not hearken unto Me, and will not do all these commandments; and if ye shall reject My statutes, and if your soul abhor Mine ordinances, so that ye will not do all My commandments, but break My covenant; I will do this unto you . . ." (Lev. 26:14–43). ". . . Cursed be he that confirmeth not the words of this law to do them. And all the people shall say: Amen." (Deut. 27:15–26; 28:15–66)

The Koranic phrase "for I am easy to be turned and merciful" recalls the biblical: "Pardon, I pray Thee, the iniquity of this people according unto the greatness of Thy lovingkindness, and according as Thou hast forgiven this people, from Egypt even until now. And the Lord said: 'I have pardoned according to thy word' " (Num. 14:19–20)! Compare also: "For Thou, Lord, art good, and ready to pardon, And plenteous in mercy unto all them that call upon Thee" (Ps. 86:5).

VERSES 156–57

> Verily, those who misbelieve and die while still in misbelief, on them is the curse of God, and of the angels, and of mankind altogether; to dwell therein for aye; the torment shall not be lightened for them, nor shall they be looked upon.

A similar expression is found in the following two biblical passages: "See now that I, even I, am He, And there is no God with Me; I kill, and I make alive; I have wounded, and I heal; And there is none that can deliver out of My hand" (Deut. 32:39). "And they shall go forth, and look Upon the carcasses of the men that have rebelled against Me; For their worm shall not die, Neither shall their fire be quenched; And they shall be an abhorring unto all flesh" (Is. 66:24). Likewise the Talmud states: "the thoroughly wicked will forthwith be inscribed definitively as doomed to Gehinnom."[1] Wrongdoers . . . "after twelve months their body is consumed and their soul is burnt and the wind scatters them under the soles of the feet of the righteous."[2]

Those "who rejected the Torah and denied the resurrection of the dead, . . . and those who 'spread their terror in the land of the living,' and who sinned and made the masses sin, like Jeroboam the son of Nebat and his fellows — these will go down to Gehinnom and be punished there for all generations . . ."[3]

[1] B. R. H. 16b.

[2] *Ibid.*, 17a.

[3] *Ibid.*

VERSE 159

> Verily, in the creation of the heavens and the earth, and the alternation of night and day, and in the ship that runneth in the sea with that which profits man, and in what water God sends down from heaven . . . and in the shifting of the winds, . . . are signs to people who can understand.

The expression "the ship that runneth in the sea" recalls the biblical expression, "The way of a ship in the midst of the sea" (Prov. 30:19). Similarly does the Psalmist declare: "They that go down to the sea in ships, That do business in great waters — These saw the works of the Lord, and His wonders in the deep;" . . . . "Let them give thanks unto the Lord for His mercy, And for His wonderful works to the children of men" (Ps. 107:23, 31)![1]

The belief that rain and wind are a manifestation of the power of the true God abounds in Jewish tradition.[2] Thus, Amos declares: "For, lo, He that formeth the mountains, and createth the wind . . . the Lord, the God of hosts, is His name." The prophet Jeremiah pronounces: "Are there any among the vanities of the nations that can cause rain? Or can the heavens give showers? Art not Thou He, O Lord our God, and do we not wait for Thee? For Thou hast made all these things" (Jer. 14:22).

The Talmud, too, attributes the phenomenon of rainfall to divine power,[3] "Because it is put on a level with the resurrection of the dead, therefore, it[4] was inserted in the benediction of the resurrection."[5]

[1] Cf.: השמים מספרים . . . כל פעל ה' למענהו, לקילוסו. דבר אחר שהכל מקלסין אותו על פעולתו ועל מעשהו וכל מעשיו מקלסים אותו (שוחר טוב, פי"ט, ג).

[2] See notes to 2:20, 27, 111.

[3] Cf. the second benediction in the *Shemone 'Esre*: אתה גבור . . . משיב הרוח ומוריד הגשם; and compare מחליף את הזמנים in the Prayer Book with the Koranic expression "and the alternation of night and day." See also Is. 55:10–11, כי כאשר ירד הגשם והשלג מן השמים ושמה לא ישוב כי אם הרוה את הארץ והולידה והצמיחה ונתן זרע לזרע ולחם לאוכל . . . כן יהיה דברי אשר יוצא מפי . . . .

[4] The formula "Thou causest wind to blow," cited in the *Daily Prayer Book*.

[5] B. Ber. 33a.

VERSE 160

> Yet there are some amongst mankind who take to themselves peers other than God; they love them as they should love God; while those who believe love God more. O that those who are unjust could only see, when they see the torment, that power is altogether God's! Verily, God is keen to torment.

Some translators render the word *andād*[1] as "objects of worship," which may refer to "idols" or to "the leaders who lead their followers into evil."[2]

The expression here about man's love for Allah is reminiscent of numerous biblical passages. The injunction to love God is a cardinal principle in Judaism and it occupies an essential place in the *Shema'*.[3] The commandment "And thou shalt love the Lord thy God . . ." (Deut. 6:5, 11:1) is considered in the Talmud as the first commandment.[4] The Psalmist expresses the same idea in his own language: "As the hart panteth after the water brooks, So panteth my soul after Thee, O God (Ps. 42:2)."[5]

The idea that those who follow other gods will be punished severely by God is also expressed in the Midrash: "(When) the men of Israel depart from their Creator and trust in the statutes of the nations, they are bad, accursed, and bitter, and there is no benefit in them for the world. Just as the waters of the rivers (are) the food of the waters of the sea, so are (the sinners destined to be) fuel for Gehinnom."[6]

Muḥammad never specified the time at which the Day of Judgment would take place. He is sure of its coming and of the punishment of the sinners. Similarly to the Psalmist's expression that with God one day means a thousand years: "For a thousand years in Thy sight are but as yesterday when it is past, And as a watch in the night" (Ps.

[1] Peers=انداد.

[2] Ali, *op. cit.*, p. 73; cf. 2:20 and B. Sanh. 74a concerning idolatry.

[3] שמע ישראל יי אלהינו יי אחד . . . ואהבת את יי אלהיך . . .; cf. notes to 2:1–2.

[4] Cf. Deut. 10:12 and the prayer in the *Siddur*: "Enlighten our eyes in Thy Torah, and let our hearts cleave to thy commandments, and unify our hearts to love and reverence Thy Name" (אהבה רבה . . .).

[5] Cf. B. Ber. 10b.

[6] P.R.E., p. 63.

90:4), Muḥammad, too, states in 22:46, "They will bid thee hasten on the torment, but God will never fail in his promise; for, verily, a day with thy Lord is as a thousand years of what ye number."[7]

[7] A similar idea is also found in 32:4, "He governs the affair from the heaven unto the earth; then shall it ascend to him in a day, the measure of which is a thousand years of what ye number." Compare B. Sanh. 97a and consult Ibn Ezra's commentary on Ps. 90:4.

VERSE 167

O ye who do believe! eat of the good things wherewith we have provided you, and give thanks unto God if it be Him ye serve. He has only forbidden for you what is dead, and blood, and flesh of swine, and whatsoever has been consecrated to other than God.

In 5:4 Muḥammad adds the following to the above forbidden things: "that which dies of itself . . . and the strangled and the knocked down, and that which falls down, and the gored, and what wild beasts have eaten — except what ye slaughter in time — and what is sacrificed to idols, and dividing carcases by arrows."[1]

All these prohibitions are found in the Bible and in rabbinic literature.[2] The Bible rules against eating that which dies of itself, and advises that one give it . . . "unto the stranger that is within thy gates, that he may eat it" (Deut. 14:21). The reason for the prohibition is given in the same verse: "for thou art a holy people unto the Lord thy God." The talmudic law also prohibits the meat of an animal that has not been slaughtered according to the Jewish law. According to the *Sifra*,[3] Moses was holding the animal[4] and showed it to Israel, saying "this you may eat and this you may not eat."

In Jewish tradition there is a specific branch of law concerning food which had been consecrated or intended to be consecrated to idol worship. The law prohibits wine which has remained under the sole care of idol-worshippers long enough to have been dedicated to idols, even if such a dedication is not formally established.[5]

Ṭabarī, commenting on the Koranic expression, "and (has forbidden) whatsoever has been consecrated to other than God," states that whenever they (Arab idolators) slaughtered an animal to offer a sacrifice to their gods, they named the animal by the name of the god to whom they sacrificed.[6] This corresponds to the mishnaic

[1] Cf. 3:87, "All food was lawful to the children of Israel save what Israel made unlawful to himself before that the law was revealed." Cf. 6:119; 16:115; 22:35–36.

[2] *Yoreh De'ah*, chs. 13–17; Maimonides מורה נבוכים ח"ג, פמ"ט; B. Ḥul. 39a, b.

[3] מלמד שהיה משה אוחז החיה ומראה להם לישראל ואומר להם זו תאכלו וזו לא תאכלו (ספרא, שמיני, ע"מז, ב [W]); cf. B. Ḥul. 42a and Gen. 9:4; 32:33.

[4] Referring to the biblical phrase in Deut. 14:4: "These are the beasts which ye may eat."

[5] Maimonides, *Mishneh Torah*, ch. 11 re יין נסך; cf. notes to 2:216.

[6] Ṭabarī, Vol. II, p. 258: لانهم كانوا اذا ارادوا ذبح ما قربوه لالتهم سموا اسم التهم التى قربوا ذلك لها.

prohibition that "if a man slaughtered in honour of mountains or of hills or of seas or of rivers or of wildernesses, what he slaughters is invalid."[7]

Similarly to the Jewish law[8] that if "ravenous hunger seize a man he may be given even unclean things to eat . . .," Muḥammad, too, states that if in time of emergency[9] or by compulsion a man eats some of the unlawful things, it is no sin.[10]

Muḥammad, greatly influenced by Jewish law, prohibits food used by Arab idolators, and orders abstention from "flesh of swine"[11] and "what is dead and blood!"[12] According to Torrey, Muḥammad evidently intended "in a general way to imitate them (the Jews). Conditions and customs in Arabia necessitated some differences, however. The laws of Israel are now superseded by the Muslim enactments . . .[13] He insists, however, both here and in other passages, that these prohibitions were not *originally* given, but were of the nature of punishment."[14]

The Koranic idea that the forbidden food in the Mosaic law was a punishment for the Jews for being rebellious, is undoubtedly of Christian influence. St. Justin Martyr in his *Dialogue with Trypho* writes that circumcision "is not essential for all men, but only for the Jews, to mark you off for the suffering you now so deservedly endure."[15] And he goes on to say that the Jews were "forbidden to eat certain

[7] Mishnah Ḥul. 2:8 [D]. The Talmud interprets the mishnaic sentence as follows: דאמר לגדא דהר (חולין מ, ע"א).

[8] Cf. Hirschberg, *op. cit.*, pp. 197–8: יהודי חג'אז נזהרו ממאכלות אסורות. אכילת בשר גמל נחשבה לסימן שמד והתאסלמות. וכן לא היו אוכלים את החֵלֶב, אלא מוכרים אותו לערבים. דבר זה חשב מוחמד — שלא בצדק — לעבירה על מצוות התורה . . . מובן שהיהודים לא אכלו בשר חזיר, נבילות וטריפות, ומהם קבל מחמד את האיסורים הללו. Cf. also, 4:158; 16:119.

[9] 6:146. [10] *Ibid.*; cf. ספק נפשות דוחה את השבת (משנה יומא, פג, ע"א).

[11] The pig is the only one singled out in the Koran. (6:146 خنزير.) The prohibition of the flesh of the donkey or ass came later. Rivlin, *Gesetz* . . . , pp. 67 ff.; Leszynsky, *op. cit.*, p. 26.

[12] In 6:146 the prohibition is against "dead (of itself), or blood that has been shed, or the flesh of swine — for that is a horror — or an abomination that is consecrated to other than God." The expression فانه رجس recalls the phrase in Gen. 43:32, כי תועבה. Compare the laws of נבלה, טרפה, B. Ḥul. 43a; cf. Yahuda, in *Goldziher Memorial Volume*, pp. 303 f.

[13] 5:7, "the food of those to whom the Book has been given is lawful for you, and your food is lawful for them." Cf. 6:147.

[14] Torrey, *op. cit.*, pp. 151–52; cf. 3:87, 4:159 and Geiger, *op. cit.*, pp. 135–37.

[15] *Writings of Saint Justin Martyr*, ed. by Thomas B. Falls, Christian Heritage, Inc., New York, 1948, p. 175.

kinds of meat, so that when you ate and drank you would keep God before your eyes, for you have always been disposed to forget Him."[16]

This idea, however, is in contradiction to the Midrash and other rabbinic sources which emphasize that the prohibition was not a punishment for misbehavior but rather a willingness on the part of the Jews to indulge more in the precepts of the Lord.[17]

Regarding the phrase, "consecrated to other than God," Palmer remarks that "At the time of slaughtering an animal the Muslims always repeat the formula *bismi'llâh*, in the name of God." This is similar to the talmudic law of pronouncing a benediction before the slaughtering of an animal for food or sacrifice.[18] This law extends to the pronouncement of a benediction before partaking of food.[19] In killing the animal the Moslem, like the Jew,[20] must be careful that the jugular vein of the throat be cut and not the spinal cord.[21]

The expression *Inna 'llaha ghafūrun raḥīm* recalls the liturgical expressions *'Adonai moḥel wesoleaḥ* and *'El raḥum weḥannun.*[22] The Talmud also states that when the Israelites were slaughtering their Passover sacrifices, the Levites would recite the *Hallel.*[23]

Hirschfeld commenting on 3:87 — "Bring the law and recite it, if ye speak the truth" — writes: "It is, therefore, not quite clear what Muhammad meant by this remark, except that he wished to parade his intimate acquaintance with the Pentateuch, and the passages in Gen. 9:4 and 32:33[24] in particular."[25] According to Baiḍāwī, Jacob

[16] *Ibid.*, p. 177; cf. M. Zucker, ברורים בתולדות הוכוחים הדתיים שבין היהדות והאיסלם, in *Festschrift Armand Kaminka*, Wien, 1937, pp. 31–48; I. Goldziher, "Über Mohammedanische Polemic gegen Ahl al-Kitāb," *ZDMG*, Vol. XXXII, p. 372; Steinschneider, *op. cit.*, p. 34.

[17] ... מתחילת ברייתו של עולם היה הכל מותר שנאמר כירק עשב נתתי לכם את כל,
... ומשעמדו ישראל על הר סיני הרבה להם תורה ומצוות ליתן להם שכר טוב (תנחומא, שמיני, יג [B])
Cf. Moshe Zucker, חלקו של ר' סעדיה גאון בפולמוס ממחרת השבת, in *PAAJR*, Vol. XX (1952), pp. 25–6.

[18] Palmer, p. 21 n.; B. Ber. 35a; *Yoreh De'ah*, ch. 1; B. Ḥul. 17b; B. Pes. 7b.

[19] B. Ber. 35a; cf. Nu. 18:14, כל חרם בישראל לך יהיה; and Talmud Yerushalmi, ברכות, פ"ח, ה"ז.

[20] Maimonides, *Mishneh Torah*, הלכות שחיטה ch. 1.

[21] Bu., Vol. IV p. 14, الذكاة في الحلق واللبّة.

[22] ה' מוחל וסולח, אל רחום וחנון, ان الله غفور رحيم.

[23] B. Pes. 64a.

[24] Gen. 32:33: על כן לא יאכלו בני ישראל את גיד הנשה אשר על כף הירך עד היום הזה כי נגע בכף־ירך יעקב בגיד הנשה.

[25] Hirschfeld, *New Researches* . . ., p. 114.

suffered from a severe pain in the sciatic nerve. He made a vow that if he were cured he would never eat the food he liked best and that[26] was what he liked most. Hence the prohibition of the sinew of the thigh.[27] The Koranic expression, "bring the law and recite it," recalls the well-known talmudic phrase *nete sefer weneḥeze.*[28] It is not unlikely that Muḥammad used a common expression which prevailed among the Jews in Medina, in order to show them that not only was he well versed in the Torah but that he alone possessed the true revelation.[29] He, thus, challenged them to deny his statement.

[26] *I. e.*, the sciatic nerve.

[27] Baiḍāwī, Vol. I, p. 80:
وقيل كان به عرق النسا فنذر ان شفى لم ياكل احب الطعام اليه وكان ذلك احب اليه.

[28] ניתי ספר ונחזה; B. Ḳid. 30a, ניתי ספר תורה ואימנינהו; cf. B. Shab. 49a, וליתי ספר תורה ולימני.

[29] 3:106; 20:112; 75:16.

VERSE 172

> Righteousness is not that ye turn your faces towards the east or the west, but righteousness is, one who believes in God, and the last day, and the angels, and the Book, and the prophets, and who gives wealth for His love to kindred and orphans, and the poor, and the son of the road, and beggars, and those in captivity; and who is steadfast in prayer, and gives alms; and those who are sure of their covenant when they make a covenant; and the patient in poverty, and distress, and in time of violence; these are they who are true, and these are those who fear.

The basic tenets of Islām and their relation to Judaism have been discussed elsewhere. They are represented by those who express faith in Allah;[1] in the Last Day;[2] in the angels;[3] in the Book;[4] in the prophets;[5] as well as by those who take care of the needy,[6] of the wayfarer,[7] and of those in captivity;[8] also by those who are steadfast in prayer,[9] give charity[10] and abide by the covenant.[11]

Similar attempts to enumerate the essentials of true piety are found in the Bible and in the Talmud. Thus, according to the rabbis, King David reduced the essential precepts to eleven,[12] as enumerated in Ps. 15: "Lord, who shall sojourn in Thy tabernacle? Who shall dwell upon Thy holy mountain? He that walketh uprightly, and worketh righteousness, And speaketh truth in his heart; That hath no slander upon his tongue, Nor doeth evil to his fellow, Nor taketh up a reproach against his neighbour; In whose eyes a vile person is despised, But he honoureth them that fear the Lord; He that sweareth to his own hurt, and changeth not; He that putteth not out his money on interest,

[1] 2:12, 101, 109, 111, 256.

[2] يوم الدين, 2:74, 160.

[3] 2:28–30.

[4] 2:1, 48–51, 209; 3:2.

[5] 2:254; 3:75.

[6] 2:1–2, 211.

[7] 2:1–2, note 61.

[8] 2:1–2, 211, 273, 280.

[9] 2:1–2, 239, 240; 3:7.

[10] 2:1–2, 211, 273, 280.

[11] 2:1–2, 87.

[12] "Leading virtues." Cf. B. Mak. 24a.

Nor taketh a bribe against the innocent. He that doeth these things shall never be moved." Came Habakkuk "and based them all on one (principle), as it is said, '*But the righteous shall live by his faith* (Hab. 2:4).' "[13]

The Koranic verse also recalls Isaiah 1:11, 17, where God abhors "the multitude of your sacrifices," and requests: "Seek justice, relieve the oppressed, Judge the fatherless, plead for the widow."

[13] *Ibid.*

VERSES 173–75

> O Ye who believe! Retaliation is prescribed for you for the slain: the free for the free, the slave for the slave, the female for the female; yet he who is pardoned at all by his brother, must be prosecuted in reason, and made to pay with kindness. That is an alleviation from your Lord, and a mercy; and he who transgresses after that for him is grievous woe. For you in retaliation is there life, O ye possessors of minds! it may be ye will fear.

In the *Jāhilīyah* period, retaliation was not only against the person who committed the crime but against the next of kin as well.[1] the new religion, however, prescribed that retaliation (*qiṣaṣ*) is only against the one who committed the crime. This innovation by Muḥammad recalls the biblical law in Deut. 24:16: "The fathers shall not be put to death for the children, neither shall the children be put to death for the fathers; every man shall be put to death for his own sin." Sa'adia Gaon, too, states that in the pre-Islāmic period the Arabs retaliated not only against the criminal but also against his relatives, and it was later prohibited by God.[2] The Koranic recommendation to be lenient in retaliation and to accept ransom instead, is not in accord with the Bible which prohibits ransom in the case of murder.[3] It is possible that Muḥammad expresses here the biblical idea of "an eye for an eye" (Exod. 21:24 and Lev. 24:20), which is based on the principle that the punishment must be equal to the crime committed and prohibits doing more harm than the criminal had done.[4]

[1] Th. W. Juynboll, *Handbuch des islamischen Gesetzes* . . ., Leiden-Leipzig, 1910, p. 289.

[2] This remark, which is attributed to Sa'adia Gaon, is quoted in Ibn Bal'ām's commentary on the Pentateuch: ולקד אחסן רבנו סעדיה ז"ל פי קו' אן אלנץ אנמא עני בדכר הדא ואן כאן מחכמא פי אלעקל לאן אלערב כאנת תחכם פי גהליתהא במתל הדא אעני אן יקתל אלקריב באלקריב פנהי אללה ען מתל דלך. Solomon Fuchs, *Studien über Abu Zakaria Jachja Ibn Bal'ām*, Berlin, 1893, p. xxi.

[3] Num. 35:31: "Moreover ye shall take no ransom for the life of a murderer, that is guilty of death; but he shall surely be put to death." Cf. Num. 35:33 and Maimonides, *Guide* . . . (Friedländer ed.), p. 344.

[4] Maimonides, *ibid.*, "injuries that cannot be reproduced exactly in another person, are compensated for by payment." Cf. 4:94.

VERSES 179–81

> O ye who believe! There is prescribed for you the fast as it was prescribed for those before you; haply ye may fear. A certain number of days, but he amongst you who is ill or on a journey, then (let him fast) another number of days. And those who are fit to fast (but do not) may redeem it by feeding a poor man; but he who follows an impulse to a good work it is better for him; and if ye fast it is better for you, if ye did but know.

At first Muḥammad accepted the Day of Atonement[1] as a day of fast. It was known as *'Ashūrā'*,[2] meaning the tenth day and corresponding to the Jewish Day of Atonement, which occurs on the tenth of *Tishri*. Muḥammad later[3] substituted for it the month of Ramaḍān,[4] and required every Moslem to fast a whole month.

Torrey thinks that the fast of Ramaḍān is "very probably patterned on the Lenten fast of the Christians."[5] He adds, however, that "the *manner* of fasting, abstaining altogether during the day, and eating and drinking after sundown was Jewish."[6]

It is probable that Muḥammad took for his pattern the Jewish month of *'Elul* which precedes *Rosh Hashanah* and *Yom Kippur*, a month devoted to repentance and asking for forgiveness.[7] Perhaps

[1] יום הכפורים or עשור. See Maimonides, יד החזקה on הלכות עשור. Cf. Bu., Vol. I, p. 498: قدم النبى... المدينة فراى اليهود تصوم يوم عاشوراء... فصامه فامر بصيامه....

[2] From the Hebrew עשור, which connotes the Day of Atonement; cf. Rashi on Exod. 18:13. *'Ashūrā'* coincided with the fast of *Yom Kippur*. Hirschberg, *op. cit.*, p. 196; Wensinck, *op. cit.*, pp. 12, 136–37.

[3] *'Ashūrā* was never abolished and is still practiced today as a voluntary fast but for a different reason; cf. Nöldeke-Schwally, Vol. I, p. 179; A. Sprenger, *Das Leben . . .*, Vol. III, p. 539; Margoliouth, *Mohammed and Mohammedanism*, p. 250; Geiger, *op. cit.*, p. 37.

[4] Cf. Simon Duran (*op. cit.*, p. 14), who claims that Muḥammad substituted it for the Jewish Day of Atonement: ולפי שהוא (יוה"כ) צום ותשובה תקן להם שלשים צומות.

[5] Torrey, *op. cit.*, p. 131; cf. Rivlin, *op. cit.*, p. 11; and Duran, *op. cit.*, p. 14.

[6] *Ibid.*, p. 138; cf. Hirschberg, *op. cit.*, p. 196: הערבים היו רגילים לראות את הצום כאבל, ולפיכך השתוממו בראותם כי אצל היהודים יום הכפורים חג הוא ונשיהם מתקשטות בו...

[7] ואף שהתשובה טובה בכל עת מ"מ חדש אלול הוא מובחר ומוכן יותר שמקובל תשובתו משאר ימות השנה (אברהם דאנציג, חיי אדם, כלל קלז, כח, ע"ב). See also Zohar (הצא דף נ"ח):

we have here an allusion to the forty days which Moses spent on the Mountain and to the day he descended, i. e. on the Day of Atonement.[8] Ramaḍān is considered a month devoted to prayer for redemption and deliverance from sin.[9] The idea of fasting[10] as an expression of submission to the divine Being is Jewish.[11] The practices and ceremonies that Moslems must observe during the month of Ramaḍān are likewise traceable to Jewish sources. Thus, a Moslem, like a Jew on *Yom Kippur*, must abstain during his fast from food, drink, falsehood and foul talk.[12] Though fasting is one of the pillars of Islām, excessive fasting is prohibited. Similarly one who is ill or of old age or on a journey, or a pregnant woman may be excused and is permitted to keep the fast at another time.[13] Likewise when one eats or drinks, forgetting that he is fasting, the fast is not broken.[14]

ובכתה את אביה ואת אמה ירח ימים — דא הוא ירחא דאלול, דביה סליק משה לטורא למבעי רחמא. The suggestion that Muḥammad, in establishing the fast of Ramaḍān, had in mind "the fast of the tenth" mentioned in Zech. 8:19, rather than "the fast of the tenth" of Lev. 16:29 is untenable, since the Zechariah reference is to *Ṭebet*, the tenth *month* of the Hebrew calendar, commemorating the destruction of the Temple, whereas in Leviticus the reference is to the tenth *day* of the month.

[8] Rashi on Exod. 18:13: כך שנינו בספרי ומהו ממחרת למחרת רדתו מן ההר. According to the Bible: "(Moses) was there with the Lord forty days and forty nights; he did neither eat bread, nor drink water" (Exod. 34:28). Compare 2:91, notes on Moses and verse 7:138: "And when we appointed for Moses thirty nights, and completed them with ten (more), so that the time appointed by his Lord was completed to forty nights." See also: ובראש חדש אלול אמר הקב"ה למשה עלה אלי ההרה (פדר"א, פמ"ו).

[9] Rivlin, *op. cit.*, p. 15; M. Plessner, "Ramaḍān," *E.I.*, 1929, Vol. III, p. 1111.

[10] Cf. 2:183 f.; Bu., Vol. I, p. 473 quotes the Prophet, in the name of Abū Huraira, that "the odour of the mouth of one fasting is tastier in the estimation of God than the odour of musk."

[11] Hirschberg, *op. cit.*, p. 197: ממקור אחד אפשר להסיק, כי מוחמד היה צם בכל יום שני וחמישי; וכן יש לשער כי ידע את צום ט' באב. Cf. Wensinck, *op. cit.*, pp. 125 ff.; F. (S. D.) Goitein, "Zur Entstehung des Ramaḍān," in *Der Islam*, Vol. XVIII (1929), pp. 189 f.; Wellhausen, *Reste* . . . , 2nd edition, p. 97.

[12] Bu., Vol. I, p. 475. Abstaining from cohabitation during the fast of Ramaḍān also recalls the Jewish observance on יום הכפורים eve; cf. Lev. 23:27–33; C. C. Berg, "Ṣawm," *E. I.*, Vol. III, p. 202; Th. Juynboll, *op. cit.*, p. 114; Th. Nöldeke, *Neue Beiträge* . . . , p. 36.

[13] Bu., Vol. III, p. 202. The provision to fast at another time for one who is sick or who is on a journey resembles the biblical prescription in Num. 9:9–13 about the "second Passover," פסח שני; cf. Torrey, *op. cit.*, p. 138; B. Yom. 83b.

[14] Bu., Vol. I, p. 471: "اذا نسى فاكل وشرب فليتمّ صومه....".

The Koranic phrase, "God desires for you what is easy," recalls the talmudic statement that the Sages declared not to "trouble the community unduly."[15]

The exact date on which the Koran was revealed is stated by Muḥammad to be in the month of Ramaḍān, in the Night of al-Qadr.[16] "The Night of Power is better than a thousand months! The angels and the Spirit descend therein, by the permission of their Lord with every bidding" (97:3–4). In Jewish tradition, too, the date of the giving of the Torah is fixed. It was the sixth day of the month of *Siwan*, the date of the Feast of Weeks.[17] The Midrash also speaks of thousands of angels that ascended with God upon Sinai to witness the revelation of the Torah.[18]

[15] B. Ta'an. 14b אין מטריחין את הציבור יותר מדאי and שאין גוזרין גזירה על הציבור אלא אם כן רוב ציבור יכולין לעמוד בה (ב"ק ע"ט, ע"א). Cf. Talmud Yerushalmi, Rosh H. 1, 4.

[16] Cf. 44:2; 97:1. Re the calendar in Islām, see Rivlin, *op. cit.*, pp. 3–7.

[17] According to Jewish tradition, Moses received the second tablets from God on *Yom Kippur*. Rashi to Exod. 31:18. Goitein, in his article on Ramaḍān in *Der Islam*, XVIII, calls attention to the parallelism between Muḥammad's mission and the handing of the second tablets of the law to Moses on the tenth day of the month. He claims that Ramaḍān, the successor to '*Ashūrā*', was at first a fast lasting ten days and not a whole month (2:184), which paralleled the practice of the Jews to observe ten days of penance preceding the Day of Atonement. Cf. ואז עלה בר"ח אלול ונשתהה שם עם יום כפור שהיה גמר כפרה . . . ישראל היו נוהגים כל אותם הימים צום ותענית ויום אחרון שבכלם דהיינו בעשרה בתשרי גזרו בתענית ולנו בתענית ולפיכך נקבע אותו יום דהיינו יום הכפורים לכפרה לעולם . . . וחייב כל אדם עכ"פ להכין את עצמו ליום שיכנס למשפט לפני ה' בר"ה שלשים יום קודם בתשובה ותפלה ויתן כל לבו רק בעבודת ה' (חיי אדם, כלל קלז). See also אליהו רבה, פרק ו, ח"א and אמר הקב"ה לישראל עשו תשובה באילו עשרת הימים בין ראש השנה ליום הכיפורים ואני מזכה אתכם ביום הכיפורים. . . . ולמה עשרה. כנגד עשרת ימי תשובה. ואם עשיתם תשובה בהם ואתם באים לפני יום הכיפורים ואפילו יש (לכם) עונות מן הארץ ועד השמים אני מלבינם כשלג (פסיקתא רבתי, בחדש השביעי, פ"מ, ע קס"ט, [F]).

[18] *Exod. Rab.* 29,9; cf. Obermann, *op. cit.*, p. 91.

VERSE 182

> When My servants ask thee concerning me, then, verily, I am near; I answer the prayer's prayer whene'er he prays to me. So let them ask me for an answer, and let them believe in me; haply they may be directed aright.

Similar words are found in the Bible: "The Lord is nigh unto all them that call upon Him, To all that call upon Him in truth. He will fulfil the desire of them that fear Him; He also will hear their cry, and will save them" (Ps. 145:18–19).

The Koranic verse recalls also the words of Isaiah: "Seek ye the Lord while He may be found, Call ye upon Him while He is near" (Is. 55:6).[1]

[1] Cf. 2:1–2, 77.

VERSE 183

> Lawful for you on the night of the fast is commerce with your wives; they are a garment unto you, and ye are a garment unto them. God knows that ye did defraud yourselves, wherefore He has turned towards you and forgiven you; so now go in unto them and crave what God has prescribed for you, and eat and drink until a white thread can be dinstinguished by you from a black one at the dawn. Then fulfil the fast until the night, and go not in unto them, and be at your devotions in the mosques the while. These are the bounds that God has set, so draw not near thereto. Thus does God make manifest His signs to men, that haply they may fear.

Within Jewish tradition the expression, "Ye shall afflict your souls" (Lev. 16:29), entails five prohibitions: eating and drinking, bathing, anointing, wearing shoes and sexual intercourse.[1] Muḥammad here pronounces fasting and sexual intercourse as prohibited for the days and not for the nights. This is contrary to talmudic law which prohibits cohabitation on the eves of the fast days of *Yom Kippur* and the *Ninth of 'Ab*, since the nights are counted as part of the fast days themselves.

Muḥammad identifies daybreak in the manner prescribed in the Mishnah: "So soon as one can distinguish between blue and white (thread)."[2] However, the Koranic statement is in connection with fasting, whereas the talmudic expression deals with the time of reciting the *Shema'*. Also, the identification mark in the Koran is between "white and black," whereas in the Mishnah it is between "blue and white."

[1] Mishnah Yom. 8:1

[2] Mishnah Ber. 1:2 [D].

VERSE 185

> They will ask thee about the phases of the moon; say, 'They are indications of time for men and for the pilgrimage.' And it is not righteousness that ye should enter into your houses from behind them, but righteousness is he who fears; so enter into your houses by the doors thereof and fear God; haply ye may prosper yet.

A counterpart is found in Talmud Yerushalmi, where the moon is an indication of the time for holidays[1] and pilgrimages.[2] Similarly, do we find in the Midrash that the moon serves as an indicator for pilgrimages and festivals.[3]

[1] Cf. Gen. 1:14; Ps. 104:19: עשה ירח למועדים שמש ידע מבואו.

[2] עשה ירח למועדים שמש ידע מבואו, משמש ידע מבואו עשה ירח למועדים (תלמוד ירושלמי, ר"ה, פ"ב, ה"א).

[3] ויאמר אלהים יהי מאורות . . . ר' יוחנן פתח עשה ירח למועדים. אר"י לא נברא להאיר אלא גלגל חמה בלבד, א"כ למה נבראת לבנה למועדים . . . והיו לאותות אלו שבתות, ולמועדים אלו שלש רגלים . . . (בראשית רבה פ"ו, א). Cf. [F] פסיקתא רבתי פט"ו, ע"א and [B] פסיקתא דר"כ פסקא ה, עמ"ב.

VERSE 186

> Fight in God's way (cause) with those who fight with you, but transgress not (by beginning the fight yourselves); verily, God loves not those who do transgress.

According to Zamakhsharī, the prohibition to commence a fight or to wage war applies to those who might attack people incapable of fighting, such as women, old men and children. This prohibition included also war against those with whom a covenant had been made.[1]

The Bible, too, states: "When thou drawest nigh unto a city to fight against it, then proclaim peace unto it . . . And if it will make no peace with thee, but will make war against thee, then thou shalt besiege it . . . but the women, and the little ones, and the cattle . . . shalt thou take for a prey unto thyself" (Deut. 20:10–14). Zamakhsharī's view is also expressed in the Mishnah:[2] "*ye draw nigh unto battle this day against your enemies* — and not against your brethren."[3]

[1] Zamakhsharī, Vol. I, p. 132:
[ولا تعتدوا] بابتداء القتال او بقتال من نهيتم عن قتاله من النساء والشيوخ والصبيان والذين بينكم وبينهم عهد.

[2] Mishnah Soṭ. 8:1 [D].

[3] Cf. 2:187 and שלש פרסטיגיות שלח יהושע לארץ ישראל עד שלא יכנסו לארץ מי שהוא רוצה להפנות יפנה להשלים ישלים לעשות מלחמה יעשה גרגשי פינה והאמין לו להקב"ה והלך לו לאפריקי עד בואי ולקחתי אתכם אל ארץ כארצכם זו אפריקי גבעונים השלימו וכי השלימו יושבי גבעון את ארץ ישראל שלושים ואחד מלך עשו מלחמה ונפלו (תלמוד ירושלמי, שביעית, פ"ו ה"א). See, also, Maimonides, 6, 1, הלכות מלכים.

VERSE 187

> Kill them wherever ye find them, and drive them out from whence they drive you out; for sedition is worse than slaughter; but fight them not by the Sacred Mosque until they fight you there; then kill them, for such is the recompense of those that misbelieve.

That "sedition is worse than slaughter" is expressed in identical words in the *Sifre* on Deut. 23:8.[1] The Talmud likewise deals with the seducer more severely than with other criminals: "For all whom the Torah condemns to death no witnesses are hidden to entrap them, excepting for this one (seducer)."[2] If the seducer is a layman he is stoned. But if he be a prophet he is strangled.[3]

The Koranic statement not to fight at the Sacred Mosque recalls the biblical verse in Exod. 21:14 that "if a man come presumptuously upon his neighbour, to slay him with guile; thou shalt take him from Mine altar, that he may die." A specific example of the custom of the guilty to seek refuge at the altar, in order to escape death, is found in I Kings 2:28: ". . . And Joab fled unto the Tent of the Lord, and caught hold on the horns of the altar." The presumption behind this practice was that no religious man would desecrate the altar by committing murder upon it. To the Moslems, Mecca served as "a city of refuge" (Num. 35:6).

The statement in 2:186, "fight in God's way," and the phrase here, "kill them wherever you find them," may have their antecedents in the biblical verses dealing with *milḥemet mizwah*[4] and *milḥemet reshut*[5] which are found in Exod. 17:14–16[6] and in Deut. 20:1.[7]

The Talmud states: "(A war) which is (designated) voluntary according to the Rabbis is commanded according to R. Judah, and (a war) which is (designated) commanded according to the Rabbis is

[1] ללמדך שמחטיא האדם קשה לו מן ההורגו.

[2] Mishnah Sanh. 67a; cf. notes to 2:213.

[3] *Ibid.*; cf. Deut. 13:2–13.

[4] *Sifre* on Deut. 19:19; B. Sanh. 20b.

[5] B. Soṭ 44b; *Sifre, ibid.*

[6] ויאמר יהוה אלא משה כתב זאת זכרון בספר ושים באזני יהושע כי מחה אמחה את זכר עמלק מתחת השמים. ויבן משה מזבח ויקרא שמו יהוה נסי. ויאמר כי יד על־כס יה מלחמה ליהוה בעמלק מדר דר (שמות י״ז, י״ד–ט״ז).

[7] כי תצא למלחמה על איבך וראית סוס ורכב עם רב ממך לא תירא מהם כי יהוה אלהיך עמך המעלך מארץ מצרים (דברים כ, א).

obligatory according to R. Judah. Raba said: The wars waged by Joshua to conquer (Canaan) were obligatory in the opinion of all; the wars waged by the House of David for territorial expansion were voluntary in the opinion of all; where they differ is with regard to (wars) against heathens so that these should not march against them. One calls them commanded and the other voluntary, the practical issue being that one who is engaged in the performance of a commandment is exempt from the performance of another commandment."[8]

Jihād (Holy War)[9] is one of the main pillars of Islām,[10] and he "who loses his life in the struggle enters Paradise as a martyr of the faith."[11]

[8] B. Soṭ. 44b. The biblical injunction "When thou drawest nigh unto a city to fight against it, then proclaim peace unto it" (Deut. 20:10), is referred to in *Yalkuṭ Shim'oni* as מלחמת רשות, which, according to the Talmud, needs the approval of the Sanhedrin (B. Sanh. 20b).

[9] Bu., Vol. II, pp. 198–99: "show me a deed which is equal to *jihād*. He said, I can not find one" دلني على عمل يعدل الجهاد قال لا اجده. Cf. 22:76, and 60:2 "and fight strenuously for God," وجاهدوا في الله حق جهاده. See also notes to 2:125 and *SHEI*, p. 89.

[10] Ph. Hitti, *op. cit.*, pp. 136 f.

[11] G. von Grunebaum, *op. cit.*, p. 9; cf. H. U. W. Stanton, *The Teaching of the Qur'ān*, London, 1919, p. 65; and Bu., Vol. II, p. 206: "He who dies in *jihād* enters paradise," فقال عمر للنبى... اليس قتلانا في الجنة وقتلاهم في النار قال بلى....

VERSE 193

> The pilgrimage[1] is (in) well-known months: whosoever then makes it incumbent on himself (let him have neither) commerce with women, nor fornication, nor a quarrel on the pilgrimage; and whatsoever of good ye do, God knoweth it; then provide yourself for your journey; but the best provision is piety. Fear ye me ye who possess minds.

The Bible states: "Three times thou shalt keep a feast unto Me in the year. The feast of unleavened bread shalt thou keep; seven days thou shalt eat unleavened bread, as I commanded thee, at the time appointed in the month Abib — for in it thou camest out from Egypt; and none shall appear before Me empty; and the feast of harvest, the first-fruits of thy labours, which thou sowest in the field; and the feast of ingathering, at the end of the year, when thou gatherest in thy labours out of the field. Three times in the year all thy males shall appear before the Lord God" (Exod. 23:14–17). "Three times a year shall all thy males appear before the Lord thy God in the place which He shall choose; on the feast of unleavened bread, and on the feast of weeks, and on the feast of tabernacles; and they shall not appear before the Lord empty; every man shall give as he is able, according to the blessing of the Lord thy God which He hath given thee" (Deut. 16:16–17).[2] In the Talmud we find the following: "Beth Shammai says: The pilgrimage offering must be worth (at least) two pieces of silver and the Festal offering one ma'ah of silver." But Beth Hillel says: "the pilgrimage-offering must be worth (at least) one ma'ah of silver and the festal sacrifice two pieces of silver."[3]

The Koran, following the biblical injunction regarding pilgrimage, prescribes that every Moslem, except those physically and financially unable, visit Mecca at least once in his lifetime; and, again, as in the biblical practice, an offering to God[4] must be rendered at the pilgrimage: "And proclaim amongst men the Pilgrimage; let them come to

[1] حج; Hebrew חג. Cf. Jud. 21:19; I Kings 8:2. The *Ḥajj* is to be undertaken at the time of the new moon of the twelfth month *Dhu'lḥijjah.*

[2] Later on, after the destruction of the first temple in 586 B.C.E., when the Jews were no longer able to travel to Jerusalem, the Synagogue was established. S. Zeitlin, *The History of the Second Commonwealth*, Philadelphia, 1933, p. 52.

[3] Cf. Mishnah Ḥag. 2a.

[4] Mishnah Yom. 83b.

you on foot and on every slim camel, from every deep pass, that they may witness advantages for them, and may mention the name of God for the stated days over what God has provided them with of brute beasts, then eat thereof and feed the badly off, the poor" (22:29).[5]

A prohibition against cohabitation during the days of the pilgrimage is not known in Jewish law. It is possible that the Koranic prohibition against dealing with women,[6] fornication and quarrel, stem from the talmudic command, "a man should purify himself for the festival."[7]

In early days the *Ḥajj* was associated with great fairs. "These fairs were probably the main thing to Muḥammad's contemporaries, as they still are to many Muslims. For the significance of the religious ceremonies had even then lost its meaning for the people. The following may be stated. A main part of the ceremony was the *wuḳūf* 'the halt' in the plain of 'Arafāt; in Islām the Ḥadjdj without *wuḳūf* is invalid. This can only be explained as the survival of a pre-Muslim notion. Houstma has compared the *wuḳūf* with the stay of the Israelites on Mount Sinai. The latter had to prepare themselves for this by refraining from sexual intercourse (Ex. 19.15) and the washing of their garments (Exod. 19.10, 14). Thus they waited upon their god (נכונים, 11, 15). In the same way the Muslims refrain from sexual intercourse, wear holy clothing and stand before the deity (وقف=כון=stand) at the foot of a holy mountain."[8]

The institution of *Ḥajj* has been serving as a major influence upon Moslems congregating in Mecca from all over the world. Rich and poor fraternize in comity on the common ground of faith. Each pilgrim enters "the holy precincts as a *muḥrim* (wearing a seamless garment) and performs the seven-fold circumambulation of the Ka'bah (*ṭawāf*) and the seven-fold course (*sa'y*) between the adjacent al-Ṣafa mound and the Marwah eminence lying opposite. The *ḥajj* proper begins with the march to 'Arafah, which lasts from the seventh to the eighth of dhu-al-Ḥijjah. The halts (*wuqūf*) take place at the outlying sanctuaries of 'Arafah, namely, al-Muzdalifah and Mina. The stone-

[5] Compare Exod. 34:23 and עני וידו רחבה קורא אני עליו איש כמתנת ידו עשיר וידו מעוטה קורא אני עליו כברכת ה׳ אלהיך (תלמוד ירושלמי חגיגה פ"א, ה"ה).

[6] Bu., Vol. I, p. 408: "They did not mix with them (wives)," .... قلت كيف يخالطهنّ الرجال قال لم يكن يخالطهُنّ. Cf. notes to 2:179–81.

[7] B. R. H. 16b, חייב אדם לטהר את עצמו ברגל.

[8] Wensinck, E. I. (1927) Vol. II, p. 200; cf. B. Shab. 87a.

throwing ceremony takes place on the way to the valley of Mina at Jamrat al-'Aqabah. With the sacrifice at Mina of a camel or of a sheep or other horned domestic animal (Koran 22:34–37), which always takes place on the tenth of dhu-al-Ḥijjah and is celebrated throughout the Moslem world as 'Īd al-Aḍḥa (the festival of sacrifice), the whole ceremony formally ends. After the shaving of the head the garment (*iḥrām*) is discarded and the *iḥlāl* (secular condition) resumed."[9]

[9] Hitti, *op. cit.*, pp. 133–34. As to the Jewish origin of the practices of the *ḥajj* see Dozy, *op. cit.*, pp. 120 f.

VERSE 196

> And when ye have performed your rites, remember God as ye remember your fathers, or with a keener memory still.

This verse alludes, according to Rivlin,[1] to the Jewish practice of reciting the *Ḳaddish*[2] by the Reader or mourner at the close of each section of a public service.[3] To remember God after performing "the rites," may also refer to the word *'Amen*[4] which is included in the *Ḳaddish*, or to the custom in the Synagogue of having the assembly of worshippers respond to the prayer: " 'Amen, may God's great Name be praised for ever and ever."[5] According to the Talmud, "He who responds 'Amen!' with all his might has the sentence against him annulled." Similarly, the Islamic tradition maintains that "a correct observance of the ritual of prayer brings about the cancellation of sin. When the Imām says, 'Not of those with whom thou art angered nor of those who go astray,' say 'Amen,' for whosoever says 'Amen' at the same time as the angels shall have his past sins remitted him."[6]

[1] Rivlin, *op. cit.*, p. 109.

[2] Lit. "Holy." It is a brief prayer, written in Aramaic, magnifying and hallowing the great name of God.

[3] B. Ber. 21b; cf. Rivlin, *op. cit.*, p. 109 n, who refers to Juynboll, *op. cit.*, p. 78: "Vor dem Ruk'u, sowie vor und nach jedem Sudjūd hat man ein Takbīr auszusprechen. Das Kaddisch beginnt mit יתגדל, was wörtlich mit Takbīr übereinstimmt."

[4] Cf. notes to 2:1–2, note 28; Ps. 89:53, ברוך יהוה לעולם אמן ואמן.

[5] B. Shabb. 119b אמן יהא שמיה רבא מברך; cf. B. Ber. 16b: "Rab on concluding his prayer added the following: May it be Thy will (הכי יהי רצון), O Lord our God, to grant us long life . . . , a life in which Thou shalt fulfil all the desires of our heart for good!" This prayer is now a part of the Sabbath prayers and recited when the New Moon is announced. Cf. ברוך יהוה אלהי ישראל מן העולם ועד העולם ואמר כל העם אמן הללו־יה (תהלים ק״ו, מ״ח).

[6] Quoted by Taylor, *op. cit.*, pp. 198–99.

VERSE 206

> What can they expect but that God should come unto them in the shadow of a cloud, and the angels too? But the thing is decreed, and unto God do things return.

Sa'adia Gaon, in his translation of the biblical phrase in Lev. 23:43, "... to dwell in booths ...,"[1] employs the identical words[2] used in the Koran.[3] The Talmud refers to the *booths* as "clouds of glory."[4] Identical descriptions are employed by Rashi[5] and in the tannaitic literature.[6]

[1] כי בסכות הושבתי.

[2] في ظلال من غمامى.

[3] *I. e.* "in the shadow of a cloud," في ظلال من الغمام.

[4] B. Suk. 11b. This view is not accepted by R. 'Akiba who maintains: "they made for themselves real booths" (*ibid*).

[5] Rashi on Lev. 23:43, ענני כבוד.

[6] The opinions of Rabbi Eliezer and Rabbi Akiba are reversed in the *Sifra*. In the latter, R. Akiba maintains, that the booths were "clouds of glory." ר' אליעזר אומר סוכות ממש היו, ר' עקיבא אומר בסוכות ענני הכבוד היו (ספרא, אמור עק"ג, [W]). Cf. ילקוט שמעוני, בא, רמז רט.

VERSE 209

> Men were one nation once, and God sent prophets with good tidings and with warnings, and sent down with them the Book in truth, to judge between men in that wherein they disagreed.

According to some Moslem commentators the expressions, "men were one nation once,"[1] refers to the ten generations from Adam to Noah,[2] whose people followed the true faith and were like one single religious community. This thought is likewise expressed in Jewish tradition,[3] which maintains that from Adam to Enosh all people worshipped the one true God and only in the time of Enosh[4] did idolatry emerge.[5]

[1] كان الناس امة واحدة.

[2] Zamakhsharī, Vol. I, p. 143:
فان قلت متى كان الناس امّة واحدة متفقين على الحق — قلت عن ابن عباس . . . . انه كان بين آدم وبين نوح عشرة قرون على شريعة من الحقّ فاختلفوا. Cf. Baiḍāwī, *ad loc.*

[3] Compare Mishnah Aboth 5:2: "(There were) ten generations from Adam to Noah, in order to make known how long-extended is long-suffering with him; for all those generations were repeatedly acting provokingly, until He brought upon them the waters of the flood."

[4] See *Targum Jonathan* and *Gen. Rab.* 23, 6; compare also Maimonides, עבודת כוכבים, 1, 1; cf. Gen. 4:26.

[5] Rashi to Gen. 4:26: אז הוחל: לשון חולין לקרא את שמות האדם ואת שמות העצבים בשמו של הקב״ה לעשותן אלילים ולקרותן אלהות. The expression הוחל is from חולין, *i. e.* profane. See, however, Ibn Ezra and Sforno, *ad loc.*, who claim that הוחל is derived from תחלה, and the meaning is that this was the beginning of worshipping the true God.

VERSE 211

> They will ask thee what they are to expend in alms: say, 'Whatsoever good ye expend it should be for parents and kinsmen, and the orphan and the poor, and the son of the road; and whatsoever good ye do, verily, of it God knows.'

The place of charity[1] in Islām is discussed in 2:1-2 and elsewhere.[2] In Jewish tradition the laws pertaining to obligatory "alms," i. e. the one-tenth of the yearly produce and the unharvested edges of the fields and orchards, were supplemented by other laws in the Bible, e. g., "If there be among you a needy man, . . . thou shalt not harden thy heart, nor shut thy hand . . . lend him sufficient for his need" (Deut. 15:7–8). Islāmic tradition, too, elaborates on the Koranic *Zakāh*[3] and urges helping "the distressed one who is in need," "as well as the giving of charity in secret.[4]

The sequence in the Koranic verse implies that "parents and kinsmen" have priority with regard to alms. The same is true in the case of the orphan and the widow.[5] This corresponds to Jewish law.[6] The Talmud provides that: "If an orphan applied for assistance to marry, a house must be rented for him, a bed must be prepared for him and (he must also be supplied with) all (household) objects (re-

[1] *Ṣadaqah*, صد قة.

[2] Cf. notes on 2:172, 246, 272, 273, 280; 3:128 and T. H. Weir, "Ṣadaka," *E. I.*, Vol. IV, pp. 33 f.

[3] Bu., Vol. I, p. 377: "in the produce derived from the watering of heaven and springs or in what is watered by water running on the surface of the ground is one-tenth . . ." فيما سقت السّماء والعيون او كان عثريّا العشر وما سُقى بالنّضح نصف العُشر.
Cf. Deut. 26:12: "When thou hast made an end of tithing all the tithe of thine increase in the third year, which is the year of tithing, and hast given it unto the Levite, to the stranger, to the fatherless, and to the widow, that they may eat within thy gates, and be satisfied."

[4] Bu., Vol. I, pp. 359 f. Cf. notes 53–64 to 2:1–2.

[5] Bu., Vol. III, p. 485; cf. Al-Ghazālī, *Iḥyā 'Ulūm al-Dīn* (Cairo, 1326 A.H.), Vol. I, pp. 149 f.; T. W. Juynboll, *op. cit.*, pp. 109 f.

[6] Maimonides, הלכות מתנות עניים פ"י, הט"ז: וכן הנותן מזונות לאביו ולאמו הרי זה בכלל צדקה, וצדקה גדולה היא שהקרוב קודם.

quired for) his use, and then he is given a wife in marriage . . ."[7] The rabbis add: "You are commanded to maintain him and supply him even with a horse and a servant (if he were used to such luxuries), but you are not commanded to make him rich."[8]

Regarding "the son of the road," Jewish tradition, too, puts great stress on the obligation to take care of the wanderer and to provide him with board and lodging as well as an escort in case of danger.[9]

[7] B. Ket. 67b. According to the Bible, the giving of צדקה approximates a loan to God. "He that is gracious unto the poor lendeth unto the Lord, And his good deed will He repay unto him." Prov. 19:17; cf. *Lev. R.* 34, 15; B. B. B. 9b. The Koran, too, states: "Verily, those who give in charity, men and women, who have lent to God a goodly loan, — it shall be doubled for them, and for them is a generous hire" (57:17).

[8] B. Ket. 67b; *Sifre* on Deut. 15:6.

[9] *Sifre* to Deut. 21:7: שלא בא לידינו ופטרנוהו בלא לוייה ולא ראינוהו והנחנהו. Cf. B. Soṭ. 48b and תלמוד ירושלמי, סוטה, פ"ט, ה"ו.

VERSE 213

> They will ask thee of the sacred month, — of fighting therein. Say, 'Fighting therein is a great sin; but turning folks off God's way, and misbelief in Him and in the Sacred Mosque, and turning His people out therefrom, is a greater sin in God's sight; and sedition is a greater sin than slaughter.'

The Talmud too, discusses the problem of waging war on the Sabbath. According to the rabbis: "Gentile cities must not be besieged less than three days before the Sabbath; yet once they commence they need not leave off. And thus did Shammai say: *until it fall*, even on the Sabbath."[1]

Idolatry or sedition is considered by Muḥammad, as in Jewish tradition,[2] to be a graver offense than fighting at the prohibited time and worse than slaughter. According to the Mishnah, "exile comes upon the world because of idolatry and incest and the shedding of blood."[3] The Talmud further stipulates: "in every (other) law of the Torah, if a man is commanded: 'Transgress and suffer not death' he may transgress and not suffer death, excepting idolatry, incest (which includes adultery), and murder."[4]

[1] B. Shab. 19a.

[2] Cf. notes to 2:187.

[3] Mishnah Ab. 5:9 [D].

[4] B. Sanh. 74a.

VERSE 216

> They will ask thee about wine and *el mâisar*,[1] say, 'In them both is sin and profit to men; but the sin of both is greater than the profit of the same.'

The Bible prohibits the drinking of wine and of other intoxicating beverages only in the case of priests and judges.[2] The Koranic prohibition of drinking wine applies only to the time of prayer,[3] which corresponds to the talmudic law "that a drunken person is forbidden to say the *Tefillah*."[4] Wine was considered in the talmudic period to be an intoxicating drink[5] and was used moderately even for benediction.[6] However, though the Jews looked upon wine as a serious evil,[7] its usage in a temperate form was encouraged in the Bible.[8]

[1] المَيسِر. A form of gambling, "the prize being a young camel, which was slaughtered and given to the poor." Palmer, p. 29 n.

[2] Lev. 10:9. Perhaps we have here an allusion to Deut. 28:39: "Thou shalt plant vineyards and dress them, but thou shalt neither drink of the wine, nor gather the grapes; for the worm shall eat them." Compare الخمر with וחמר in Onkelos, Deut. 29:5.

About the reason for Muḥammad's prohibition of wine, see *Zion*, V, 209–10 and notes 8–9. Also, R. Hai Gaon in תשובות הגאונים (Assaf, Editor), Jerusalem, 1929, §§ 10, 11, and ספר האשכול (הוצאת ח. אלבק), ע' 74.

[3] 4:46.

[4] B. Ber. 31a. Cf. Nöldeke-Schwally, *op. cit.*, p. 182 n.

[5] שאין לך דבר שמביא יללה על האדם אלא יין (ברכות מ, ע"א). Cf. תנחומא, נח, כג [B]: בכל מקום שאתה מוצא יין אתה מוצא כשלון.

[6] אין מברכין על היין . . . עד שנתן לתוכו מים (ברכות נ, ע"ב).

[7] See the story of Noah in Gen. 9:20–24 and רמז לו שקודם שישתה אדם מן היין הרי הוא תם ככבש זו שאינה יודעת כלום וכרחל לפני גוזזיה נאלמה שתה כהוגן הרי הוא גבור כארי ואומר אין כמותי בעולם. כיון ששתה יותר מדאי נעשה כחזיר מתלכלך במי רגלים ובדבר אחר. נשתכר נעשה כקוף עומד ומרקד ומשחק ומוצא לפני הכל נבלות הפה ואינו יודע מה יעשה (תנחומא, נח, י"ג, ע"א).

[8] Ecc. 10:19 ". . . And wine maketh glad the life . . ." Cf. Torrey, *op. cit.*, p. 152.

VERSE 220

> Wed not with idolatrous women until they believe, for surely a believing handmaid is better than an idolatrous woman, even though she please you. And wed not to idolatrous men until they believe, for a believing slave is better than an idolater, even though he please you.

Compare: Ezra 9:13–14: "And after all that is come upon us for our evil deeds, and for our great guilt, seeing that Thou our God hast punished us less than our iniquities deserve, and hast given us such a remnant, shall we again break Thy commandments, and make marriages with the people that do these abominations? wouldest not Thou be angry with us till Thou hadst consumed us, so that there should be no remnant, nor any to escape?"

The Mishnah prohibits inter-marriage with Nethinim[1] for all time, whether they be males or females.[2] Accordingly, "a female . . . Nethinah (is prohibited) to an Israelite[3] and a daughter of an Israelite to a Nethin."[4]

The rabbis interpret Lev. 18:21, "And thou shalt not give any of thy seed to set them apart to Molech . . .," to mean "an Israelite who has intercourse with a Cuthean woman and begets from her a son for idolatry."[5]

[1] Descendants of the Gibeonites who deceived Joshua (Josh. 9:3 f.).

[2] Mishnah Yeb. 78b.

[3] "Who is forbidden on the ground of the sanctity of Israel to marry such types."

[4] Mishnah Yeb. 20a.

[5] B. Meg. 25a; cf. *Targum Jonathan* to Lev. 18:21 and B. Sanh. 64a.

VERSE 222

> They will ask thee about menstruation: say, 'It is a hurt.' So keep apart from women in their menstruation, and go not near them till they be cleansed; but when they are cleansed come in to them by where God has ordered you; verily, God loves those who turn to Him, and those who keep themselves clean.

According to the Talmud "menstruation" is one of the ten curses inflicted on Eve for eating of the fruit of the forbidden tree (Gen. 3:6).[1] The Koranic expression, "it is a hurt," recalls the biblical words: "Unto the woman He said: 'I will greatly multiply thy pain and thy travail; in pain thou shalt bring forth children . . ." (Gen. 3:16).

Ṭabarī, referring to the Koranic words, "and go not near them until they be clean," writes that Moslem commentators differ about the exact meaning of this sentence. Some maintain that the true meaning is to refrain from sexual intercourse, whereas others hold that any proximity to a woman during the menstruation period is prohibited.[2] Such an interpretation is also found in the Talmud: "Said I to her, 'My daughter! how was he (the husband) to thee in thy days of menstruation?' 'God forbid!' she rejoined; 'he did not touch me even with his little finger.' "[3] The Koranic phrase, *lā taqrabūhunna*,[4] is similar to the Hebrew, *lo tiḳrab*[5] (Lev. 18:19). Likewise the term

[1] Cf. אדר"נ, chapter 1; *Pereḳ Adam ha-Rishon*, in *T.S.*, Vol. II, p. 97.

[2] Ṭabarī, Vol. II, p. 217:

اختلف اهل التاويل في تاويل قوله فاتوهن من حيث امركم الله فقال بعضهم معنى ذلك فاتوا نسائكم اذا تطهرن من الوجه الذى نهينكم عن اتيانهن منه في حال حيضهن....

[3] B. Shab. 13b; יורה דעה § 195, לא יגע בה. Cf. Lev. 18:19: "And thou shalt not approach unto a woman to uncover her nakedness, as long as she is impure by her uncleanness." See also Lev. 15:19–30. The biblical prohibition is in agreement with most Moslem commentators who claim that Muḥammad prohibited actual cohabitation during the period of menstruation. Compare Ṭabarī (*ibid.*) and Wensinck, "Die Entstehung der muslimischen Reinheitsgesetzgebung," *Der Islam*, Vol. V (Strassburg, 1914), pp. 62–80.

[4] لا تقربوهنّ.

[5] לא תקרב.

"clean,"[6] used for purification and recovery, corresponds to the Hebrew *Ṭahor*[7] (Lev. 15:13, 28).

The expression, *fa'tazalū*[8] (go not near), recalls the Hebrew *paraṣh*[9] (Lev. 15:31),[10] used in connection with the biblical and talmudic prohibition to approach women during their menstruation: "Rabbi Jeremiah observed, . . . that they shall separate from their wives near their periods."[11]

[6] يطهرن.

[7] טהר.

[8] فاعتزلوا.

[9] פרש.

[10] Cf. Rashi, *ad loc.*: והזרתם — אין נזירה אלא פרישה; also, Onkelos, *ad loc.*, ותפרשון. Compare Ibn Ezra, *ad loc.*, והרחקתם; and see B. Ket. 61a.

[11] B. Nid. 63b.

VERSE 223

> Your women are your tilth, so come into your tillage how you choose; but do a previous good act for yourselves, and fear God, and know that ye are going to meet Him; and give good tidings unto those who do believe.

That "women" are "tilth" is also noted in the Talmud: "Esther was merely natural soil (which is tilled)."[1] The comparison of a woman with tilth occurs, also, in the El-Amarna tablets.[2] Similarly, the comparison between "sexual intercourse" and "plowing" is well known in rabbinic literature.[3] The famed heretic and founder of the Karaite movement, 'Anan ben David,[4] interprets the biblical sentence, ". . . in plowing time and in harvest thou shalt rest" (Exod. 34:21), to mean abstention from cohabitation on the Sabbath.[5] Comparisons between the "woman" and the "field" abound in the Talmud: "If one has married a woman and has not found in her virginity (and) she says, 'After thou hadst betrothed me (to thyself) I was violated and thy field has been inundated . . .' "[6] In the Song of Songs (4:12) the woman is described as "A garden shut up," and as "A spring shut up, a fountain sealed."

The expression here, *fa'atū ḥarthakum*[7] (so come into your tillage), recalls the biblical phrase: ". . . go in, I pray thee, unto my handmaid . . ." (Gen. 16:2).[8] Likewise, the phrase, "how you choose," is comparable to the talmudic dictum: ". . . a man may do whatever he pleases with his wife (at intercourse)."[9] The latter view is not shared by R. Joḥanan b. Dahabai.[10]

[1] B. Sanh. 74b.

[2] D. H. Müller, *Semitica*, Vol. I, p. 33; cf. O. Weber, *Die Literatur der Babylonier und Assyrier*, Leipzig, 1907, p. 307; S. Poznanski, in *Studies in Jewish Literature in honor of Kaufmann Kohler*, Berlin, 1913, p. 241.

[3] Talmud Yerushalmi, Yeb. 1, 1: חמש חרישות חרש וחמש נטיעות נטע.

[4] Lived in Babylonia and died c. 800 C. E.

[5] Ibn Ezra on Exod. 34:21: אמר ענן . . . כי זה על משכב האשה. והלא תכסהו בושה. כי אם אמרנו כי ביד הגבר החריש. הלא במלת קציר יחריש.

[6] B. Ket. 16a.

[7] فاتوا حرثكم.

[8] Cf. Gen. 16:4, ויבא אל הגר; and Gen. 29:21, ואבואה אליה.

[9] . . . אלא כל מה שאדם רוצה לעשות באשתו עושה, משל לבשר הבא מבית הטבח רצה לאכלו במלח אוכלו צלי אוכלו מבושל אוכלו שלוק אוכלו וכן דג הבא מבית הצייד . . . (נדרים כ, ע״ב)

[10] *Ibid.*

Some of the Jewish practices regarding marriage are found in the Ḥadīth. Bukhārī's statement not to force marriage against the woman's will,[11] is in accord with the talmudic statement: "One may not give his daughter in betrothal when a minor (but must wait) until she grows up and says 'I want So-and-So.' "[12]

[11] Bu., Vol. III, p. 430: ولا تنكح البكر حتى تستاذن.
Cf. S. Bialoblocki, *Materialien zum Islamischen und Jüdischen Eherecht,* Giessen, 1928, p. 54 f.

[12] B. Ḳid. 41a.

VERSE 224

> Make not God the butt of your oaths, that ye will keep clear and fear and make peace amongst men, for God both hears and knows.

Almost all of the ten commandments in the Decalogue[1] have their counterpart in the Koran. In Sura 17 verses 23–41 Muḥammad commands, among others: "Put not with God other gods;" "ye shall not serve other than Him;" "kindness to one's parents;" "give thy kinsman his due and the poor and the son of the road;"[2] "draw not near to fornication;" "slay not the soul that God has forbidden you, except for just cause;"[3] and "draw not near to the wealth of the orphan."

The Koranic phrase, "Make not God the butt of your oaths," is comparable to the biblical: "Thou shalt not take the name of the Lord thy God in vain" (Exod. 20:7).[4] Muḥammad likewise commands his followers not to invoke the name of God in a false oath.

The phrase, "Make peace amongst men," seems to be a replica of the statement in *Sifre* that peace is essential for the dead as well as for the living.[5]

[1] Exod. 20:2–18 and Deut. 5:6–18: אנכי יהוה אלהיך . . . לא יהיה לך אלהים אחרים על פני . . . לא תעשה לך פסל . . . לא תשתחוה להם . . . לא תשא את שם יהוה אלהיך לשוא . . . זכור את יום השבת לקדשו . . . כבד את אביך ואת אמך . . . לא תרצח. לא תנאף. לא תגנב. לא תענה ברעך עד שקר. לא תחמד בית רעך. לא תחמד אשת רעך . . . Cf. 2:172. In 50:25 the expression, الذى جعل مع الله الها آخر, is comparable to Exod. 20:20, . . . לא תעשון אתי. Similarly, لا يسمع ولا يبصر in 19:43 is identical with Deut. 4:28, לא יראון ולא ישמעון. See also Rivlin, *op. cit.*, p. 118 and notes to 2:1–2, 77, 211, etc.

[2] Cf. Bu., Vol. IV, p. 109—Respect for father and mother; Bu., Vol. IV, p. 128—"Thou shalt not hate one another"; Bu., Vol. IV, p. 117—"Be merciful to men."

[3] Cf. פקוח נפש; also, וחי בהם (he shall live by them), Lev. 18:5. In Judaism Sabbath laws are suspended in the case of danger to human life. According to the rabbis, man shall live by the laws but shall not die because of them, B. Yom. 85a; cf. B. Ket. 5a.

[4] Cf. B. Shab. 119b, 120a; Mishnah Sheb. 3:10 [D].

[5] Cf. וקראת אליה לשלום גדול השלום שאפילו מתים צריכים שלום, גדול השלום שאפילו במלחמה של ישראל צריכים שלום, גדול השלום שדרי רום צריכים שלום שנאמר עושה שלום במרומיו. גדול השלום שחותמים (בו) ברכת כהנים. ואף משה היה אוהב שלום שנאמר ואשלח מלאכים ממדבר קדמות . . . דברי שלום (*Sifre* on Deut. 20:10). Also *Sifre* on Num. 6:26: גדול השלום ששקול כנגד כל מעשה בראשית.

VERSE 226

> Those who swear off from their women, they must wait four months; but if they break their vow God is forgiving and merciful.

The rabbis, too, set a limit to the time during which a husband may have no intercourse with his wife: "If a man vowed to have no intercourse with his wife, the School of Shammai say: (She may consent) for two weeks. And the School of Hillel say: For one week (only). Disciples (of the Sages) may continue absent for thirty days against the will (of their wives) while they occupy themselves in the study of the Law; and labourers for one week . . ."[1] If the man oversteps the time limit, he is obliged either to grant his wife a divorce or revoke his vow.[2] This is in line with Baiḍāwī's comment on the second part of the verse: "they retract their oaths by revoking it."[3]

The expression, "those who swear off from their women," recalls the biblical phrase in Deut. 24:1, "if she find no favour in his eyes."[4]

[1] Mishnah Ket. 5:6 (D).

[2] B. Ket. 61b.

[3] Baiḍāwī, Vol. II, p. 56: رجعوا في اليمين.

[4] Cf. Samuel Rosenblatt, "The Relation Between Jewish and Muslim Laws Concerning Oaths and Vows," in *PAAJR*, Vol. VII (1935–36), pp. 229–43.

VERSE 228

> Divorced women must wait for themselves three courses; and it is not lawful to them that they hide what God has created in their wombs, if they believe in God and in the last day. Their husbands will do better to take them back in that (case) if they wish for reconciliation; for, the same is due to them as from them; but the men should have precedence over them. God is mighty and wise.

This verse and verse 233 are similar to the talmudic laws. According to the rabbis, a divorced woman is not allowed to be married within ninety days of the date of the divorce. This is done in order to ascertain pregnancy, since it is presumed to take three months[1] to detect pregnancy.[2] The Mishnah, too, states: "widows may not (again) be betrothed or married before three months have passed . . ."[3] Though the Koran, as in Judaism, gives the right of divorce only to the husband, divorce legislation in Islām as a whole differs greatly from Jewish practice.[4]

[1] Deduced from Gen. 38:24: "And it came to pass about three months after . . ."

[2] B. Nid. 8b.

[3] Mishnah Yeb. 4:10 (D). Geiger, however, states: "und merkwürdig ist II:230, wo es heisst, der Mann dürfe, nachdem er die Frau (zum zweiten Male) verstossen, sie nicht wieder heirathen, es müsste sie denn ein Anderer schon geheirathet und wieder verstossen haben, in direktem Widerspruche mit 5 M, 1 ff.," *op. cit.*, p. 196.

It is worth noting that the list of the near relatives with whom marriage is not permitted according to the Koran (4:26–27) tallies with the list enumerated in Lev. 18:6–18; 20:11–21. Muḥammad, however, unlike the biblical law, disallows marriage with a niece. Cf. R. Roberts, *The Social Laws of the Qorān*, London, 1925, p. 14; Torrey, *op. cit.*, p. 149.

[4] The Koran does not require the granting of "a bill of divorce" (2:229), as prescribed in the Bible and in the Talmud. See B. Giṭ. 21b: בכתיבה מתגרשת ואינה מתגרשת בכסף. A written document, however, is required in monetary transactions, 2:283. For an elaborate discussion of the close relationship between Jewish and Moslem laws of marriage and divorce see Bialoblocki, *op. cit.*, pp. 25 f., and D. B. Macdonald, *The Development of Muslim Theology, Jurisprudence and Constitutional Theory*, London, 1903, pp. 67 f.

VERSE 233

> Mothers must suckle their children two whole years for one who wishes to complete the time of suckling; and on him to whom it is born its sustenance and clothing are incumbent; but in reason, for no soul shall be obliged beyond its capacity. A mother shall not be forced for her child; nor he to whom it is born for his child. And the same (is incumbent) on the heir (of the father). But if both parties wish to wean, by mutual consent and counsel, then it is no crime in them. And if ye wish to provide a wet-nurse for your children, it is no crime in you when you pay what you have promised her, in reason. Fear God, and know that God on what ye do doth look.

A prescribed time for childrens' suckling is also found in the Talmud, which states that a baby sucks and may continue to suck until twenty-four months old. " 'From that age onwards he is to be regarded as one who sucks an abominable thing.' "[1]

"If she (the mother) was divorced, he (her husband) cannot compel her; but if (the child) knows her (and refuses to be nursed by any other woman), (her husband) pays her the fee and may compel her to suckle it in order (to avert) danger."[2]

[1] B. Ket. 60a, כיונק שקץ. Compare Josephus, *Antiquities*, 2, 9; and 31:13, "and his (child's) weaning is in two years."

[2] B. Ket. 59b.

VERSE 239

> Observe the prayers, and the middle prayer, and stand ye attend before God.

The Koranic phrase, to "observe the prayer," recalls the talmudic expression *leḳayyem miẓwat tefillah.*[1] In 20:14 the term *aqāma ṣ-ṣalāh*[2] is similar to the Hebrew *la'amod bitefillah.*[3] The Arabic term for prayer *ṣalāh*[4] is identical with the Aramaic *ẓelota.*[5] "Stand ye attend before God" recalls the Mishnaic phrase: "None may stand up to say the *Tefillah* save in sober mood."[6]

According to Islāmic tradition: "The prayer in the midst of the congregation stands twenty-five degrees higher than the prayer one performs in his house or in the market place."[7] Similarly, the Talmud states: "A man's prayer is heard (by God) only in the Synagogue . . . How do you know that the Holy One, blessed be He, is to be found in the Synagogue? For it is said: *God standeth in the congregation of God* (Ps. 82:1). And how do you know that if ten people pray together, the Divine Presence is with them? For it is said '*God standeth in the congregation of God*' (and a congregation consists of not less than ten)."[8]

[1] לקיים מצות תפלה; cf. notes to 2:1–2, 172, 211, 246 and elsewhere. The Hebrew, *Tefilla* (prayer), which is derived from the root פלל "to judge", is taken as "self-examination" or as "an invocation of God to judge." See Gen. 21:17; 25:21; 28:20; 32:11; 35:3; Deut. 9:25–26.

[2] اقام الصلوة.

[3] לעמוד בתפלה; B. Sanh. 44b: כל המאמץ עצמו בתפילה. See, also, Geiger, *op. cit.*, p. 84; Rivlin, *Gesetz* . . . , p. 93; Mittwoch, *op. cit.*, p. 16; Torrey, *op. cit.*, p. 138n.; and 2:229–30 لا يقيما. Cf. B. Ber. 30a.

[4] صلوة; cf. William Rudolph, *Die Abhängigkeit des Qorans von Judentum und Christentum*, Stuttgart, 1922, p. 56; A. J. Wensinck, "Ṣalāt," *EI*, Vol. IV, pp. 99 f.

[5] צלותא.

[6] Mishnah Ber. 5:1: אין עומדין להתפלל אלא מתוך כובד ראש.

[7] Taylor, *op. cit.*, p. 200; cf. note 28 to 2:1–2.

[8] B. Ber. 6a; cf.: תפלת הצבור נשמעת תמיד ואפילו היו בהם חוטאים אין הקב"ה מואס בתפלתם של רבים לפיכך צריך אדם לשתף עצמו עם הצבור (רמב"ם, יד החזקה, הלכות תפלה, פ"ח, ה"א). See also Mishnah Meg. 4:3, B. Sanh. 2b and Juynboll, *op. cit.*, p. 81.

VERSE 240

> And if ye fear, then afoot[1] or on horseback; but when ye are in safety remember God, how He taught you while yet ye did not know.

A similar verse is found in 3:188: "who remember God standing and sitting or lying on their sides, and reflect on the creation of the heavens and the earth," to which Baiḍāwī comments that Muḥammad directed his followers to pray in any of these three postures depending upon their strength. That is, pray standing and if unable, sitting; and if still unable (to pray), leaning on one side.[2]

The Talmud, too, prescribes the position for prayer:[3] "If one was riding on an ass and the time arrived for saying *Tefillah*, if he has someone to hold his ass, he dismounts and prays, if not, he sits where he is and prays."[4] As in Judaism,[5] so in Islām, prayer may be shortened in time of emergency,[6] and in purification before prayers, sand[7] may be substituted for water in time of need.[8]

[1] "That is, if ye are in danger, say your prayers, as best you can, on foot or horseback, not staying so as to endanger your lives," Palmer, p. 33 n.; cf. 4:46; 10:13.

[2] Baiḍāwī, Vol. I, p. 93:
وقيل معناه يصلون على الهيئات الثلاث حسب طاقتهم... صل قائما فان لم تستطع فقاعدا فان لم تستطع فعلى جنب.

[3] Cf. Mishnah Ber. 4:5 [D].

[4] B. Ber. 30a.

[5] ההולך במקום סכנה מתפלל תפלה קצרה (משנה ברכות כ"ח, ע"ב). אבוה דשמואל כי אתי באורחא לא מצלי תלתא יומי (עירובין, ס"ה, ע"א).

[6] 4:102: "And when ye knock about in the earth, it is no crime to you that ye come short in prayer." Cf. Geiger, *op. cit.*, p. 86: "vergleich den ganz gleichen Ausdruck שוט בארץ." See notes to 2:1–2, 147, 172, 182, 196, etc.

[7] 5:8: "But if ye are sick, or on a journey, or if one of you comes from the privy, or if ye have touched women and cannot find water, then take fine surface sand and wipe your faces and your hands therewith," cf. Bu., Vol. I, p. 98 and B. Ber. 15a: מי שאין לו מים לרחוץ ידיו מקנח ידיו בעפר ובצרור ובקסמית.

[8] In 5:8, the Koran prescribes the following: "O ye who believe! when ye rise up to prayer wash your faces, and your hands as far as the elbows, and wipe your heads, and your feet down to the ankles. And if ye are polluted, then purify yourselves." Such a practice was prescribed in Exod. 30:19 for Aaron and his sons to "wash their hands and their feet thereat." The Talmud refers to this practice

VERSE 244

> Dost thou not look at those who left their homes by thousands, for fear of death; and God said to them "Die," and then He quickend them again? Verily, God is Lord of grace to men, but most men give no thanks.

Ezekiel[1] relates that the spirit of God had placed him in a valley that was filled with human bones, all very dry and numerous. Then the word of God came forth asking: Can these bones return to life? Ezekiel replied: Thou, Lord, thou knowest. God said: Prophesy over these bones, in the name of God, that He will enclose them with veins, flesh and skin, and the spirit of life, that they all come back to life. Ezekiel prophesied. A storm and noise of moving bones were heard; the bones neared each to its parts, and they were clothed with skin and flesh. God then asked Ezekiel to call upon the wind from the four corners and blow into those killed ones. The winds brought the spirit, and a very large army arose, standing upon their feet. God then said to Ezekiel: These bones are the children of Israel. They had said: Our hopes are lost, our bones are dried up.[2]

---

as קידש ידיו ורגליו (B. Yom. 30b). Cf. B. Zeb. 19b: "Our Rabbis taught: How is the precept of 'sanctification' (fulfilled)? (The priest) places his right hand on his right foot and his left on his left foot, and sanctifies them (so that he washes his hands and feet simultaneously, by pouring water on each pair with his fore hand). R. Jose son of Judah said: He places both his hands on each other and on his two feet lying on each other, and sanctifies them." See also Rivlin, *op. cit.*, p. 90.

[1] Ezek. 37:1–14; cf. notes to 2:260, 261, 262.

[2] Cf. B. Shab. 88b and B. Sanh. 92b: מתים שהחיה יחזקאל עלו לארץ ישראל ונשאו נשים והולידו בנים ובנות. Also Geiger, *op. cit.*, p. 190n: "Auch arab. Ausleger wissen davon, jedoch halb träumend, sowie Ismail ben Ali im Namen des Ibn Taleb angiebt, es sei dies in den Zeiten des Richters (?) حزقيل, der nach برسياس, Sohn des Caleb, diese Stelle bekleidet habe, vorgefallen (Mar. Prodr. IV, 83)." According to Moslem writers, Ezekiel was one of the judges of Israel.

VERSE 246

> Who is there that will lend to God a good loan? He will redouble it many a double; God closes His hand and holds it out, and unto Him shall ye return.

A similar verse is found in Sura 3:177: "God heard the speech of those who said, 'Verily God is poor and we are rich.' "[1] Baiḍāwī, commenting on the latter verse, writes that this was said by the Jews when they heard the words, 'Who then will lend a hand to God a good loan?' It is related that the Prophet once sent a letter from Abū Bakr to the Jewish tribe Banū Qainuqā' inviting them to accept Islām and to observe prayer and to give alms and to lend to God a good loan. When Pinḥās B. 'Azurā said, 'Then God must be poor, if He desires a loan!' Then Abū Bakr slapped him saying, 'Were it not for the covenant that is between us, I would have cut off your head.' Then Pinḥās complained to the Prophet, claiming that he had not said it. Then this text was revealed which gave its meaning, that it is not hidden from God, and that He has prepared punishment for them on account of it.[2]

Talmudic law, too, reacts to people who are critical of the law of charity. The rabbis say ". . . The critic (of Judaism) may bring against you the argument, 'If your God loves the poor, why does He not support them?' If so, answer him, 'So that through them we may be saved from the punishment of Gehinnom.' This question was actually

[1] Compare: "And the Lord said unto Moses: 'Is the Lord's hand waxed short? now shalt thou see whether My word shall come to pass unto thee or not' " (Num. 11:23).

[2] Baiḍāwī, Vol. I, p. 92:

قالته اليهود لما سمعوا من ذا الذى يقرض الله قرضا حسنا وروى انه عليه الصلاة والسلام كتب مع ابى بكر رضى الله تعالى عنه الى يهود بنى قينقاع يدعوهم الى الاسلام واقام الصلاة وايتاء الزكاة وان يقرضوا الله قرضا حسنا فقال فنحاص بن عازوراء ان الله فقير حتى سأل القرض فلطمه ابو بكر رضى الله عنه على وجهه وقال لولا ما بيننا من العهد لضربت عنقك فشكاه الى رسول الله ....وجحد ما قاله فنزلت والمعنى انه لم يخف عليه وانه اعد لهم العقاب عليه.

Cf. M.C.B. p. 128.

put by Turnus Rufus (Roman Governor of Judea) to R. Akiba: 'If your God loves the poor, why does He not support them?' He replied, 'So that we may be saved through them from the punishment of Gehinnom.' 'On the contrary,' said the other, 'it is this which condemns you to Gehinnom. I will illustrate by a parable. Suppose an earthly king was angry with his servant and put him in prison and ordered that he should be given no food or drink, and a man went and gave him food and drink. If the king heard, would he be angry with him? And you are called 'servants,' as it is written, '*For unto me the children of Israel are Servants*' (Lev. 25:55). R. Akiba answered him: 'I will illustrate by another parable. Suppose an earthly king was angry with his son, and put him in prison and ordered that no food nor drink should be given to him, and someone went and gave him food and drink. If the king heard of it, would he not send him a present? And we are called 'sons,' as it is written: *Sons are ye to the Lord your God* (Deut. 14:1)."[3]

The Koranic idea that giving charity makes man God's creditor may refer to the biblical verse in Prov. 19:17: "He that is gracious unto the poor lendeth unto the Lord, And his good deed[4] will He repay unto him."[5] Muḥammad, probably aware of this Jewish precept, emphasized the importance of righteousness[6] in helping the poor and the needy. This is clear from other verses: "Verily, those who give in charity, men and women, who have lent to God a godly loan, — it shall be doubled for them, and for them is a generous hire" (57:17). Similar words are also found in 64:17; 73:21 and in 30:38, ". . . but what ye put out in alms, desiring the face of God — these it is who shall gain double."[7]

In Sura 3:177 Muḥammad also states: "We will write down."[8] This recalls the liturgical phrase in the prayer of the Eighteen Benedictions on the High Holy Days: "O inscribe all Thy children of Thy covenant for a happy life."[9]

[3] B. B. B. 10a.

[4] Cf. Toyozo W. Nakarai, "The Prophetic Concept of Righteousness," in *The Shane Quarterly*, Vol. XIII (1952), pp. 51–57.

[5] Cf. B. B. B. 10a, b; *Lev. Rab.* 34,15; Horovitz, *HUCA*, pp. 212 f.

[6] صدقة; cf. notes to 2:1–2, 211, 240.

[7] Cf. Geiger, *op. cit.*, p. 16, where he mistakenly relates 3:177 to 5:69: "the Jews say, 'God's hand is fettered'."

[8] Cf. 3:46: "So write us down with those which bear witness."

[9] Cf.: בראש השנה יכתבון וביום צום כפור יחתמון (תפלת מוסף) . . . כתבנו בספר חיים טובים (אבינו מלכנו . . . מחזור ראש השנה).

VERSES 247–48

> Dost thou not look at the crowd of the children of Israel after Moses' time, when they said to a prophet of theirs, 'Raise up for us a king, and we will fight in God's way?' He said, 'Will you perhaps, if it be written down for you to fight, refuse to fight?' They said, 'And why should we not fight in God's way, now that we are dispossessed of our homes and sons?' But when it was written down for them to fight they turned back, save a few of them, and God knows who are evildoers. Then their prophet said to them, 'Verily, God has raised up for you Tâlût as a king;' they said, 'How can the kingdom be his over us; we have more right to the kingdom than he, for he has not an amplitude of wealth?' He said, 'Verily, God has chosen him over you, and has provided him with an extent of knowledge and of form. God gives the kingdom unto whom He will; God comprehends and knows.'

Muḥammad does not specify the name of the prophet who was asked to "raise up for us a king." The reference is undoubtedly to Samuel who anointed Saul[1] "to be prince over His inheritance" (I Sam. 10:1). Moslem commentators, however, disagree about the name of the prophet. Some maintain it was Samuel or Joshua[2] and others think it was Simeon.[3]

Regarding the birth of Samuel, Ṭabarī[4] relates an interesting

[1] In Arabic, Ṭālūt طالوت. Cf. B. Heller, "Ṭālūt," *EI*, Vol. IV, 1931, pp. 642–43; Ṭabarī, Vol. II, pp. 357 f.; Gustav Weil, *Biblische Legenden der Muselmänner*, pp. 192–208.

[2] Baiḍāwī, Vol. I, p. 61: هو يوسع او شمعون او سمويل.

[3] Cf. Zamakhsharī, *ad loc.*; Horovitz, *Koranische Untersuchungen*, pp. 39 f.

[4] Ṭabarī, Vol. II, p. 354:

كانت بنو اسرائيل يقاتلون العمالقة وكان ملك العمالقة جالوت وانهم ظهروا على بنى اسرائيل .... وكانت بنو اسرائيل يسالون الله ان يبعث لهم نبيا يقاتلون معه وكان سبط النبوة قد هلكوا فلم يبق منهم الا امراة حبلى فاخذوها فحبسوها في بيت رهبة ان تلد جارية فتبدلها بغلام .... فجعلت المراة تدعو الله ان يرزقها غلامًا فولدت غلاما فسمته شمعون فكبر الغلام فارسلته يتعلم التوراة في بيت المقدس وكفله شيخ ... فلما بلغ الغلام ان يبعثه الله نبيا

legend: After Moses' death, the Israelites fought the Amalekites, and lost. Whereupon the Israelites besought God to send them a prophet who would lead them to victory. In the struggle with the Amalekites the tribe of Levi, which was the tribe of prophets, was, however, completely annihilated save for one pregnant woman. The Israelites took the woman and locked her up in a convent, so that in case she gave birth to a girl they would exchange the child for a boy. The woman prayed to God to grant her a son. Her plea was fulfilled, and she named the boy Simeon. When Simeon grew up, she sent him to study in the sanctuary where he also rendered services to an old man. When the boy reached maturity, the angel Gabriel called him one night. The boy, who slept in the same place with the old man, inquired of the latter if he had called him. The old man replied in the negative and ordered the boy to lie down again. This was repeated three times. On the third time, Gabriel revealed himself to the boy and told him to return to his people and serve as a prophet.

This story is a mixture of Jewish, Christian and Moslem traditions. The reference to the convent is obviously Christian. The reference to Gabriel is undoubtedly Moslem. The story about the boy in the sanctuary hearing the voice of God calling him several times recalls the tale in I Samuel, Chapter 3.

As to the name Simeon, it is to be traced to the story of Leah, Jacob's wife, who called her second son Simeon,[5] "because the Lord hath heard[6] that I am hated" (Gen. 29:33). This reason is also given by Ṭabarī, who comments that "she called him Simeon because God hearkened to her prayer."[7]

Moslem literature abounds in legends about King Saul. Some commentators explain that Ṭālūt (Saul) is derived from the Arabic *Ṭul* (long), because Saul was tall.[8]

The Koranic expression, "has provided him with an extent of knowledge and of form," is explained by Ṭabarī as meaning "head and

اتاه جبريل والغلام نائم الى جنب الشيخ ... فدعاه بلحن الشيخ يا شماول فقام الغلام فزعا الى الشيخ فقال يا ابتاه دعوتنى فكرِهَ الشيخ ان يقول لا .... فقال يا بنى ارجع فنم .... فلما كانت الثالثة ظهر له جبريل فقال اذهب الى قومك فبلغهم رسالة ربك .....

[5] שמעון.

[6] From the Hebrew, שמע.

[7] Ṭabarī, Vol. II, p. 354.

[8] Zamakhsharī, Vol. I, p. 165 and Baiḍāwī, Vol. I, p. 61: وزعموا انه من طول. Cf. Grünbaum, *op. cit.*, pp. 185–87; Horovitz, *HUCA*, pp. 162–63; Nöldeke-Schwally, *op. cit.*, Vol. I, p. 184. See also notes to 2:249, 250.

shoulders above the people."[9] This has its origin in the Bible (I Sam. 9:2): "and there was not among the children of Israel a goodlier person than he: from his shoulders and upward he was higher than any of the people."

Ṭabarī also relates that God said to Samuel, after the latter had prepared oil to anoint the king, "that a man will appear in your house and if the oil will begin to flow over, you will know that this man is appointed by Me to be king in Israel."[10] He adds another Moslem tradition that God gave Samuel a cane and told him that if the man's height would measure up to the cane, it was a sign that he was the appointed king.[11]

Moslem commentators attribute the people's objection to the choice of Saul as king to his inferior ancestry. They maintain that from the tribe of Levi prophets emerged and from that of Judah came kings, but as for Saul, he was of the tribe of Benjamin and therefore was qualified neither for kingdom nor for prophecy.[12] This tradition recalls Saul's own words to Samuel: " 'Am not I a Benjamite, of the smallest of the tribes of Israel? and my family the least of all the families of the tribe of Benjamin? wherefore then speakest thou to me after this manner?' " (I Sam. 9:21.)

It is possible that the sentence, "Will you perhaps, if it be written down for you to fight, refuse to fight?" refers to the comment by the rabbis[13] that he who becomes merciful at the wrong time will become cruel at the end.[14]

[9] Ṭabarī, Vol. II, p. 354:

قال ان الله اصطفاه عليكم وزاده بسطه في العلم والجسم قال واجتمع
بنو اسرائيل فكان طالوت فوقهم من منكبيه فصاعداً ....

[10] *Ibid.*, Vol. II, p. 355:

فقال الله انظر القرن الذى فيه الدهن في بيتك فاذا دخل عليك
رجل فنشّ الدهن في القرن فهو ملك بنى اسرائيل.

[11] *Ibid.*, Vol. II, p. 359:

فقال السدى اتى النبي .... بعصا تكون مقدارا على طول الرجل
الذى يبعث فيهم ملكا فقال ان صاحبكم يكون طوله هذه العصا
فقاسوا انفسهم بها فلم يكونوا مثلها فقاسوا طالوت بها فكان مثلها.

[12] *Ibid.*, Vol II, 353–54; cf. Zamakhsharī and Baiḍāwī, *ad loc.*

[13] Based on the biblical verse in I Sam. 15:9: "But Saul and the people spared Agog." Cf. אל תהי צדיק הרבה (קהלת ז, ט"ז); B. Yom. 22b; *Ecc. Rab.* 7,16.

[14] ר' שמעון בן לקיש אומר כל מי שנעשה רחמן במקום אכזרי סוף שנעשה אכזרי במקום רחמן
שנאמר (ש"א, כ"ב, י"ט) ואת נוב עיר הכהנים הכה לפי חרב ולא תהא נוב כזרעו של עמלק.

VERSE 249

> Then said to them their prophet, 'The sign of his kingdom is that there shall come to you the ark with the *shechina* in it from your Lord, and the relics of what the family of Moses and the family of Aaron left; the angels shall bear it.' In that is surely a sign to you if ye believe.

In Moslem tradition this ark[1] was sent down from heaven to Adam. In its wanderings it finally came to the Israelites who considered it extremely precious,[2] and carried it whenever they went into battle. In the wars led by Moses the enemy captured the ark from the Israelites. At the coronation of Ṭālūt (Saul)[3] the ark, in sight of all the Israelites, was brought back by the angels and placed at the feet of Ṭālūt. Thereupon all Israel acknowledged king Saul as anointed by God himself.[4]

This tradition seems to spring from two distinct but unrelated Jewish sources. Rebecca, in outfitting Jacob to get the blessing from his father Isaac instead of Esau, dressed Jacob in the beautiful clothes that had been entrusted to her care (Gen. 27:15). According to Jewish commentators these clothes had been presented to Adam by God himself. The rabbinic sources vary as to how these clothes reached Esau. One source maintains that when Esau noticed Nimrod wearing the clothes God had made for Adam, he murdered him and

[1] التابوت is identical with the Hebrew תבה or Aramaic תיבותא. The expression here, "shall come to you (before) the ark," recalls the Mishnaic phrase, "He that goes before the Ark" (Mishnah Ber. 5:4). Similarly, the term سكينة is identical with the Hebrew שכינה.

[2] Zamakhsharī, Vol. I, p. 166.

[3] The king who, according to verse 247, was not wanted by the people.

[4] Zamakhsharī, Vol. I, p. 166:
وقيل كان مع موسى ومع انبياء بنى اسرائيل بعده يستفتحون به فلما غيّرت بنو اسرائيل غلبهم عليه الكفار فكان في ارض جالوت فلما اراد الله ان يملّك طالوت اصابهم ببلاء حتى هلكت خمس مدائن فقالوا هذا بسبب التابوت بين اظهُرِنا فوضعوه على ثورين فساقهما الملائكة الى طالوت. Cf. 2:250, 253.

robbed him of the clothes.[5] Another source, however, claims that Adam received these clothes from God in order to function as high priest. By heredity they came down to Noah, and from him to Shem his oldest son, who was a priest to the Almighty God. Shem, in surrendering the priestly privileges to Abraham, also surrendered his priestly clothes to him. From Abraham the clothes came to Isaac, thence to Esau, his first born. Rebecca, Esau's mother, thus became the custodian of these clothes. When Esau sold his birth-right to Jacob, Rebecca rightly assumed that the clothes thereafter belonged to Jacob, and she instructed him to wear them when he went to secure the blessing from his father.[6]

Moslem commentators interpret the *relics* ("of what the family of Moses and the family of Aaron left") to mean the tablets, the broken tablets, the jar of manna (which Moses told Aaron "to lay . . . up before the Lord, to be kept throughout your generations"),[7] Moses' rod,[8] and Aaron's rod and hat.[9] Again we have here an admixture of Jewish and non-Jewish sources.[10]

As for the second source of the tradition concerning the ark, we find the following: "So I made an ark of acacia-wood . . . and put the tables in the ark which I had made; and there they are, as the Lord commanded me" (Deut. 10:3–5). According to Talmud Yerushalmi[11] there were four tablets in the ark: the first, the broken ones, and the second set. The *Sifre*[12] comments that this ark, which went along with Israel in their encampments, housed the broken

[5] עשו . . . ראה את הכתנת שעשה הקב"ה לאדם ולחוה על נמרוד וחמד אותה בלבו והרגו ולקח אותה ממנו (פדר"א, פכ"ד). As for Moslem legends about Nimrod, see B. Heller, "Namrūd," *EI*, Vol. III, 1930, pp. 843 f.; Bernard Chapira, "Légendes Bibliques Attribuées à Ka'b el-Aḥbār," *R.E.J.*, Vol. LXIX (1919), pp. 86–107; D. Sidersky, *Les Origines des Légendes Musulmanes*, Paris, 1933, pp. 31–35. Cf. notes to 2:260.

[6] אדם הראשון היה בכורו של עולם . . . לבש בגדי כהונה . . . כיון שמת מסרן לשת . . . לנח . . . לשם . . . לאברהם . . . יעקב . . . שלא היה בכור (במדבר רבה, פ"ד, ו). Cf. 2:118.

[7] Exod. 16:33–34.

[8] Exod. 17:5.

[9] Zamakhsharī, Vol. I, p. 166.

[10] Dov Heller, שאול מלך ישראל באגדות המושלמים, in *Haẓofeh*, 1926, pp. 138–39.

[11] וארבעה לוחות היו בו שנים שבורים ושנים שלימים דכתיב, אשר שברת ושמתם בארון (תלמוד ירושלמי סוטה, פ"ח, ה"ג).

[12] וארון ברית י"י נוסע לפניהם ארון זה שיצא עמהם במחנה היו בו שברי לוחות (*Sifre* on Num. 10:33).

tablets. The Talmud Yerushalmi[13] adds that there were two arks with Israel in the desert; one in which the Torah was placed and the other containing the broken tablets. The former was in the Tabernacle, the latter went out in front of the armies. A precedent was established by the two sons of Eli, who took the gold-coated ark and carried it in front of the Jewish armies in their battle with the Philistines. The ark was later captured by the Philistines, and the Jewish armies were dispersed.[14] The Moslem tradition, however, has it that the Amalekites, and not the Philistines, captured the ark.[15]

[13] שני ארונות היו מהלכין עם ישראל במדבר אחד שהיתה התורה נתונה בתוכו ואחד שהיו שברי לוחות נתונין בתוכו זה שהיתה התורה נתונה בתוכו היה מונח באוהל מועד . . . זה שהיו שברי לוחות נתונין בתוכו היה נכנס ויוצא עמהן (תלמוד ירושלמי שקלים, פרק ו׳, ה״א).

[14] *'Eliahu Rab.* 11,10.

[15] Cf. I Sam., chapters 3, 4, 5.

VERSE 250

> And when Tâlût set out with his soldiery, he said, 'God will try you with a river, and he who drinks therefrom, he is not of mine; but whoso tastes it not, he is of mine, save he who laps it lapping with his hand.'

According to Ṭabarī, Saul (Ṭālūt) put his forces in water in order to test them, since they had complained about the shortage of water. He then urged them to pray to God to make a river flow between them and their enemies.[1]

The Koranic story of Saul is confused with the biblical story about Gideon, who camped with his forces beside 'En-harod (the well of Harod) (Judg. 7:1), where God said to Gideon: " 'The people are yet too many; bring them down unto the water, and I will try them for thee there; and it shall be, that of whom I say unto thee: This shall go with thee, the same shall go with thee; and of whomsoever I say unto thee: This shall not go with thee, the same shall not go.' So he brought down the people unto the water; and the Lord said unto Gideon: 'Every one that lappeth of the water with his tongue, as a dog lappeth, him shalt thou set by himself; likewise every one that boweth down upon his knees to drink.' And the number of them that lapped, putting their hand to their mouth, was three hundred men; but all the rest of the people bowed down upon their knees to drink water. And the Lord said unto Gideon: 'By the three hundred men that lapped will I save you, and deliver the Midianites into thy hand; and let all the people go every man unto his place' " (Judg. 7:4–7).

Ṭabarī's statement that the soldiers were tried because they complained that there was no water to drink, is undoubtedly a reference to the Israelites' complaint in the desert: "Wherefore the

[1] Ṭabarī, Vol. II, pp. 369–70:
وقيل ان طالوت قال ان الله مُبتليكم بنهر لانهم شكوا الى طالوت قلة المياه بينهم وبين عدّوهم وسألوه ان يدعو الله لهم ان يجرى بينهم وبين عدوهم نهرًا فقال لهم طالوت حينئذ ما اخبر عنه انه قاله من قوله ان الله مبتليكم بنهر ذكر من قال ذلك .... ذكره عن طالوت انه قال لجنوده اذ شكوا اليه العطش فاخبر ان الله مُبتليكم بنهرٍ ....

Cf. notes to 2:247, 249, 250.

people strove with Moses, and said: 'Give us water that we may drink.' And Moses said unto them: 'Why strive ye with me? wherefore do ye try the Lord?' " (Ex. 17:2.)[2]

[2] Cf. Hans v. Mžik's "Die Gideon-Saul Legende und die Überlieferung der Schlacht bei Badr" in *Festschrift Joseph Ritter v. Karabaček*, pp. 63 f.

VERSE 251

> And they drank from it save a few of them, and when he crossed it, he and those who believed with him, they said, 'We have no power this day against Jâlût (Goliath) and his soldiery,' those who thought that they should meet their Lord said, 'How many a small division of men have conquered a numerous division, by the permission of God, for God is with the patient."

Muḥammad seems to have had some knowledge (though not exact) of David's words to Saul as recorded in the Bible: "Thy servant smote both the lion and the bear; and this uncircumcised Philistine shall be as one of them, seeing he hath taunted the armies of the living God" (I Sam. 17:36).[1]

[1] Cf. P. Jensen, "Das Leben Muhammeds und die David-Sage," in *Der Islam* (Berlin-Leipzig, Vol. 12, 1922), pp. 84–97.

VERSE 253

> And they put them to flight by the permission of God, and David killed Jâlût, and God gave him the kingdom and wisdom, and taught him of what He willed.

This story is related in detail by Ṭabarī with some deviations from the biblical[1] narrative: i. e., a) David desired the king's daughter as a prize for fighting Goliath; b) following Goliath's death, many people claimed to have killed him; some brought his sword and some brought parts of his body, but King Saul announced that the real victor was the one who brought Goliath's head, and then David came and produced the Philistine's head.[2]

Zamakhsharī,[3] commenting on this Koranic verse, states that when David was on his way to kill (Goliath), he found three stones. Each one pleaded with him to use it in order to slay Goliath.

Ṭabarī connects the three stones with the three patriarchs, i. e. Jacob, Isaac and Abraham.[4]

Mas'ūdī[5] states that all three stones became one in David's bag. Grünbaum[6] traces the latter legend to Gen. 28:11: "and he (Jacob)

[1] I Sam., chapter 17; cf. 2:251.

[2] Ṭabarī, Vol. II, p. 375:

... فاتى بداود الى طالوت فقاضاه ان قتله ان ينكحه ابنته .... ولما رجعوا الى طالوت ادعى الناس قتل جالوت فمنهم من ياتى بالسيوف وبالشيء من سلاحه او جسده وخبأ داود رأسه فقال طالوت من جاء برأسه فهو الذى قتله فجاء به داود ....

[3] Zamakhsharī, Vol. I, p. 168:

وقد مرّ في طريقه بثلثة احجار دعاه كل واحد منها ان يحمله وقالت له انك تقتل بنا جالوت.

[4] Ṭabarī, Vol. II, p. 375:

فمرّ بحجر فقال يا داود خذنى فاجعلني في مخلاتك تقتل بي جالوت واني حجر يعقوب ... ومشى .... اذ مر بحجر آخر فقال يا داود خذني ... تقتل بي جالوت فانى حجر اسحق ... فبينما هو مشي اذ مرّ بحجر فقال ... فانى حجر ابراهيم ....

[5] Mas'ūdī, Vol. I, p. 107, quoted by Grünbaum, *op. cit.*, p. 192.

[6] *Ibid.*

lighted upon the place and tarried there all night, because the sun was set; and he took one of the stones[7] of the place, and put it under his head, and lay down in that place to sleep." Rashi, commenting on the latter verse, tells that the stones began quarrelling for the honor of having Jacob's head rest upon them, whereupon God made them all into *one* stone.[8]

The legend of the stones as related in Zamakhsharī, Ṭabarī and Mas'ūdī is found in the Midrash where it is related that David selected five stones to honor God, Aaron and the three patriarchs.[9]

[7] Literally, "of the stones of the place," מאבני המקום.

[8] Rashi, *ad loc.*: וישם מראשותיו. עשאן כמין מרזב סביב לראשו שירא מפני חיות רעות התחילו מריבות זו את זו זאת אומרת עלי יניח צדיק ראשו וזאת אומרת עלי יניח מיד עשאן הקב"ה אבן אחת וזהו שנאמר ויקח את האבן אשר שם מראשתיו. Cf., also: חמשא ניסין אתעבידו לאבונן ליעקב . . . ניסא תליתיא אבניא דנסב יעקב אבונן ברמשא ושוי יתהון תחות יסודי רישיה וכיון דקם בצפרא ואשכח דכולהון לאבן חדא והיא אבנא דאקים קיימא קמא ואריק משח על רישיה (תרגום ירושלמי, בראשית כ"ח, י).

[9] ויבחר לו חמשה חלקי אבנים אחד לשמו של הקב"ה ואחד לשמו של אהרן ושלשה לשלשת אבות העולם (ילקוט שמעוני, שמואל א, רמז קכז). Cf. L. Ginzberg, *Legends of the Jews*, Vol. IV, p. 87: "The stones turned into one pebble," and "came of their own accord." See also האבנים היו מתלקטות מאליהן (ילקוט, *ibid.*).

VERSE 254

> These apostles have we preferred one of them above another. Of them is one to whom God spake; and we have raised some of them degrees; and we have given Jesus the son of Mary manifest signs, and strengthened him by the Holy Spirit. And, did God please, those who came after them would not have fought after there came to them manifest signs. But they did disagree, and of them are some who believe, and of them some who misbelieve, but, did God please, they would not have fought, for God does what He will.

This verse contradicts verses 2:130 and 3:78 where Muḥammad states: "we will make no distinction between any of them." Wellhausen,[1] relying on Baiḍāwī, suggests that Jesus is considered in the Koran to have eclipsed all Jewish prophets. However, as Torrey already indicates, there is no reason for such a "hasty contention."[2] On the contrary, Baiḍāwī states that Moses and Muḥammad were the only ones who spoke with God, whereas his reference to Jesus is in connection with the miracles he performed.[3] Elsewhere[4] we have shown that to Muḥammad, Abraham and Moses were the two great leaders who served as examples for developing the religion of Islām.[5] This view is corroborated in 3:30, where Muḥammad states: "Verily, God has chosen Adam, and Noah, and Abraham's people, and Imrân's people above the world . . . ."

It seems that here, too, Muḥammad is under the influence of

[1] *Reste* . . . , p. 205: "Jüdische Gesinnung verrät es nicht, dass Jesus im Quran hoch über alle Propheten des Alten Testamentes gestellt wird," quoted in Torrey, *op. cit.*, p. 75.

[2] *Ibid.*: "Nowhere in the Koran is there any trace of a wish to give 'Isā ibn Maryam especially high rank among the prophets." Cf. note 4 to 2:136.

[3] Baiḍāwī, Vol. I, p. 63:

وهو موسى عليه الصلاة والسلام وقيل موسى ومحمد عليهما الصلاة والسلام — كلم الله موسى ليلة الحيرة وفي الطور ومحمدا .... ليلة المعراج .... بان فضله على غيره (محمد) وقيل ابراهيم ... وقيل ادريس .... وجعل معجزاته (عيسى) سبب تفضيله.

[4] 2:91.

[5] 2:125.

Jewish tradition which considers Moses the greatest of all prophets.[6] The rabbis discuss the various degrees[7] of all prophets,[8] and conclude that that of Moses was the highest.[9]

[6] וכל שהיה מתנבא מעין נבואתו של משה היה (שמות רבה, פמ"ב, ח). Cf. B. Yeb. 49b: "All the prophets looked into a dim glass (imagining like Isaiah that they saw the Deity), but Moses looked through a clear glass." See also Horovitz, "Nabī," *ZDMG*, Vol. LV, pp. 519 f.; Tor Andrae, *Die Person Muhammeds in Lehre und Glauben seiner Gemeinde*, Stockholm, 1918, pp. 32 f.; Nöldeke-Schwally, *op. cit.*, Vol. I, pp. 159 f.

[7] א"ר ברכיה כל הנביאים כולן ראו הכבוד מתוך תשע מראות ומשה רבינו מתוך מראה אחת. כל הנביאים לא היו שומעין את הקול אלא לפי כוחן שנ' קול ה' בכח אבל משה רבנו היה שומעו כתקונו, שנ' וישמע את הקול, הקול כמות שהוא (משנת רבי אליעזר 115–116; ויקרא רבה, פ"א, יד).

[8] כל נביא ונביא ניתן בו רוח־הקדש כל אחד לפי כחו (ילקוט שמעוני איוב, רמז תתקט"ז); and: א"ר אחא אפילו רוח הקדש ששורה על הנביאים אינה שורה אלא במשקל, יש שמתנבא ספר אחד ויש שנים (ויקרא רבה, פט"ו, ב).

[9] שמות רבה, פמ"ב, ז; ויקרא רבה, פ"א, טו.

VERSE 256

> God, there is no god but He, the living, the self-subsistent. Slumber takes Him not, nor sleep. His is what is in the heavens and what is in the earth. Who is it that intercedes with Him save by His permission? He knows what is before them and what is behind them, and they comprehend not aught of His knowledge but of what He pleases. His throne extends over the heavens and the earth, and it tires Him not to guard them both, for He is high and grand.

Compare Isaiah 45:5–8: "I am the Lord, and there is none else, Beside Me there is no God . . . That they may know from the rising of the sun, and from the west, That there is none beside Me; I am the Lord, and there is none else; I form the light, and create darkness; I make peace and create evil; I am the Lord, that doeth all these things." Also the following: "Behold, unto the Lord thy God belongeth the heaven, and the heaven of heavens, the earth, with all that therein is" (Deut. 10:14). "He . . . doth neither slumber nor sleep" (Ps. 121:4); ". . . The heaven is My throne, and the earth is My footstool . . ." (Is. 66:1); "For the Lord your God, He is God of gods, and Lord of lords, the great God, the mighty . . ." (Deut. 10:17).

A similar idea is also found in the Midrash: "The Holy One, blessed be He, is One and there is no god but He, neither man, nor animals nor His serving angels know His whereabouts. He is all over."[1]

The Koranic idea that the intercessor requires the sanction of the Lord is to be found in Jewish lore. According to the Aggada, God revealed to Abraham his intention to destroy Sodom in order to provoke him to intercede.[2] Similarly, God encouraged Moses to intercede for the people of Israel.[3]

[1] אחד ואין לו תמורה ולא שני כנגדו . . . ואין אדם יודע היכן הוא מקומו והחיות אין יודעות היכן הוא מקומו ולא המלאכים המהללים שמו יודעין היכן הוא . . . (מדרש תמורה, עק״ל, תוספת לאגדת בראשית). Cf. notes to 2:1–2, 101, 109.

[2] תדע לך שבזמן שהבריות חוטאין ומכעיסין לפניו והוא כועס עליהן. מה הקב״ה עושה חוזר ומבקש להם סניגור שילמד עליהן זכות ונותן שביל לפני הסניגור . . . וכן כשחטאו הסדומיים גלה לאברהם ללמד עליהן זכות שנא׳ וה׳ אמר המכסה אני מיד התחיל אברהם ללמד עליהן סניגוריא (תנחומא וירא, כד, ע״ב).

[3] והנה עם קשה עורף הוא ועתה הניחה לי ויחר אפי בהם ואכלם. וכי משה היה תופס בהקב״ה שהוא אומר הניחה לי. אלא למה״ד למלך שכעס על בנו והכניסו לקיטון ומתחיל לבקש להכותו והיה המלך מצעק מן הקיטון הניחה לי שאכנו. והיה פדגוג עומד בחוץ. אמר הפדגוג המלך ובנו לפנים בקיטון למה הוא אומר הניחה לי, אלא מפני שהמלך מבקש שאלך ואפייסנו על בנו לכך הוא מצעק הניחה לו. כך אמר הקב״ה למשה ועתה הניחה לי אמר משה מפני שהקב״ה רוצה שאפייס על ישראל לפיכך הוא אומר ועתה הניחה לי. מיד התחיל לבקש עליהם רחמים (שמות רבה, פמ״ב, י).

VERSE 260

> Do you not look at him who disputed with Abraham about his Lord, that God had given him the kingdom? When Abraham said, 'My Lord is He who giveth life and death,' he said, 'I give life and death.' Abraham said, 'But verily, God brings the sun from the east, do thou then bring it from the west?' And he who misbelieved was dumbfounded, for God does not guide unjust folk.

This verse and verses 21:69–70; 29:14–25; 37:81–99, stressing Abraham's faith in one God and his constant struggle against idolatry, are taken from Jewish sources. The legends concerning the relations between the impious Nimrod and the youth Abraham are many and are recorded in different versions in the Midrash: "Abraham then took a hatchet in his hand, and broke all his father's gods, and when he had done breaking them he placed the hatchet in the hand of the biggest god among them all, and he went out. Terah (Abraham's father), having heard the crash of the hatchet on the stone, ran to the room of the idols, and he reached it at the moment when Abraham was leaving it, and when he saw what had happened, he hastened after Abraham, and he said to him, 'What is this mischief thou hast done to my gods?' Abraham answered: 'I set savory meat before them, and when I came nigh unto them, that they might eat, they all stretched out their hands to take of the meat, before the big one had put forth his hand to eat. This one, enraged against them on account of their behavior, took the hatchet and broke them all, and, behold, the hatchet is yet in his hands, as thou mayest see.'

"Then Terah turned in wrath upon Abraham, and he said: 'Thou speakest lies unto me! Is there spirit, soul, or power in these gods to do all thou hast told me? Are they not wood and stone? and have I not myself made them? It is thou that didst place the hatchet in the hand of the big god, and thou sayest he smote them all.' Abraham answered his father, and said: 'How, then, canst thou serve these idols in whom there is no power to do anything? Can these idols in which thou trustest deliver thee? Can they hear thy prayers when thou callest upon them?' After having spoken these and similar words, admonishing his father to mend his ways and refrain from worshipping idols, he leapt up before Terah, took the hatchet from the big idol, broke it therewith, and ran away.

"Terah hastened to Nimrod, bowed down before him, and besought him to hear his story, about his son who had been born to him fifty years back, and how he had done to his gods, and how he had spoken.

'Now, therefore, my lord and king,' he said, 'send for him that he may come before thee, and do thou judge him according to the law, that we may be delivered from his evil.' When Abraham was brought before the king, he told him the same story as he had told Terah, about the big god who broke the smaller ones, but the king replied, 'Idols do neither speak, nor eat, nor move.' Then Abraham reproached him for worshipping gods that can do nothing, and admonished him to serve the God of the universe."[1] The King then replied: "Do you not know that I am the Lord of the Universe, the creation, the sun and the moon?" . . . God then endowed Abraham with wisdom and he spoke up: "Naturally the sun always rises in the East and sets in the West. If you are the creator of the universe, command the sun tomorrow to rise in the west and to set in the east, only then will I testify to your lordship . . ."[2]

The Koranic words also recall the biblical sentence: "Then the nations that are left round about you shall know that I the Lord have builded the ruined places, and planted that which was desolate; I the Lord have spoken it, and I will do it" (Ezek. 36:36).[3]

[1] Louis Ginzberg, *The Legends of the Jews*, Vol. I, pp. 214–15.

[2] וירא תרח את אשר עשה לו אברם בנו וילך ויגד לנמרוד ויאמר ילד יולד לי זה חמשים שנה וזאת אשר עשה לאלוהי . . . וישלח נמרוד ג׳ אנשים ויביאו את אברם לפניו . . . ויען אברם את המלך כדברים אשר דבר אל אביו. ויאמר האלוה הגדול אשר היה אתם בבית עשה להם את אשר שמעת. ויאמר המלך אל אברם היש בהם כח לדבר ולאכול ולעשות ככל אשר דברת. ויען אברם . . . ואם אין בהם כח למה תעבדם ולמה לא תעבדו אלהי כל הארץ אשר ברא אתכם . . . כמעשה הזה . . . חטאו אבותינו . . . ויבא ה׳ עליהם את מי המבול . . . ויאמר נמרוד לאברהם וכי אין אתה יודע שאני הוא אדון של כל המעשים והחמה והלבנה והכוכבים והמזלות ובני האדם מלפני יוצאין כולן . . . באותה שעה נתן הקב״ה בינה לאברהם ואמר לו אברהם אדוני המלך מנהגו של עולם . . . החמה יוצאת ממזרח ושוקעת במערב למחר תהא מצוה את החמה שתצא ממערב ותשקע במזרח ואף אני מעיד בך שאדון כל המעשים אתה . . . (ספר ילקוט ספורים ומדרשים, נח י״ג, ז׳). Cf. also the following: אמר אילו הרגני אמרפל לא הייתי עפר. ואולי שרפני נמרוד לא הייתי אפר (בראשית רבה וירא פמ״ט, כג); ואמר ליה אנא יי דאפקית יתך מאתון נוריהון מאור דכשדאי (תרגום ירושלמי בראשית ט״ו, ז); וכשהוציאו מאור כשדים נשתחוו כל אותם המלכים על כפות רגליו של אברהם אבינו והיו קוצצים ארזים ועשו לו בימה גדולה והושיבוהו בראשה והיו מביאים בניהם ומשליכין בחיקו ואומרים תלמדינו דרכיך לבטוח בחי וקיים לעדי (בית המדרש ה, ע׳ 40, מדרש דאברהם אבינו).

[3] Cf. Horovitz, *Kor. Unt.* . . ., p. 40: "Die erste — eingeführt mit alam tara ilā — und dritte spielen in der Zeit des Ibrāhīm, während die zweite weder Namen noch Ort nennt. A. Müller, *ZDMG* XLII, 80 hat sie aus der im äthiopischen Baruchbuch 5, 6 ff., erzählten Episode herleiten wollen, M. Schreiner ib. 436 aus der Geschichte des Ḥōnī ha-me'aggēl (Ta'anīt 23a)." See also notes to 2:261, 262.

VERSE 261

> Or like him who passed by a village,[1] when it was desolate and turned over on its roofs, and said, 'How will God revive this after its death?' And God made him die for a hundred years, then He raised him, and said, How long hast thou tarried?' Said he, 'I have tarried a day, or some part of a day.' He said, 'Nay, thou hast tarried a hundred years; look at thy food and drink, they are not spoiled, and look at thine ass; for we will make thee a sign to men. And look at the bones how we scatter them and then clothe them with flesh.' And when it was made manifest to him, he said, 'I know that God is mighty over all.'

According to Geiger,[2] this Koranic story refers to Nehemiah 2:13: "And I went out by night by the valley gate, even toward the dragon's well, and to the dung gate, and viewed the walls of Jerusalem, which were broken down, and the gates thereof were consumed with fire."

There is, however, a closer resemblance between the Koranic story and the legend in the Talmud about Ḥoni, the Circle-drawer: "R. Joḥanan said: This righteous man (Ḥoni) was throughout the whole of his life troubled about the meaning of the verse, *A Song of Ascents, When the Lord brought back those that returned to Zion, we were like unto them that dream* (Ps. 126:1). Is it possible for a man to dream continuously for seventy years? One day he was journeying on the road and he saw a man planting a carob tree; he asked him, How long does it take (for this tree) to bear fruit? The man replied: Seventy years. He then further asked him: Are you certain that you will live another seventy years? The man replied: I found (ready grown) carob trees

[1] Ali, *op. cit.*, p. 122, renders قرية "a town."

[2] Geiger, *op. cit.*, p. 192: "Noch eine andere Erzählung beziehen die arabischen Ausleger, nach Maracci's (Prod. IV, 85) Versicherung, auf Esra . . . wo von Einem erzählt wird, er sei vor einer zerstörten Stadt vorübergegangen, an ihre Belebung zweifelnd; Gott aber liess ihn sterben, dann nach 100 Jahren wieder aufleben und ertheilte ihm, der einen Tag sich aufgehalten zu haben glaubte, die Versicherung, dass schon 100 Jahre verflossen seien, wovon der Beweis sei, dass seine Speise und sein Trank zu Grunde gegangen, sein Esel zerfallen sei. Siehe da sammelte Gott die Gebeine des Esels, bekleidete sie mit Fleisch, so dass der Mann bekannte: Gott ist über Alles mächtig! Die Fabel rührt, wie Mar. richtig bemerkt, her von dem Ritte, den Nehemias nach dem zerstörten Jerusalem machte (Neh. 2:12 ff.), der ja so oft mit Esra verwechselt wird."

in the world; as my forefathers planted these for me so I too plant these for my children. Ḥoni sat down to have a meal and sleep overcame him. As he slept a rocky formation enclosed upon him which hid him from sight and he continued to sleep for seventy years. When he awoke he saw a man gathering the fruit of the carob tree and he asked him, Are you the man who planted the tree? The man replied: I am his grandson. Thereupon he exclaimed: It is clear that I slept for seventy years . . ."[3]

The phrase, "And look at the bones how we scatter them and then clothe them with flesh," recalls the words in Ezekiel, Chapter 37, relating to the vision of Ezekiel concerning the dry bones in the valley.[4]

[3] B. Ta'an. 23a.

[4] Cf. 2:244, 260, 262.

VERSE 262

> And when Abraham said, 'Lord show me how thou wilt revive the dead,' He said, 'What dost thou not yet believe?' Said he, 'Yea, but that my heart may be quieted.' He said, 'Then take four birds, and take them close to thyself; then put a part of them on every mountain; then call them, and they will come to thee in haste; and know that God is mighty, wise.'

This story, hinging upon the narrative in Genesis 15:11–18, probably springs from a Jewish legend which runs as follows: "But though he believed the promise given him with full and abiding faith, Abraham desired to know by what merit of theirs his descendants would maintain themselves. Therefore, God bade him bring a sacrifice of an heifer of three years old, a she-goat of three years old, a ram of three years old, a turtle dove and a young pigeon, thus indicating to Abraham the various sacrifices that should be brought in the Temple to atone for the sins of Israel. 'But what will become of my descendants after the Temple is destroyed?' asked Abraham. God replied and said: 'If they read the order of sacrifices, as they will be stated in the Scriptures, I will account it to them as if they had offered the sacrifices and I will forgive their sins.' God then revealed to Abraham the course of Israel's history in connection with the other nations on earth.

"Abraham took these animals, omitting the birds, and divided them. The birds he did not divide in order to show that Israel will remain whole. When the birds of prey came down upon the carcasses, Abraham drove them away. Dividing the birds symbolized the advent of the Messiah, who will cut the heathen into pieces. And as the Messianic time was made known unto Abraham, so also was the time of the resurrection of the dead made known to him. When Abraham laid the halves of the pieces over against each other, the animals became alive again, as the birds flew over them."[1] The idea that God brought the birds back to life is also found in Sa'adia Gaon's Commentary.[2]

[1] *Midrash Hagadol* 16, 17: אבא חנן אומר אף הראהו תחיית המתים שנא' ויקח לו את כל אלה וירד העיט על הפגרים ביקש לפזרן ולאבדן, וישב אותם אברם, נטל את האברים ונתנן זה בזה וכיון שירד עליהן הצפור חיו ופרחו והלכו להן שנאמר וישב אתם אברם ואין וישב אלא שהפריחה אותן הרוח שנאמר כי רוח ה' נשבה בו, ואומר ישב רוחו יזלו מים, quoted in T. S., Vol. III, pp. 650 f.; cf. P.R.E., pp. 198–99 and 148 ,משנת רבי אליעזר.

[2] Gen. 15:11; cf. Geiger, in כרם חמד, Vol. V, p. 180, who calls attention to this Koranic sentence. See also *T.S.*, *ibid.*, note 124.

Geiger believes that this verse shows that Muḥammad, in identifying himself with Abraham,[3] presents the latter not only as one who preached against idolatry, but also as the expounder of the doctrine of the Resurrection of the dead. Not certain about this doctrine,[4] Abraham, according to Muḥammad, prayed to God for tangible proof and became convinced when he saw that the divided birds[5] came together and were revived.[6]

[3] Cf. notes to 2:91, 244, 260–61.

[4] Baiḍāwī, Vol. I, p. 65:

قيل لما قال نمروذ انا احيى واميت قال له احياء الله تعال برد الروح الى بدنها فقال نمروذ هل عاينته فلم يقدر ان يقول نعم وانتقل الى تقرير آخر ثم سأل ربه ان يريه ليطمئن قلبه على الجواب ان سئل عنه مرة اخرى.

Cf. Geiger, *op. cit.*, p. 125, English edition, p. 100: "It is said that, after Nimrod had said: 'I make alive and I kill' (II.260), Abraham answered: 'Quickening is brought about by the return of the spirit to the body'. Nimrod replied: 'Hast thou then seen that?' Abraham could not answer in the affirmative and passed over to another argument. On this he prayed to the Lord for some revelation, in order that his mind might be easy about an answer to this question, if it were put to him again."

[5] Cf. Gen. 15:9 f.

[6] A view which, according to Geiger, is foreign to Judaism, "die freilich dem Judenthume fremd ist," *ibid.* See however, P.R.E., pp. 198 f., and *T.S.*, Vol. III, p. 667, note 197 שהראהו גם תחיית המתים. Cf. 2:262.

VERSE 271

> The devil promises[1] you poverty and bids you sin, but God promises you pardon from Him and grace, for God both embraces and knows.

Zamakhsharī interprets "the devil promises you" to mean that the devil tells you that being charitable will lead to poverty, but God promises grace.[2] This interpretation seems to be in harmony with the preceding and succeeding Koranic verses which actually deal with charity.[3] Jewish tradition, as shown elsewhere, abounds in statements relating to the importance of charity.[4] The rabbis stress that good deeds not only do not make one poorer[5] but, on the contrary, they bring a person prosperity[6] and protect him from adversity:[7] "He who gives a small coin to a poor man obtains six blessings, and he who addresses to him words of comfort obtains eleven blessings."[8]

[1] يعدكم.

[2] Zamakhsharī, Vol. I, p. 177:
ويقول لكم ان عاقبة انفاقكم ان تفتقروا .... ويغريكم على البخل ومنع الصدقات ... [والله يعدكم] فى الانفاق [مغفرة] لذنوبكم وكفارة لها.
Cf. Baiḍāwī, *ad loc.*

[3] Cf. 2:265: "Kind speech and pardon are better than almsgiving followed by annoyance, and God is rich and clement"; and compare: "Better is a dinner of herbs where love is, Than a stalled ox and hatred therewith" (Prov. 15:17); "Better is a dry morsel and quietness therewith, Than a house full of feasting with strife" (Prov. 17:1); "Better is a handful of quietness, Than both the hands full of labor and striving after wind" (Ecc. 4:6). See also 2:269, 272.

[4] Cf. notes to 2:1–2, 211, 246, 272–73.

[5] Maimonides, הלכות מתנות עניים 10, 2: לעולם אין אדם מעני מן הצדקה ואין דבר רע ולא היזק נגלל בשביל הצדקה שנא' והיה מעשה הצדקה שלום.

[6] כל הרודף אחר צדקה הקב"ה ממציא לו מעות ועושה בהן צדקה (תלמוד ירושלמי פאה פ"א, ה"א) and (ב"ב, ט, ע"ב).

[7] B. Ta'an. 9a: וא"ר יוחנן מאי דכתיב עשר תעשר, עשר בשביל שתתעשר.

[8] B. B. B. 9b.

VERSE 272

> Whatever expense ye expend, or vow ye vow, God knows it; but the unjust have no helpers. If ye display your almsgiving, then well is it; but if ye hide it and bring it to the poor, then is it better for you, and will expiate for you your evil deeds; for God of what ye do is well aware.

A similar idea is also found in the Talmud which states that he who gives charity in secret is greater than Moses, "for of Moses it is written, *For I was afraid because of the anger and the wrath* (Deut. 9:19), and of one who gives charity (secretly) it is written, *A gift in secret subdues anger* (Prov. 21:14).[1]

Maimonides, in his Mishneh Torah,[2] constructed out of the numerous talmudic precepts "an ethical ladder of eight successive rungs (of charity). The first and highest level was helping the poor man to sustain himself."[3]

The Koranic assurance that giving charity in secret "will expiate for you your evil deeds,"[4] recalls the talmudic statement that charity will deliver the donor "from an unnatural death" and "from the punishment of Gehinnom."[5]

[1] B. B. B. 9b: גדול העושה צדקה בסתר יותר ממשה רבינו. Cf. B. Ḥag. 5a: מאי אם טוב אם רע . . . זה הנותן צדקה לעני בפרהסיא, and 2:1–2, 211, 246, 271.

[2] הלכות מתנות עניים, פ"י.

[3] A. A. Neuman, *op. cit.*, Vol. II, p. 170.

[4] ويكفّر عنكم من سياتكم.

[5] B. B. B. 10a: שמצילתו מדינה של גיהנם.

VERSE 273

> Thou (Muḥammad) art not bound to guide them; but God guides whom He will; and whatever good ye expend it is for yourselves, and do not expend save craving for God's face.

The last phrase here recalls the Psalmist's prayer: "As for me, I shall behold Thy face in righteousness;[1] I shall be satisfied, when I awake, with Thy likeness."[2] The Midrash comments that this teaches that even transgressors who have no other merits but that of giving charity,[3] are privileged to face the *Shekinah* (the Spirit of the Omnipresent as manifested on earth).[4]

[1] בצדק.

[2] Ps. 17:15.

[3] צדקה. Cf. notes on 2:1–2, 172, 211, 246, 271, 272, 280; 3:128.

[4] ללמדך שאפילו רשעים ואין בהם אלא זכות של צדקה בלבד זוכין ומקבלין פני שכינה (שוחר טוב, יז, סה).

VERSES 276–77

> Those who devour usury shall not rise again, save as he riseth whom Satan hath paralysed with a touch; and that is because they say 'selling is only like usury,' but God has made selling lawful and usury unlawful; and he to whom the admonition from his Lord has come, if he desists, what has gone before is his: his matter is in God's hands. But whosoever returns (to usury) these are the fellows of the Fire, and they shall dwell therein for aye. God shall blot out usury, but shall make almsgiving profitable, for God loves not any sinful misbeliever.

Similarly to the biblical[1] statement, the Koran also states, "And what ye put out to usury that it may increase with the wealth of men, it shall not increase with God . . ." (31:39).[2]

According to Islām, usury is prohibited in the case of a Moslem dealing with a fellow-believer, but not when dealing with a non-Moslem. Also, the term usury applies not only to money transactions but to any barter or business transaction where profit results.[3]

The same idea is expressed in the Bible: "Thou shalt not lend upon interest to thy brother; interest of money, interest of victuals, interest of any thing that is lent upon interest. Unto a foreigner thou mayest lend upon interest; but unto thy brother thou shalt not lend upon interest; that the Lord thy God may bless thee in all that thou puttest thy hand unto, in the land whither thou goest in to possess it" (Deut. 23:20–21).[4]

The rabbis in discussing the prohibition of usury state: "He who lends money on usury denies God . . . he makes the Torah a laughing

[1] Exod. 22:24: "If thou lend money to any of My people, even to the poor with thee, thou shalt not be to him as a creditor; neither shall ye lay upon him interest."

[2] Cf. 3:125; cf. Torrey, *op. cit.*, p. 148.

[3] The Arabic word for usury is *ribā* الربى (an excess) corresponding to the Hebrew רבית.

[4] Cf. Ezek. 22:12; Ps. 15:5; Prov. 28:8.

stock and Moses a fool."[5] "Usury is like the sting of a serpent."[6] "A man should rather sell his daughter than borrow on usury."[7]

[5] אמר רבי יסא בוא וראה כמה סמיות עיני מלוי רבית... ללמדך שכל המלוה בריבית כופר בעיקר רבי שמעון בן אלעזר אומר יותר ממה שכופרין בעיקר כופרין שעושין התורה פלסטרן ואת משה טיפש ואומרין אילו היה יודע משה שכך היינו מרויחין לא היה כותבו (תלמוד ירושלמי בבא מציעא, פ"ה, ה"ח).

[6] לא תנשוך את העני כשם שנשך הנחש את האדם ועקרו לו ולתולדותיו... לא תהיה כנחש... כל מי שנוטל רבית מעלה עליו הכתוב כאלו עשה את כל הרעות והעבירות שבעולם (שמות רבה, לא, ג).

[7] ליתא ניחא לאיניש דליזבין ברתיה ולא ליזיף בריביתא... לסוף שמוכר את עצמו (ערכין ל, ע"ב).

VERSE 280

> And if it be one in difficulties, then wait for easy circumstances; but that ye remit it as alms[1] is better for you, if ye did but know.

Moses, in caring for the underprivileged, prescribes: "If thou lend money to any of My people, even to the poor with thee, thou shalt not be to him as a creditor; neither shall ye lay upon him interest" (Ex. 22:24). ". . . thou shalt not go into his (debtor's) house to fetch his pledge . . . And if he be a poor man, thou shalt not sleep with his pledge; thou shalt surely restore to him the pledge when the sun goeth down" (Deut. 24:10–13).

According to Rashi, assisting the poor is obligatory[2] and a poor man should get preference in assistance over one who is better off.[3] Nor should the poor man be treated in a slighting manner.[4] Rather should the creditor put himself in the position of the needy.[5] When the debt falls due, the creditor must not insist on the pledge and should evince special consideration and kindness.[6]

The rabbis insisted that if a creditor sees the debtor approaching, he should cross to the other side of the street in order not to cause him embarrassment.[7]

[1] Cf. 2:1–2, 211, 246, 272, 273; 3:128.

[2] Rashi on Exod. 22:24: אם כסף תלוה את עמי. רבי ישמעאל אומר כל אם ואם שבתורה רשות חוץ מג׳ וזה א׳ מהן.

[3] *Ibid.*: עני ועשיר עני קודם.

[4] *Ibid.*: שלא תנהוג בו מנהג בזיון בהלוואה שהוא עמי.

[5] *Ibid.*: לא תתבענו בחזקה אם אתה יודע שאין לו אל תהי דומה עליו כאלו הלויתו אלא כאלו לא הלויתו כלומר לא תכלימהו.

[6] *Ibid.*, verse 25: אם חבל תחבל. כל לשון חבלה אינו משכון בשעת הלואה אלא שממשכנין את הלוה כשמגיע הזמן ואינו פורע.

[7] כי אתא רב דימי אמר מנין לנושה בחברו מנה ויודע שאין לו שאסור לעבור לפניו ת״ל לא תהיה לו כנושה (בבא מציעא, עה, ע״ב).

VERSE 282

O ye who believe! if ye engage to one another in a debt for a stated time, then write it down, and let a scribe write it down between you faithfully; nor let a scribe refuse to write as God taught him, but let him write, and let him who owes dictate; but let him fear God his Lord, and not diminish therefrom aught; but if he who owes be a fool, or weak, or cannot dictate himself, then let his agent dictate faithfully, and let them call two witnesses out from amongst their men.

The Koranic requirement of two witnesses recalls the biblical injunction that "at the mouth of two witnesses, or at the mouth of three witnesses, shall a matter be established" (Deut. 19:15).[1] The trustworthiness of the witnesses, who are present at the act, must be unimpeachable and they shall be in full agreement with each other as to their testimony.

According to Moslem commentators,[2] the Koranic expression, "from amongst their men,"[3] refers to the faithful and excludes disbelievers and slaves.[4] This is in agreement with Maimonides' view about testimony of witnesses.[5]

[1] Deut. 19:15: על פי שנים עדים ... יקום דבר; cf. B. Sanh. 9b and Ibn Ezra on Deut. 17:6 and Deut. 19:15.

[2] Zamakhsharī, Vol. I, p. 182: "Non-Jews and slaves are not qualified as witnesses."

[3] من رجالكم.

[4] Ṭabarī, Vol. III, p. 75:
واما قوله من رجالكم فانه يعنى من احراركم المسلمين دون عبيدكم ودون احراركم الكفار ....

[5] Maimonides, עדות פ"ט, ה"א; cf. B. Sanh. 9b: "... he is a wicked man (and therefore disqualified from acting as witness) ..." See also Exod. 23:1.

VERSE 286

> God will not require of the soul save its capacity. It shall have what it has earned, and it shall owe what has been earned from it. Lord, catch us not up, if we forget or make mistake; Lord, load us not with a burden, as Thou hast loaded those who were before us. Lord, make us not to carry what we have not strength for, but forgive us, and pardon us, and have mercy on us. Thou art our Sovereign, then help us against the people who do not believe!

The Koranic idea that God does not "require of the soul save its capacity" is also found in the Talmud, where the rabbis urge not to impose "a restriction upon the community unless the majority of the community will be able to stand it."[1] Similarly, the Midrash states that the punishment to be meted out by God to the wicked will be commensurate with their actions.[2] As for "it shall have what it has earned . . .," the Psalmist, too, states: "Behold, he travaileth with iniquity; Yea, he conceiveth mischief, and bringeth forth falsehoods. He hath digged a pit, and hollowed it, And is fallen into the ditch which he made" (Ps. 7:15–16).

The second part of this Koranic verse recalls the Psalmist who, in a similar vein exclaims: "Who can discern errors? Clear Thou me from hidden faults."[3] If Thou, Lord, shouldest mark iniquities, O, Lord, who could stand?"[4]

[1] B. B. Ḳ. 79b.

[2] ואף כל הדורות אם אדם יחטא ידין אותו מעין חטאו . . . (אגדת בראשית, ע״ח).

[3] Ps. 19:13; cf., שוחר טוב, יט, סה: אמר לו הקב׳ה לדוד מה את בעיה אמר לו: שגיאות מי יבין. אמר ליה הא שרי והא שביק לך שגייתא דעבדינן.

[4] Ps. 130:3; cf. Sabbath Prayer Book.

SURA III

VERSE 2

> He has sent down to thee the Book[1] in truth, confirming what was before it, and has revealed the law, and the gospel before for the guidance of men, and has revealed the Discrimination.

The terms *nazzala* (sent down) and *anzala* (revealed)[2] as used here recall the biblical expressions, "and the Lord came down" (Exod. 19:20)[3] and "Go down (Moses)" (Exod. 19:21).[4] Since "go down" is connected with the giving of the Torah, it is possible that Muḥammad adopted a similar usage for his revelation.

The term Taurāt[5] for "the law" as used here, according to Geiger, refers to the Jewish revelation only, meaning the Pentateuch.[6] Later on Moslem commentators expanded the term to include also the Psalms, the prophecy of Isaiah and other prophecies, but not the Gospel.[7]

Since Muḥammad considered Moses as *the* lawgiver and listed the Psalms and other biblical prophets separately, it is natural that he should refer here to the Torah as the Pentateuch. To the Jews, too, the Torah, which in Hebrew means guidance, learning or teaching, originally referred only to the Pentateuch. As time went on the term Torah embraced not only the Pentateuch and the whole Bible[8]

[1] Cf. 2:1–2.

[2] Cf. انزل, 2:3 and elsewhere.

[3] וירד יהוה על הר סיני.

[4] רד העד בעם.

[5] توراة.

[6] Geiger, *op. cit.*, p. 44: ". . . er hierunter bloss den Pentateuch verstanden haben will indem er (Muḥammad) unter den jüdischen Propheten nach den Patriarchen bloss den Moses als Gesetzgeber gelten lässt."

[7] Geiger, *ibid.*, p. 45 n. (quoting Ahmed ben Abd Elhelim, from Maracc. Prodromi, I, p. 5):

ولفظ التوراة قد عرف انه الكتب يراد جنس الشى يقراها اهل الكتاب فيدخل في ذلك الزبور ونبوة اشعيا وساير النبوات خلا الانجيل.

Cf. Horovitz, *HUCA.*, p. 194.

[8] תורה, נביאים וכתובים (תנ"ך).

but the entire gamut of Jewish religious literature. The Moslem commentators, who went beyond the Pentateuch in defining Torah, followed the accepted view of the Jews in Arabia and referred to the Torah as the whole Hebrew Bible.

Regarding *Injīl*,[9] Ali claims that the term "does not signify, as supposed by Muir and others, the New Testament."[10] He goes on to say that "the Qur-ān nowhere suggests that the original *Injīl*, the revelation of Jesus Christ, existed at the time of the Holy Prophet."[11] The term, Ali claims, "stands for the Evangel or the *Gospel*, and signifies literally *good tidings*."[12] However, most scholars agree that the word refers to the revelation of God to Jesus which later on encompassed the whole New Testament.[13]

[9] الانجيل.

[10] Ali, *op. cit.*, p. 140 n.

[11] *Ibid.*

[12] *Ibid.*

[13] For a detailed discussion of this term see Th. P. Hughes, *Dictionary of Islam*, London, 1885, *s. v. Injīl*, p. 211; and Jeffery, *The Qur'ān as Scripture*, pp. 66–67.

VERSE 4

> Verily, God, there is nothing hidden from Him in the earth, nor in the heaven; He it is who fashions you in the womb as He pleases. There is no God but He, the mighty, the wise.

Baiḍāwī, commenting on the word "hidden," writes: "Nothing, which comes to pass in the world, be it universal or particular, faith or unbelief."[1] The idea that nothing is hidden from God is stressed frequently in rabbinic literature. The Midrash states that the wicked think that God does not see when they sin because He is separated from them by seven heavens . . . but God . . . sees everybody and everything.[2]

As to the phrase, "who fashions you in the womb as He pleases," compare: "Thus saith the Lord that made thee, and formed thee from the womb" (Is. 44:2). "Before I formed thee in the belly I knew thee" (Jer. 1:5). "For Thou hast made my reins; Thou hast knit me together in my mother's womb" (Ps. 139:13). "Did not He that made me in the womb make him?" (Job 31:15)

Similarly, the Talmud states: ". . . Come and observe how the capacity of human beings falls short of the capacity of the Holy One, blessed be He. It is in the capacity of a human being to draw a figure on a wall, but he cannot invest it with breath and spirit, bowels and intestines. But the Holy One, blessed be He, is not so; He shapes one form in the midst of another, and invests it with breath and spirit, bowels and intestines. And that is what Hannah said: *There is none holy as the Lord, for there is none beside Thee, neither is there any ẓur* (*rock*) *like our God*" (I Sam. 2:2).[3]

[1] Baiḍāwī, Vol. I, p. 70:
اى شيءٍ كائن في العالم كليّا كان او جزئيا ايمانا او كفرا.
Cf. M.C.B. p. 3.

[2] לפי שהרשעים אומרין אין הקב"ה רואה כשאנו חוטאין כי רחוק הוא ושבעה רקיעים בינינו וביניו שנאמר עבים סתר לו ולא יראה. וכן דוד אמר עליהם ויאמרו לא יראה יה ולא יבין אלהי יעקב והקב"ה אומר להם רשעים שבעולם הנוטע אוזן הלא ישמע וגו' הלא הוא מביט לכל דבר שנאמר הן כל ראתה עיני שמעה אזני ותבן לה (אגדת בראשית, ע"ט). Cf. אתה יודע רזי עולם (יומא, פ"ז ע"ב); and: לפניך נגלו כל תעלומות והמון נסתרות שמבראשית . . . הכל גלוי וידוע לפניך יי אלהינו, צופה ומביט עד סוף כל הדורות (מחזור – מוסף ראש-השנה, זכרונות).

[3] B. Ber. 10a. Cf. Ps. 22:11.

It is interesting that the Koran uses the term *ṣawwara*[4] for "fashion" or "shape," instead of *khalaqa*.[5] The former is identical with the biblical *yaẓar*,[6] which is used in connection with the creation of man.[7]

4 صوّر.

5 خلق.

6 יצר.

7 Gen. 2:7–8, 19; Ps. 33:15; Jer. 1:5: בטרם אצורך בבטן ידעתיך; B. Ber. 60b: ברוך אשר יצר את האדם בחכמה; B. Yoma 85a: מהיכן הולד נוצר מראשו.

VERSE 5

> He it is who has revealed to thee the Book, of which there are some verses that are decisive, they are the mother[1] of the Book . . .

The Koranic expression, "some verses are decisive,"[2] is comparable to the Hebrew *'Otiyot Maḥkimot*.[3] Similarly the expression, "they are the mother of the Book,"[4] recalls the talmudic *'Em Lamiḳra'*.[5] As for the word "decisive," compare the Talmud:[6] "*Miḳra* is determinant."[7]

[1] Palmer, *ad loc.*, *i. e.* "the fundamental part of it."

[2] ايات محكمات.

[3] Cf. Hirschberg, *op. cit.*, p. 215; I. Wolfensohn, *Ka'b al-Aḥbār und seine Stellung in Ḥadīṯ und in der islamischen Legendenliteratur*, Berlin, 1933, p. 45; Horovitz, *HUCA*, pp. 188 f.

[4] هن امّ الكتاب.

[5] B. Sanh. 4a: אם למקרא, אם למסורת.

[6] "'*Miḳra* has a mother,' or these in preference to *Miḳra* . . . *i. e.* the *reading* of the sacred text according to the *Ḳere* קרי, the established vocalization has an authentic origin, hence well-founded, as distinct from the *Masorah* (מסורה), the *Kethib* כתיב the traditional text of consonants without vowels." *Ibid.*, p. 10, n. 4.

[7] *Ibid.*: כולהו סבירא להו יש אם למקרא. Cf. B. Suk. 6b: יש אם למסורת . . . יש אם למקרא.

VERSE 7

> 'O Lord! pervert not our hearts again when Thou hast guided them, and grant us mercy from Thee, for Thou art He who grants. O Lord! Thou shalt gather together man unto the day wherein is no doubt. Verily, God will not depart from His promise.'

The first half of this Koranic verse recalls the Jewish daily prayer: "O our Father, merciful Father, ever compassionate, have mercy upon us; O put it into our hearts to understand and to discern, to mark, learn and teach, to heed, to do and to fulfill in love all the words of instruction in thy Torah."[1]

The idea in the second part of this Koranic verse that God will "gather together men unto the day" is also expressed in the Talmud: "In times to come, the Holy One, blessed be He, will take a scroll of the Law in His embrace and proclaim: 'Let him who has occupied himself herewith, come and take his reward.' Thereupon all the nations will crowd together in confusion, as it is said: *All the nations are gathered together, etc.* (Is. 43:9). The Holy One, blessed be He, will then say to them: 'Come not before Me in confusion, but let each nation come in with its scribes.' "[2]

[1] D.P.B., p. 115.

[2] B. 'A. Z. 2a–2b.

VERSE 8

> Verily, those who misbelieve, their wealth shall not help them, nor their children, against God at all; and they it is who are the fuel of the fire.

The Psalmist exclaims: "Wherefore should I fear in the days of evil, . . . Of them that trust in their wealth, and boast themselves in the multitude of their riches? No man can by any means redeem his brother, nor give to God a ransom for him . . . And must be let alone for ever . . . For when he dieth he shall carry nothing away; His wealth shall not descend after him" (Ps. 49:6–18)[1].

The Koranic idea that "their wealth shall not help them, nor their children, against God at all," is also found in the *Sifre*.[2] Similarly, we find in the Talmud: "A son confers privileges on his father, but a father confers no privilege on a son . . . Abraham cannot deliver Ishmael, (and) Isaac cannot deliver Esau."[3]

[1] Cf. 2:5, 156–57; 3:172.

[2] *Sifre* to Deut. 32:39: ואין מידי מציל אין אבות מצילים את הבנים . . . ואפילו נותנים לו כל ממון שבעולם אין נותנים לו כפרו שנא' אח לא פדה יפדה איש ולא יתן לאלהים כפרו.

[3] B. Sanh. 104a.

VERSE 9

> As was the wont of Pharaoh's people, and those before them, they said our signs were lies, and God caught them up in their sins, for God is severe to punish.

In similar vein the Midrash relates: "When Moses and Aaron came to Pharaoh, they said to him: 'Thus saith the Lord, the God of Israel, let my people go' (Exod. 5:1), that they may serve Me. He said: I know not the Lord. 'Who is the Lord, that I should hearken unto his voice to let Israel go? I know not the Lord, and moreover I will not let Israel go' (Exod. 2:2). Aaron cast down his rod, and it became a fiery serpent. The magicians also cast down their rods, and they became fiery serpents. The rod of Aaron ran and swallowed them up with their rods . . . (Moses) put his hand into his bosom, and brought it forth leprous like snow, and the magicians also put their hands in their bosoms, and brought them forth leprous like snow. But they were not healed till the day of their death. Every plague which the Holy One, blessed be He, brought upon them, they also produced, until He brought upon them the boils, and they were not able to stand and to do likewise . . . ."[1]

[1] P.R.E., pp. 380–81; Exod. 7:9–17; cf. 2:46–47.

VERSE 11

> 'Ye have had a sign in the two parties who met; one party fighting in the way of God, the other misbelieving; these saw twice the same number as themselves to the eyesight, for God aids with His help those whom He pleases'.

Moslem exegetes consider this verse to have been composed following the battle of Badr,[1] the first major victory won by Muḥammad against the Meccans. Three miracles happened on that occasion: a) Muḥammad, at the instruction of the angel Gabriel, took a handful of gravel and threw it toward the enemy; the Meccans immediately turned their backs and fled. b) "The unbelievers thought the believers to be twice the number of the unbelievers, though the number of the latter was 1000, or twice the number of the Muslims, who numbered somewhat over 310."[2] c) God sent down three thousand angels, led by Gabriel, who routed the enemy, killing seventy of the Quraish tribe and taking that many prisoners; themselves losing fourteen men in that battle.[3]

A story involving miracles similar to the above first two miracles is related in the Talmud: "Once the Jews desired to send to the Emperor a gift and after discussing who should go they decided that Nahum of Gamzu should go because he had experienced many miracles. They sent with him a bag full of precious stones and pearls. He went and spent the night in a certain inn and during the night the people in the inn arose and emptied the bag and filled it up with earth. When he discovered this the next morning he exclaimed, This also is for the best. When he arrived at his destination and they undid his bag they found that it was full of earth. The king thereupon desired to put them all to death saying, The Jews are mocking me. Nahum then exclaimed, This is also for the best. Whereupon Elijah appeared in the guise of one of them (Romans) and remarked, Perhaps this is

[1] Baiḍāwī, Vol. I, p. 71, يوم بدر; cf. 3:160.

[2] Baiḍāwī, Vol. I, p. 71:

يرى المشركون المؤمنين مثلى عدد المشركين وكان قريبا الف او مثلى عدد المسلمين وكانوا ثلثمائة وبضعة عشر.

Cf. M.C.B., p. 9.

[3] Wherry, *op. cit.*, vol. II, p. 7 n.

some of the earth of their father Abraham, for when he threw earth (against the enemy) it turned into swords and when (he threw) stubble it changed into arrows, for it is written, *His sword maketh them as dust, his bow as the driven stubble* (Is. 41:2). Now there was one province which (the emperor had hitherto) not been able to conquer but when they tried some of this earth (against it) they were able to conquer it. Then they took him (Nahum) to the royal treasury and filled his bag with precious stones and pearls and sent him back with great honour. When on his return journey he again spent the night in the same inn he was asked, What did you take (to the king) that they showed you such great honour? He replied, I brought thither what I had taken from here. (The innkeepers) thereupon razed the inn to the ground and took of the earth to the king and they said to him, The earth that was brought to you belonged to us. They tested it and it was not found to be (effective) and the innkeepers were thereupon put to death."[4]

Concerning the third miracle, we find in the Midrash[5] that large armies of angels came sweepingly before Esau while he, with four hundred strong, went to meet Jacob for a reckoning. This comment is built upon the verse 'and Jacob sent messengers' (Gen. 32:4), who according to the Midrash were real angels.[6]

In the battle against Sisera, Deborah sang: "They fought from heaven, The stars in their courses fought against Sisera" (Judg. 5:20). This poetic conception of the heavenly help extended to Deborah against an enemy who possessed nine hundred iron chariots, has been taken literally by some commentators.[7]

Similarly, we find in 2 Kings 19:35: "And it came to pass that night, that the angel of the Lord went forth, and smote in the camp of the Assyrians a hundred fourscore and five thousand; and when men arose early in the morning, behold, they were all dead corpses."[8]

[4] B. Ta'an. 21a.

[5] בראשית רבה, וישלח, פע"ד, ד.

[6] (*Ibid.*) רבנן אמרי מלאכים ממש; cf. Rashi on Gen. 32:4, מלאכים ממש.

[7] ילקוט שמעוני, שופטים, רמז נג: כי אתא סיסרא כתיב מן שמים נלחמו כיון דנחתי כוכבי שמיא עלייהו נחות לאוקורי נפשייהו בנחל קישון.

[8] Cf. Is. 37:36: ויצא מלאך יהוה ויכה במחנה אשור מאה ושמונים וחמשה אלף וישכימו בבקר והנה כלם פגרים מתים.

VERSE 12

> Seemly unto men is a life of lusts, of women, and children, and hoarded talents of gold and silver, and of horses well-bred, and cattle, and tilth; — that is the provision for the life of this world; but God, with Him is the best resort.

Muḥammad here stresses the inferiority of worldly possessions in relation to religious attainments. According to Baiḍāwī, Muḥammad condemns those who seek these possessions but fail to attain the bliss which is with God.[1] This view is in harmony with the view expressed in the Talmud by Rabbi Simeon ben Yoḥai who, upon seeing people engaged in worldly affairs said: " 'All what they made they made for themselves; they built market-places, to set harlots in them; baths, to rejuvenate themselves; bridges, to levy tolls for them.' "[2]

Another Talmudic source gives a similar idea: "The Holy One, blessed be He, will then say to them: 'Wherewith have you occupied yourselves?' They will reply: 'O Lord of the Universe, we have established many market-places, we have erected many baths, we have accumulated much gold and silver, and all this we did only for the sake of Israel, that they might (have leisure) for occupying themselves with the study of the Torah.' The Holy One, blessed be He, will say in reply: 'You foolish ones among peoples, all that which you have done, you have only done to satisfy your own desires. You have established market-places to place courtesans therein; baths to revel in them'. . . And '*this*' is nought else than the Torah: *And* this *is the* Law *which Moses set before the children of Israel* (Deut. 4:44). They will then depart crushed in spirit."[3]

[1] Baiḍāwī, Vol. I, p. 71:

وهو تحريض على استبدال ما عنده من اللذات الحقيقية الابدية بالشهوات المخدجة الفانية.

Cf. Zamakhsharī, Vol. III, p. 195; and 3:80.

[2] B. Shab. 33b.

[3] B. 'A. Z. 2b.

VERSE 13

> Say, 'But shall we tell you of a better thing than this?' For those who fear are gardens with their Lord, beneath which rivers flow; they shall dwell therein for aye, and pure wives and grace from God.

This Koranic idea may be compared with the statement in the Ethics of the Fathers: ". . . and better is one hour of bliss, in the world to come than the whole life of this world."[1]

[1] Mishnah Ab. 4:17 (D). ויפה שעה אחת של קרת רוח בעולם הבא מכל חיי העולם הזה (ד, כב). Cf. 2:23, 3:12, 80, 127.

VERSES 25–26

> Say, 'O God, Lord of the kingdom! Thou givest the kingdom to whomsoever Thou pleasest, . . . Thou honourest whom Thou pleasest, and abasest whom Thou pleasest; in Thy hand is good. Verily, Thou art mighty over all. Thou dost turn night to day, and dost turn day to night, and dost bring forth the living from the dead, and dost provide for whom Thou pleasest without taking count.' Those who believe shall not take misbelievers for their patrons, rather than believers, and he who does this has no part with God at all, unless, indeed, ye fear some danger from them. But God bids you beware of Himself, for unto Him your journey is.

Similarly to the Koranic idea, the Bible states: "Thine, O Lord, is the greatness, and the power, and the glory, and the victory, and the majesty; for all that is in the heaven and in the earth is Thine; Thine is the kingdom, O Lord, and Thou art exalted as head above all. Both riches and honour come of Thee, and Thou rulest over all; and in Thy hand is power and might; and in Thy hand it is to make great, and to give strength unto all" (1 Chron. 29:11–12).

Hannah in her famous prayer to God utters the following words: "He raiseth up the poor out of the dust, He lifteth up the needy from the dung-hill, To make them sit with princes, And inherit the throne of glory; For the pillars of the earth are the Lord's, And He hath set the world upon them" (I Sam. 2:8).[1]

According to the Talmud: "Even a waterman[2] is appointed from heaven."[3]

Zamakhsharī comments that some books render the Koranic expression "Lord of the kingdom" as "God is the king of kings," meaning the hearts of the kings are in his hands.[4] This view corresponds to Prov. 21:1: "The king's heart is in the hand of the Lord . . . ."

[1] Cf. *Daily Prayer Book*, משפיל גאים עדי ארץ ומגביה שפלים.

[2] "Quite a menial office."

[3] B. Ber. 58a: אפילו ריש גרגיתא מן שמיא מנו ליה.

[4] Zamakhsharī, Vol. I, p. 194:
وفي بعض الكتب انا الله ملك الملوك قلوب الملوك ونواصيهم بيدي.

VERSE 28

> The day that every soul shall find what it has done of good present before it; and what it has done of evil, it would fain that there were between itself and that a wide interval. 'God bids you beware of Himself, but God is gentle with His servants.'

A similar idea is expressed in the Mishnah: "He that performs one precept gets for himself one advocate; but he that commits one transgression gets for himself one accuser. Repentance and good works are as a shield against retribution."[1]

Likewise, the Talmud states: "Perhaps thou wilt say: Who testifies against me? The stones of a man's home and the beams of his house testify against him, for it is said: *For the stone shall cry out of the wall, and the beam out of timber shall answer it*" (Hab. 2:11).[2]

[1] Mishnah Ab. 4:11 (D).

[2] B. Ḥag. 16a.

VERSE 35

> He said, 'My Lord, how can there be to me a boy when old age has reached me, and my wife is barren?' Said he, 'Thus God does what He pleaseth.'

Baiḍāwī, commenting on the phrase "when old age has reached me," states that old age had overtaken him[1] and left its mark on him. He was ninety-nine years old, and his wife ninety-eight.[2]

The Koranic sentence resembles the biblical story about Sarah who was at first barren: "And Sarah laughed within herself, saying: 'After I am waxed old shall I have pleasure, my lord being old also?' " (Gen. 18:12.) The biblical story stresses the fact that Sarah wondered how she could give birth at a time when she and Abraham had "waxed old." The Koran, however, relates this story to Abraham, and as such it may have its antecedent in the Talmud.

Referring to the biblical story, the Talmud relates: "On the day that Abraham weaned his son Isaac, he made a great banquet, and all the peoples of the world derided him . . . He went and invited all the great men of the age, and our mother Sarah invited their wives. Each one brought her child with her, but not the wet nurse, and a miracle happened unto our mother Sarah, her breasts opened like two fountains and she suckled them all. Yet they still scoffed, saying, 'Granted that Sarah could give birth at the age of ninety, could Abraham beget (child) at the age of hundred?' Immediately the lineaments of Isaac's visage changed and became like Abraham's, whereupon they all cried out, *Abraham begat Isaac*" (Gen. 25:19)![3]

[1] *I. e.* Zacharias. Cf. *Tafsīr-i-Raufi* quoted in Wherry, *op. cit.*, Vol. II, p. 16 n.

[2] Baiḍāwī, Vol. I, p. 75:

ادركني كبر السن واثّر في وكان له تسع وتسعون سنة ولامرأته ثمان وتسعون.

[3] B. B. M. 87a.

VERSE 47

> But they (the Jews) were crafty, and God was crafty,
> for God is the best of crafty ones!

According to the Bible: "Take counsel together, and it shall be brought to nought; Speak the word, and it shall not stand; For God is with us" (Is. 8:10). "There are many devices in a man's heart; But the counsel of the Lord, that shall stand" (Prov. 19:21). "There is no wisdom nor understanding Nor counsel against the Lord" (Prov. 21:30).

Baiḍāwī explains this sentence as follows: "God is the most powerful of them in plotting, and the best able to produce the mischief whence it is not expected."[1]

A parallel thought is expressed in the Midrash. Joseph's brothers said: Let's go and kill him, and the Holy Spirit[2] said: We shall see whose word will stand, Mine or yours.[3] God knows man's thoughts and metes out punishment accordingly.[4]

[1] Baiḍāwī, Vol. I, p. 76:
اقواهم مكرا واقدرهم على ايصال الضرر من حيث لا تحتسب.

[2] רוח הקדש.

[3] (B) תנחומא וישב, י"ג: אמר ר' יצחק המקרא אומר לך דרשני, מי אמר ונראה אלא הם אמרו לכו ונהרגהו, ורוח הקודש אומרת ונראה אותם, הם אמרו לכו ונהרגהו, והוא אמר והנה תסובינה אלומותיכם . . . ונראה של מי עומד שלכם או שלי. Cf. Rashi on Gen. 37:20: נראה דבר מי יקום או שלכם או שלי.

[4] (אגדת בראשית, ע"א) אמר הקב"ה חייך יודע אני מה שחשבת בלבך.

VERSE 61

Verily, the people most worthy of Abraham are those who follow him and his prophets, and those who believe; — God is the patron of the believers.

The idea of "the people most worthy of Abraham,"[1] in a spiritual sense, is mainly Christian. However, the concept is also found in Jewish tradition. Thus, the proselyte, when he brought his first-fruits[2] to Jerusalem, was entitled, like any other, to say: ". . . which the Lord swore unto our fathers to give us,"[3] since he, too, was considered spiritually a descendant of Abraham.[4] Similarly, the Mishnah states that "Whosoever possesses these three things, he is of the disciples of Abraham, our father; . . . a good eye,[5] an humble spirit and a lowly soul."[6]

[1] اولى الناس بابراهيم.

[2] בכורים; cf. Exod. 23:19.

[3] Deut. 26:3, אשר נשבע יהוה לאבותינו.

[4] Cf. Talmud Yerushalmi Bik. 1, 3; Maimonides, *Mishneh Torah*, Bik. 4, 3.

[5] *I. e.* "an eye that looks upon people with benevolence and kind feelings, free from envy and ill-will."

[6] Mishnah Ab. 5:19: כל מי שיש־בו שלשה דברים הללו הוא מתלמידיו של אברהם אבינו . . . עין טובה ורוח נמוכה ונפש שפלה . . . . According to the Bible, the stranger (גר) was entitled to the same treatment as the native Israelite (Exod. 12:49; Deut. 1:16, ושפטתם צדק בין איש ובין אחיו ובין גרו). In Jewish tradition the *ger* is also called אברהם בן אברהם. Cf. אמר הקב"ה חביב עלי שמותן של גרים כיין נסך שהוא מתנסך על גבי מזבח . . . כך הקב"ה כתב פרשה בתורה בין ישראל לגרים שאם גוזל אדם מישראל לגר דינו כגוזל מישראל . . . הא למדנו שהגרים עיקר הם בישראל . . . (במדבר רבה, פ"ח, א).

VERSE 71

> Those who sell God's covenant and their oaths for a little price, these have no portion in the future life. God will not speak to them, and will not look upon them on the resurrection day, and will not purify them; but for them is a grievous woe.

The main Koranic idea here, as well as the expression "these have no portion[1] in the future life," parallels the talmudic statement: "And these are they that have no share in the world to come: he that says that there is no resurrection of the dead prescribed in the Law, and (he that says) the Law is not from Heaven, and an Epicurean".[2]

[1] خلاق; cf. Hebrew חלק.

[2] Mishnah Sanh. 10:1 (D): אין להם חלק לעולם הבא.

VERSE 75

> And when God took the compact[1] from the prophets '(this is) surely what we have given you of the Book and wisdom. Then shall come to you the Apostle confirming what is with you. Ye must believe in him and help him.' He said moreover, 'Are ye resolved and have ye taken my compact on that (condition)?' They say, 'We are resolved.' He said, 'Then bear witness, for I am witness with you; but he who turns back after that, these are sinners.'

Baiḍāwī comments that "God took the covenant from the Prophets and their peoples and then made the mention of the Prophets serve for the mention of the peoples as well." Other commentators, however, state that "the meaning is 'the children of the prophets', with omission of the word 'children', 'the children of the prophets' being the children of Israel."[2] Baiḍāwī adds that the Jews claimed that they had a better right to be prophets than Muḥammad, since they were the true people of the Book, and prophets came from them only.[3]

The Talmud states that on Mount Sinai God revealed himself not only to the unborn prophets but to the coming generations . . . as well.[4] Similarly, the Midrash says: "The voice of the first (commandment) went forth and the heavens and earth quaked thereat, and the waters and rivers fled (dried up), and the mountains and hills were moved, and all the trees fell prostrate, and the dead who were in Sheol revived and stood on their feet till the end of all the generations, . . . and those (also) in the future who will be created, until the end of all the generations, there they stood with them on Mount Sinai."[5]

[1] Ali translates "made a covenant." *Op. cit.*, p. 167.

[2] Baiḍāwī, Vol. I, p. 79:

وقيل معناه أنه تعالى اخذ الميثاق من النبيين وأممهم واستغنى بذكرهم عن ذكر الامم ... وقيل المرد اولاد النبيين على حذف المضاف وهم بنو اسرائيل ....

Cf. M.C.B., p. 56.

[3] *Ibid.*:

... لانهم كانوا يقولون نحن اولى بالنبوة من محمد لانا اهل الكتاب والنبيون كانوا منا ....

[4] B. Sanh. 59a. Cf. B. Hor. 8b.

[5] P.R.E., pp. 324–5; cf.: [Z] אם אין נביאים הן בני נביאים הן (פסחים סו, ע"ב; תוספתא פ"ד, ב.

VERSE 84

> Verily, those who misbelieve after believing, and then increase in misbelief, their repentance shall not be accepted; these are those who err.

This Koranic idea recalls the statement in the Mishnah: "If a man said, 'I will sin and repent, and sin again and repent,' he will be given no chance to repent."[1]

[1] Mishnah Yom. 8:9 (D); cf. 2:5, 156–57; 3:8, 85, 172.

VERSE 85

> Verily, those who misbelieve and die in misbelief, there shall not be accepted from any one of them the earth-full of gold, though he should give it as a ransom. For them is a grievous woe, and helpers have they none.

That the condemned cannot redeem themselves from God's wrath through ransom is found in the Bible and in rabbinic sources: "They shall cast their silver in the streets, and their gold shall be as an unclean thing; their silver and their gold shall not be able to deliver them in the day of the wrath of the Lord; they shall not satisfy their souls, neither fill their bowels; because it hath been the stumblingblock of their iniquity" (Ezek. 7:19). "Neither their silver nor their gold shall be able to deliver them In the day of the Lord's wrath; But the whole earth shall be devoured by the fire of His jealousy; For He will make an end, yea, a terrible end, Of all them that dwell in the earth" (Zeph. 1:18).

The same idea is also found in the Midrash[1] and in the Talmud in connection with the advice given by Rabbi Joḥanan ben Zakkai to his disciples who came to see him when he was on his death-bed. They said to him: "Lamp of Israel, pillar of the right hand,[2] mighty hammer! Wherefore weepest thou? He replied: If I were being taken today before a human king who is here today and tomorrow in the grave, whose anger if he is angry with me does not last for ever, who if he imprisons me does not imprison me for ever and who if he puts me to death does not put me to everlasting death, and whom I can persuade with words and bribe with money, even so I would weep. Now that I am being taken before the supreme King of Kings, the Holy One, blessed be He, who lives and endures for ever and ever, whose anger, if He is angry with me, is an everlasting anger, who if He imprisons me imprisons me forever, who if He puts me to death puts me to death for ever, and whom I cannot persuade with words or bribe with money — nay more, when there are two ways before me, one leading to Paradise and the other to Gehinnom, and I do not know by which I shall be taken, shall I not weep?"[3]

[1] *Sifre* on Deut. 32:39: ואפילו נותנים לו כל ממון שבעולם אין נותנים לו כפרו . . . Cf. Num. 22:18.

[2] Cf. I Kings 7:21.

[3] B. Ber. 28b; cf. 3:8, 84, 172.

VERSE 106

> Ye were the best of nations[1] brought forth unto man. Ye bid what is reasonable,[2] and forbid what is wrong, believing in God. Had the people of the Book believed, it would have been better for them. There are believers among them, though most of them are sinners.

Here Muḥammad shows why his people[3] have become the best of the nations: i. e., enjoined the just, forbade the evil, and believed in God. A similar idea is expressed in the Bible and in the Midrash: "It hath been told thee, O man, what is good, and what the Lord doth require of thee: Only to do justly, and to love mercy, and to walk humbly with thy God" (Micah 6:8); R. Eliezer said: "To do justly refers to the execution of justice: to love kindness refers to acts of benignity and to walk humbly refers to the acts of burying the dead and the dowering of brides."[4]

[1] Cf. notes to 2:137 and Ali's translation, *op. cit.*, p. 174.

[2] Ali, *ibid.*, renders it "what is right."

[3] According to the Koran, the Moslems have replaced the children of Israel, who originally were preferred by God (45:15).

[4] אמר רבי אלעזר עשות משפט זה הדין, ואהבת חסד זה גמילות חסדים, והצנע לכת זה הוצאת המת והכנסת כלה, (ילקוט שמעוני, מיכה, רמז תקנה).

VERSE 114

> O ye who believe! take not to intimacy with others than yourselves; they will not fail to spoil you; they would fain ye came to trouble, — hatred is shown by their mouths; but what their breasts conceal is greater still. We have made manifest to you our signs, did ye but understand.

This parallels the several Mosaic warnings against intimate relations with the idolaters of Canaan. The natives of the land of Canaan performed many abominable deeds, — such as sacrificing their own children and indulging excessively in sensual pleasures with near of kin. Israel was not to learn such abominations or else they would, like those natives, be expelled from the Promised Land.[1]

The biblical admonition is: "They shall not dwell in thy land — lest they make thee sin against Me, for thou wilt serve their gods — for they will be a snare unto thee" (Exod. 23:33). A similar warning in the book of Deuteronomy attempts to show the lowness of the civilization of the idolaters who offer even their sons and their daughters as sacrifices to their Gods (Deut. 12:30–31).[2] The reason for not housing the idolaters is given in Deut. 20:18, "that they teach you not to do after all their abominations, which they have done unto their gods, and so ye sin against the Lord your God."[3]

[1] Cf. 16:77.

[2] Cf. B. Sanh. 63a.

[3] B. Soṭ. 35b: הא למדת שאם היו חוזרין בתשובה היו מקבלין אותן.

VERSE 127

> And vie with one another for pardon from your Lord, and for Paradise, the breadth of which is as the heaven and the earth, prepared for those who fear.

This Koranic idea is also expressed in the Talmud: "The Holy One, blessed be He, is to present to each righteous man an inheritance of three hundred ten worlds."[1] What the size of each world or its contents would be is nowhere stated. Since God has been identified with the constant creation of worlds, there is an infinity of worlds available.

Rabbi Joshua ben Levi is reported to have had the Paradise inspected. He discovered there were seven houses and each was one hundred and twenty thousand miles long, one hundred thousand miles wide, and one million miles in height.[2]

The size of the Garden of Eden is also mentioned in many rabbinic sources: "There are two gates in Paradise, made of precious stones, which are supervised by six hundred thousand angels."[3] In Midrash *Talpiyot* two Gardens of Eden are mentioned: Upper and Lower. The Lower Eden was created 1808 years before Creation, and is sixty times as large as the earth.[4] The Talmud also states that "the world is one sixtieth of the Garden (of Eden) and Garden is one sixtieth of Eden."[5]

[1] B. Sanh. 100a. עתיד הקב"ה ליתן לכל צדיק וצדיק שלש מאות ועשרה עולמות.

[2] M. Higger, *Halakoth we-'Aggadoth*, New York, 1933, chap. Gan Eden, p. 146.

[3] ילקוט שמעוני, בראשית, פ"ב, רמז כ; ילקוט ספורים ומדרשים, בראשית, פ"ו, ט.

[4] Cf. notes to 2:23; see also 3:130, 175.

[5] B. Ta'an. 10a; cf. ועולם אחד מששים בגן וגן אחד מששים בעדן (פסחים צ"ד ע"א).

VERSE 128

For those who expend in alms, in prosperity and adversity, for those who repress their rage, and those who pardon men; God loves the kind.

There are in Hebrew literature numerous notations, tales and ethical precepts concerning charity,[1] the practice of which is considered greater than the performance of sacrifices.[2] According to the rabbis, the act of charity balances all the other commandments combined.[3]

Baiḍāwī, commenting on this verse, writes that alms should be given in times of comfort or distress or under all circumstances, since man finds himself always either in a state of joy or distress. The thought is that seldom do men expend what they can, whether much or little. As for the expression, "for those who repress their rage," Baiḍāwī interprets that they restrain themselves from getting angry although they have the urge to do so. He quotes a saying of Muḥammad: "If any man repress his wrath when able to give it vent, God will fill his heart with comfort and faith."[4]

The virtue of mastering one's anger is paramount in Jewish lore. Besides the warnings in the books of the Bible against anger, there are drastic pronouncements against it in the Talmud: "Who is he that is mighty? He who subdues his (evil) inclination as it is said: He that is slow to anger is better than the mighty: and he that ruleth his spirit than he that taketh a city."[5] By "three things may a person's character be determined . . . and by his anger."[6] "Fall not into a

[1] For a detailed explanation regarding charity in Judaism see notes to 2:1–2, 172, 211, 246, 271, 273, 280.

[2] B. Suk. 49b.

[3] B. B. B. 9a. Cf.: צדקה וגמילת חסדים שקולות כנגד כל מצותיה של תורה . . . שג"ח יותר חביבה מן הצדקה. (תלמוד ירושלמי, פאה, פ"א, ה"א)

[4] Baiḍāwī, Vol. I, p. 85:
في حالتى الرخاء والشدة او الاحوال كلها اذ الانسان لا يخلو عن مسرة او مضرة والمعنى لا يخلون في حال ما بانفاق ما قدروا عليه من قليل او كثير .... وعن النبي .... من كظم غيظا وهو يقدر على انفاذه ملأ الله قلبه أمنا وايمانا.
Cf. M.C.B., p. 92.

[5] Mishnah Ab. 4:1.

[6] B. 'Erub. 65b.

passion and thou wilt not sin."[7] "He who rends his garments in his anger, he who breaks his vessels in his anger, and he who scatters his money in his anger, regard him as an idolater, because such are the wiles of the Tempter."[8]

As for the Koranic expression, "and those who pardon men," the Talmud too, states that the rabbis taught: "Those who are insulted but do not insult, hear themselves reviled without answering, act through love and rejoice in suffering, of them the Writ saith, *But they who love Him are as the sun when he goeth forth in his might* (Judges 5:31)."[9] The Talmud further emphasizes that he who forgoes retaliation, all his transgressions will be pardoned.[10]

[7] B. Ber. 29a; cf. B. Pes. 66b: כל המתיהר אם חכם הוא חכמתו מסתלקת ממנו אם נביא הוא נבואתו מסתלקת ממנו.

[8] B. Shab. 105b.

[9] *Ibid.*, 88b.

[10] B. Rosh H. 17a.

VERSE 138

> Mohammed is but an apostle; apostles have passed away before his time; what if he die or is killed, will ye retreat upon your heels? He who retreats upon his heels does no harm to God at all; but God will recompense the thankful.

This idea is also found in the Targum which states that idolaters hurt themselves rather than God.[1]

[1] *Targum Onkelos*, Deut. 32:5: ... חבילו להון לא־לה בניא־די־פלחו לטעותא. Cf. Rashi, *ad loc.*: כתרגומו חבילו להון ולא ליה: (בניו מומם) בניו היו והשחתה שהשחיתו היא מומם.

VERSE 139

> It is not for any soul to die, save by God's permission written down for an appointed time; but he who wishes for the reward of this world we will give him of it, and he who wishes for the reward of the future we will give him of it, and we will recompense the grateful.

According to Baiḍāwī, the phrase, "appointed time," means "fixed for a time," or "death shall not come before or after the fixed time."[1] Basing their reasoning on Ps. 37:23[2] and Prov. 20:24,[3] the rabbis, too, maintained: "No man bruises his finger here on earth unless it was decreed against him in heaven."[4] In Ps. 39:5 David exclaims: "*Lord make me to know mine end, And the measure of my days, what it is; 'Let me know how frail I am.'* " To this the rabbis comment that when David learned that he would die on the Sabbath, he requested God to let him die on the first of the week or on the eve of the Sabbath. Said God: " '*For a day in thy courts is better than a thousand*' (Ps. 84:11): better is to Me the one day that thou sittest and engagest in learning than the thousand burnt-offerings which thy son Solomon is destined to sacrifice before Me on the altar."[5]

The Talmud discusses three books that "are opened (in heaven) on New Year, one for the thoroughly wicked, one for the thoroughly righteous, and one for the intermediate. The thoroughly righteous are forthwith inscribed definitively in the book of life; the thoroughly wicked are forthwith inscribed definitively in the book of death; the doom of the intermediate is suspended from New Year till the Day of Atonement; if they deserve well, they are inscribed in the book of life; if they do not deserve well, they are inscribed in the book of death."[6]

[1] Baiḍāwī, Vol. I, p. 87: اى موقّتا لا يتقدم ولا يتاخر. Cf. M.C.B., p. 99.

[2] "It is of the Lord that a man's goings are established."

[3] "A man's goings are of the Lord; How then can man look to his way?"

[4] B. Shab. 30b.

[5] Cf.: "Now, every Sabbath day he (David) would sit and study all day. On the day that his soul was to be at rest (*i. e.*, depart from this world), the Angel of death stood before him but could not prevail against him, because learning did not cease from his mouth . . . . Now, there was a garden before his house; so the Angel of death went, ascended and soughed in the trees. He (David) went out to see: as he was ascending the ladder, it broke under him. Thereupon he became silent (from his studies) and his soul had repose," *ibid.*

[6] B. Rosh H. 16b. There is a parallel between the human records up in heaven

Relying upon this Talmudic declaration, R. Amnon of Mayence, famous author of the hymn *unetaneh toḳef* which is recited on the High Holy Days, writes: "As the shepherd mustereth his flock, and passeth them under his crook, so dost Thou cause to pass, number, appoint, and visit every living soul, fixing the limitations on all creatures, and prescribing their destiny. On the First Day of the year it is inscribed, and on the Fast Day of Atonement it is sealed and determined how many people shall live and die . . . who is to perish by water, who by fire."[7]

mentioned in the Talmud and the Moslem book of records. Cf. 3:148: "Say, 'If ye were in your houses, surely those against whom slaughter was written down, would have gone forth to fight even to when they are lying now; that God may try what is in your breasts and assay what is in your hearts, for God doth know the nature of men's breasts.'"

[7] Cf. *Aggadath Bereshith*, pp. 9 ff.; *'Or Zarua'*, Hilkot R. Hash. 276.

VERSE 154

> If God help you, there is none can overcome you; but if He leave you in the lurch, who is there can help you after Him? Upon God then let believers rely.

Similar expressions are found in the Psalms and in Jeremiah: "The Lord is for me; I will not fear; What can man do unto me" (Ps. 118:6)? "Many are the sorrows of the wicked; But he that trusteth in the Lord, mercy compasseth him about" (*ibid.* 32:10). "Thus saith the Lord: Cursed is the man that trusteth in man, And maketh flesh his arm, and whose heart departeth from the Lord" (Jer. 17:5).

This idea is also found in the Talmud where praise is showered on the one who puts all his faith in God.[1]

[1] B. Men. 29a.

VERSE 159

> Or when an accident befals you, and ye have fallen on twice as much, ye say, 'How is this?' Say, 'It is from yourselves. Verily, God is mighty over all.'

A counterpart is found in the Talmud: "If a man sees that painful sufferings visit him, let him examine his conduct.'[1]

[1] B. Ber. 5a.

VERSES 172–73

> Let not those who misbelieve reckon that our letting them range is good for themselves. We only let them have their range that they may increase in sin. And for them is shameful woe. God would not leave believers in the state which ye are in, until He discerns the vile from the good.[1]

Similarly to the Koranic idea the Talmud, too, states: "And to what are the wicked compared in this world? To a tree standing wholly in a place of uncleanness, but a branch thereof overhangs a place of cleanness: when the bough is lopped off, it stands entirely in a place of uncleanness. Thus the Holy One, blessed be He, makes them prosper[2] in this world,[3] in order to destroy and consign them to the nethermost rung, for it is said, *There is a way which seemeth right unto man, But at the end thereof are the ways of death* (Prov. 14:12)."[4] In another place the Talmud states that of those "who walked in perversity, it is written, *but the perverseness of the treacherous shall destroy them* (*ibid.* 11:3)."[5]

[1] Cf. 2:149, 156–57, 160; 3:127, 163, 183.

[2] Lit., "furnishes them with goodness."

[3] "Thus rewarding them for the little good they perform — lopping off the branch inclining to the place, that it may disregard in the next world."

[4] B. Ḳid. 40b. "An attempt to answer the eternal question, why the wicked prosper and the righteous suffer."

[5] B. Shab. 88b.

VERSE 179

> 'Verily, God has covenanted with us that we should not believe in an apostle until he gives us a sacrifice which fire devours.'

Ṭabārī,[1] Zamakhsharī and Baiḍāwī[2] rightly explain this to mean that the Israelites considered it a sign of the prophet's truth when a fire came down from heaven and consumed his offering. Such instances occur in the Bible and especially in postbiblical literature.

Chapter 18 in First Kings relates the story about Elijah and the prophets of Baal. The former's sacrifice was consumed by a heavenly fire whereas that of the latter was not. The consuming of an offering by a heavenly fire as proof of divine acceptance is discussed in detail in rabbinic lore.[3]

According to Christian and Moslem traditions, which undoubtedly have their roots in early Jewish traditions,[4] Abel's offering was consumed by a fire from heaven.[5]

[1] Ṭabarī, Vol. IV, p. 123:

...اليهود.... وقالوا ان الله عهد الينا ألا نؤمن لرسول حتى ياتينا بقربان تاكله النار...

[2] Baiḍāwī, Vol. IV, p. 92:

لا نؤمن لرسول حتى ياتينا بهذه المعجزة الخاصة التي كانت لانبياء بنى اسرائيل وهو ان يقرب بقربان فيقدم النبى فيدعو فتنزل نار سماوية فتاكله.

[3] *Sifra* on Leviticus p. 45b (W): כיון שראו אש חדשה שירדה משמי מרום וליחכה על המזבח את העולה ואת החלבים פתחו פיהם ואמרו שירה. Cf. B. Shab. 87b; *Seder 'Olam Rabbah*, ch. 7. *Sifre Zutta* (ed. Horovitz, p. 286) enumerates twelve times when a fire came down from heaven: six times as a good omen and six times as a bad omen: שתים עשרה פעמים ירדה אש מן השמים ששה לשבח . . .

[4] Rashi on Gen. 4:4: "Fire descended from heaven and consumed it," ירדה אש ולחכה מנחתו. Cf. Ibn Ezra, *ad loc.*

[5] Cf. V. Aptowitzer, *Kain und Abel in der Aggada der Apokryphen, der Hellenistischen, Christlichen und Mohammedanischen Literatur*, Leipzig, 1922, pp. 39, 144–46.

VERSE 191

> Lord! forgive us our sins and cover our offenses, and let us die with the righteous.[1]

A similar utterance is found in the Talmud: "Now, that wicked man (Balaam) too gave a sign for himself [that he would not enter the future world by saying, *Let me die the death of the righteous* (Num. 23:10) — meaning, If I die the death of the righteous (i. e. a natural death)], my last end will be like his (i. e. 'I will enter the world to come'); but if not (i. e., If I die a violent death), then, *behold I go unto my people* (*ibid.* 24:14) (i. e. into the Gehenna)."[2]

In 6:95 Muḥammad states: "Verily, God it is who cleaves out the grain and the datestone; He brings forth the living from the dead, and it is He who brings the dead from the living. There is God! how then can ye be beguiled?" Geiger quotes a saying attributed to Muḥammad that the dead man shall be raised in the garments in which he was buried.[3] This idea is also expressed in the Talmud: "Queen Cleopatra[4] asked R. Meir, 'I know that the dead will revive . . .[5] But when they arise, shall they arise nude or in their garments?' — He replied, 'Thou mayest deduce by an *a fortiori* argument (the answer) from a wheat grain. If a grain of wheat, which is buried naked, sprouteth forth in many robes, how much more so the righteous, who are buried in their raiment!' "[6]

[1] Cf. 2:149.

[2] B. Sanh. 105a.

[3] Geiger, *op. cit.*, p. 78: ان الميت يبعث في ثيابه التى يموت فيها.

[4] Not of 'Anthony and Cleopatra' fame. Cf. W. Bacher, *Die Agada der Tannaiten*, Strassburg, 1890, II, p. 68.

[5] Cf. Ps. 72:16: "And they (the righteous) shall (in the distant future) blossom forth out of the city (Jerusalem) like the grass of the earth."

[6] B. Sanh. 90b.

LIST OF ABBREVIATIONS

אדר"נ — אבות דרבי נתן, Ḥoreb edition.
AASOR — *Annual of the American School of Oriental Research.*
Ab. — Aboth.
A. H. — After Hi'jrah (June 20, 622 C. E.).
AJSLL — *The American Journal of Semitic Languages and Literatures.*
Ant. — Antiquities.
'Ar. — 'Arakin.
'A. Z. — 'Abodah Zarah.

B. — Babylonian Talmud.
(B) — Buber edition.
BASOR — *Bulletin of the American Society for Oriental Research.*
B. B. — Baba Bathra.
B. C. E. — Before the Common Era.
Ber. — Berakoth.
Bik. — Bikkurim.
B. Ḳ. — Baba Ḳama.
B. M. — Baba Meẓi'a.
Bu. — al-Bukhārī.

C. E. — Common Era.
I Chron. — Chronicles I.
II Chron. — Chronicles II.

(D) — Danby's translation of the Mishnah.
Dan. — Daniel.
Deut. — Deuteronomy.
D.P.B. — *The Authorized Daily Prayer Book,* by J. H. Hertz.

Ecc. — Ecclesiastes.
E I or *E.I.* — *Encyclopedia of Islam.*
E J — *Encyclopaedia Judaica.*
ERE — *Encyclopedia of Religion and Ethics.*
'Erub. — 'Erubin.
Ex. or Exod. — Exodus.
Ezek. — Ezekiel.

(F) — Friedman edition.

Gen. — Genesis.
Giṭ. — Giṭṭin.

Hag. — Haggai.
Ḥag. — Ḥagigah.
Ḥor. — Ḥorayoth.
Hos. — Hosea.
HTR — *Harvard Theological Review.*
HUCA — *Hebrew Union College Annual*; whenever the *Annual* appears with J. Horovitz's name, it is referred to Vol. II, 1925.
Ḥul. — Ḥullin.

I. C. — *Islamic Culture.*
Isa. — Isaiah.

JAOS — *Journal of the American Oriental Society.*
JBL — *Journal of Biblical Literature.*
J. E. — *Jewish Encyclopedia.*
Jer. — Jeremiah.
Josh. — Joshua.
JQR — *Jewish Quarterly Review.*
JRAS — *Journal of the Royal Asiatic Society.*
JSOR — *Journal of the Society of Oriental Research.*
Judg. — Judges.
JZWL — *Jüdische Zeitschrift für Wissenschaft und Leben.*

Ket. — Ketuboth.
Ḳid. — Ḳiddushin.
Ḳ. S. — *Ḳiryath Sefer.*

Lev. — Leviticus.
lit. — literally.

(M) — Munk edition.
Maimonides — Moses ben Maimon (1135–1204).
Mak. — Makkoth.
M.C.B. — *Chrestomathia Baidawiana*, tr. by D. S. Margoliouth.
Meg. — Megillah.
Men. — Menaḥoth.
MGWJ — *Monatschrift für Geschichte und Wissenschaft des Judentums.*
M.S.N. — Midrash Sifre on Numbers (English translation).

Ned. — Nedarim.
Neh. — Nehemiah.
Nid. — Niddah.
N.S. — New Series.
Nu. or Num. — Numbers.

OLZ — *Orientalische Literatur Zeitung.*
O. S. — old series.

PAAJR — *Proceedings of American Academy for Jewish Research.*
Par. — Parah.
Pes. — Pesaḥim.
P.H. — *The Pentateuch and Haftorahs*, by J. H. Hertz.
P.R.C. — *Pentateuch and Rashi's Commentary.*

P.R.E. — *Pirkê De Rabbi Eliezer* (English translation).
Prov. — Proverbs.
Ps. — Psalms.
פדר"א — פרקי דר' אליעזר.

R — Rab, Rabban, Rabbi.
Rab. — Rabba.
Ramban — Moses ben Naḥman Gerondi (1194–c. 1270).
Rashba — Rabbi Solomon ben Abraham Ibn Adret (1235–1310).
Rashbam — Rabbi Samuel ben Meier, c. 1085–1174.
Rashi — Rabbi Solomon ben Isaac (1040–1105).
R.E.J. — *Revue des Études Juives.*
R. H. or Rosh. H. — Rosh Hashanah.
RHR — *Revue de l'histoire des Religions.*
RSR — *Recherches des sciences religieuses.*

I Sam. — Samuel I.
II Sam. — Samuel II.
Sanh. — Sanhedrin.
S. Ch. — Soncino Chumash.
(Sch.) — Schechter edition.
Sforno, Obadiah ben Jacob, commentator (c. 1475–1550).
Shab. — Shabbath.
Sheb. — Shebi'ith.
Shebu. — Shebu'oth.
SHEI — *Shorter Encyclopedia of Islam.*
Sheḳ. — Sheḳalim.
Soṭ. — Soṭah.
ST — *Summa Theologica.*
Suk. — Sukkah.

Ta'an. — Ta'anith.
Tam. — Tamid.
Toh. — Tohoroth.
tr. — translation.
T. S. — *Torah Shlemah.*

(W) — Weiss Edition.

Yeb. — Yebamoth.
Yom. — Yoma.

(Z) — Zuckermandel edition.
ZAW — *Zeitschrift für alttestamentliche Wissenschaft.*
ZDMG — *Zeitschrift der Deutschen Morgenländischen Gesellschaft.*
Zeb. — Zebaḥim.
Zech. — Zechariah.
Zeph. — Zephaniah.
ZNW — *Zeitschrift für die neutestamentliche Wissenschaft und die Kunde der älteren Kirche.*
ZSVG — *Zeitschrift für Semitistik und verwandete Gebiete.*

TRANSLITERATION OF ARABIC LETTERS

a — ء	d — د	ḍ — ض	k — ك
b — ب	dh — ذ	ṭ — ط	l — ل
t — ت	r — ر	ẓ — ظ	m — م
th — ث	z — ز	' — ع	n — ن
j — ج	s — س	gh — غ	h — ه
ḥ — ح	sh — ش	f — ف	w — و
kh — خ	ṣ — ص	q — ق	y — ي

TRANSLITERATION OF HEBREW LETTERS

א — '	ח — ḥ	ע — '
בּ, ב — b	ט — ṭ	פּ, פ — p, f or ph
ג — g	י — i or y	צ — ẓ
ד — d	כ — k	ק — ḳ
ה — h	ל — l	ר — r
ו — w	מ — m	ש — sh, s
ז — z	ס — s	תּ, ת — t or th

Note: Transliterations employed by different authors cited in the text were left intact. This table refers to words transliterated by the author. The vowels were not indicated in the Hebrew transliteration.

BIBLIOGRAPHY

The Hebrew Bible, the Babylonian and Palestinian Talmudim as well as the midrashic material are cited in the usual manner from the standard editions. For practical reasons it was necessary to quote from the English translation of the Babylonian Talmud published by the Soncino Press (ed. by Dr. I. Epstein, 34 vols., London, 1935–48).

The Hebraic references from the Pentateuch, Targum Onḳelos, Targum Jonathan, Rashi, Ibn Ezra and Sforno are cited from *Miḳra'ot Gedolot*, Schocken Edition, Berlin, 1937. The English quotations for the whole Bible are from *The Holy Scriptures*, published by the Jewish Publication Society of America (Philadelphia, 1937), and in the case of the Pentateuch, Hertz's *The Pentateuch and Haftorahs* (London, 1938) and *The Soncino Chumash* (London, 1947) were also consulted. The Hebraic references from the Prophets and Scriptures are quoted from *Kitbe Nebiim u-Ketubim* (Cailingold's edition, London, 1935).

Palmer's translation of the Koran was adopted for this study. The passages from Zamakhsharī, Baiḍāwī, Bukharī and Ṭabarī were translated by the author and as a rule the Arabic text is cited in the notes.

The following list comprises books consulted as well as sources cited in the footnotes:

A

Aboth de Rabbi Nathan, ed. S. Schechter, London, 1877, also Ḥoreb edition.

Aggadath Bereshith, Lemberg, 1866 (includes Maseketh 'Aẓiluth and Midrash Temurah).

Aggadath Esther, ed. S. Buber, Krakau, 1897.

Aggadath Shir Hashirim, ed. Schechter, Cambridge, 1896.

Ahrens, K., "Christliches im Koran," *ZDMG*, LX (1930), pp. 15–16, 148–90.

———, *Muhammad als Religionsstifter*, Leipzig, 1935.

Albright, W. F., "Islam and the Religions of Ancient Orient," *JAOS*, LX (1940), pp. 283–301.

———, "The Names Shaddai and Abram," *JBL*, LIV (1935), pp. 173–204.

Al-Fāsī, David Ben Abraham, *Kitāb Jāmi' Al-Alfāẓ*, ed. Solomon L. Skoss, 2 vols., New Haven, 1936–45.

ALI, A. YUSUF, *The Holy Qur-an*, 2 vols., New York, 1934.

ALI, M. M., *The Holy Qur-ān*, Lahore, 1935.

———, *The Religion of Islām*, Lahore, 1926.

———, *A Manual of Ḥadith*, Lahore.

ALI, SYED AMEER, *The Spirit of Islam*, London, 1952.

ALLAM, MAHDI, "The Theory of Forgiveness as expressed in the Qur'ān," in *Manchester Literary and Philosophical Society*, Warrington, 1939, Vol. LXXXIII, pp. 63–79.

ALON, G., *Toldot Hayehudim Beeretz-Yisrael Biteḳufat Hamishnah Wehatalmud*, Tel-Aviv, 1952.

Alphabetum Siracidis, ed. Steinschneider, Berlin, 1858.

ANDRAE, TOR, *Der Ursprung des Islams und das Christentum*, Uppsala, 1926.

———, *Die Person Muhammeds in Lehre und Glauben seiner Gemeinde*, Stockholm, 1918.

———, *Mohammed: the Man and His Faith*, London, 1936.

———, *Mohammed, Sein Leben und Sein Glaube*, Göttingen, 1932.

APTOWITZER, V., "Die Paradiesesflüsse des Kurans," *MGWJ*, 1928, pp. 151–55.

———, "Zur Kosmologie der Agada," *MGWJ* (Reprint), 1929, pp. 363–70.

———, *Kain und Abel in der Aggada der Apokryphen, der Hellenistischen, Christlichen und Mohammedanischen Literatur*, Leipzig, 1922.

ARNOLD, T. W., *The Preaching of Islam*, London, 1913.

Aruch Completum. See Nathan ben Jeḥiel.

ASSAF, S., "Polemics of an Early Karaite against Rabbinism" (Hebrew), *Tarbiz*, IV (1932–33), pp. 35 ff.

————, ed. *Teshuboth Hage'onim*, Jerusalem, 1929.

B

Babylonian Talmud, Soncino edition, 34 vols., London, 1935–48. Also Ḥoreb edition (Hebrew), and Vilno edition (Hebrew), 1903.

BACHER, WILHELM, *Die Agada der Tannaiten*, 2 vols., Strassburg, 1884–90.

BAER, F., "The Political Situation of the Spanish Jews in the Age of Yehuda Halevi" (Hebrew), *Zion*, I (1935–36), pp. 6–23.

BAIḌĀWĪ, *Tafsīr* (ed. Ministry of Interior), 2 vols., Cairo, 1355 A. H.

———, *Anwāru-l-Tanzīl*, Lipsiae (ed. Vogel), 1848.

BALADHURI, AHMAD IBN YAHYA IBN JABIR, *The Origin of the Islamic State, Being a Translation from the Arabic Accompanied with Annotations, Geographic and Historic Notes.* Vol. I trans. by

Philip K. Hitti, Vol. II by F. C. Murgotten, New York, 1916–24.
BAMBERGER, B. J., *Fallen Angels*, Philadelphia, 1952.
BANETH, D. Z., "On 'Mohammed's Ten Jewish Companions'" (Hebrew), *Tarbiz*, III, 1931–32, pp. 112–16.
BARON, SALO W., *A Social and Religious History of the Jews*, 3 vols., New York, 1937.
BARTH, J., *Midraschische Elemente*, Berlin, 1903.
———, *Studien zur Kritik und Exegese des Qorans*, Strassburg, 1915.
———, *Wurzeluntersuchungen*, Leipzig, 1902.
BARTON, G. H., *Semitic and Hamitic Origins*, Philadelphia, 1934.
BASHYAẒI, E., *'Adereth 'Eliyahu*, Odessa, 1870.
BAUMSTARK, ANTON, "Jüdischer und Christlicher Gebetstypus im Koran" in *Der Islam*, Berlin, 1927, Vol. XVI, pp. 229–48.
BECKER, C. H., *Christentum und Islam*, Leipzig, 1907.
———, *Islamstudien*, 2 vols., Leipzig, 1924–32.
BELL, RICHARD, *The Origin of Islam in its Christian Environment*, London, 1926.
BENNSION, ARIEL, *The Zohar in Moslem and Christian Spain*, London, 1932.
BEN-ZEEB, I., *Hayehudim Ba'arab*, Tel-Aviv, 1931.
——— (I. WOLFENSOHN), *Ka'b al Aḥbār und seine Stellung im Ḥadīṯ und in der islamischen Legendenliteratur*, Frankfurt a/M (thesis), Gelnhausen, 1933.
BEN YEHUDA, ELIEZER, *A Complete Dictionary of Ancient and Modern Hebrew*, N. H. Tur-Sinai, ed., Jerusalem, 1952, Vol. 14, pp. 7132–35.
Bereshith Rabba, ed. J. Theodor and Ch. Albeck, Berlin, 1912–29.
Beth ha-Midrash, ed. A. Jellinek, 6 Books, 2nd ed., Jerusalem, 1938.
BIALOBLOCKI, S., *Materialien zum Islamischen und Jüdischen Eherecht*, Giessen, 1928.
BIEBLER, P. A., *Die Dschinn, Teufel und Engel im Koran*, Leipzig, 1928.
BOER, T. J. DE, *The History of Philosophy in Islam*, London, 1933.
BRAVMANN, M. M., "On the Spiritual Background of Early Islam and the History of its Principal Concepts," in *Muséon*, LXIV, 3–4, Louvain, reprint, 1951.
BROCKELMANN, CARL, *History of the Islamic Peoples*, London, 1950.
———, *Geschichte der arabischen Literatur*, Weimar, 1898–1902.
———, *Geschichte der islamischen Völker und Staaten*, Berlin, 1939.
BUHL, F., *Das Leben Muhammeds*, translated from the Danish by H. H. Schaeder, Leipzig, 1930.
BUKHĀRĪ, ABU ABDALLAH MUHAMMED IBN ISMAÎL AL-, *Les Traditions islamiques, traduites de l'arabe, avec notes et index*, par O. Houdas and W. Marçais. 4 vols., Paris, 1903–14.

BUKHĀRĪ, *Recueil des Traditions Mahométanes* (Krehl ed.), Leyde, 1862–1908.

BURCKHARDT, JOHN LEWIS, *Travels in Arabia*, London, 1829.

BURTON, R. F., *Personal Narrative of a Pilgrimage to el-Medinah and Meccah*, London, 1857.

C

CALVERLEY, E. E., *Worship in Islam*, Madras, 1925.

CARO, JOSEPH, *Beth Joseph*, Vilna, 1900.

———, *Shulḥan 'Aruk*, 4 parts, Vilno, 1875.

CASSUTO, U., *Me'Adam 'ad Noaḥ*, Jerusalem, 1953.

CHAPIRA, B., "Légendes Bibliques Attribuées à Ka'b el-Ahbar," in *Revue des Études Juives*, Vol. LXIX (1919), pp. 86 ff.

CHARLES, R. H., ed., *The Apocrypha and Pseudepigrapha of the Old Testament*, 2 vols., Oxford, 1913.

COHEN, BOAZ, "Peculium in Jewish and Roman Law," in *PAAJR*, XX (1951), pp. 135–234.

———, "Une Légende juive de Mohammet," *REJ*, LXXXVIII, 1929, pp. 1–17.

D

DANZIG, ABRAHAM, *Ḥaye 'Adam*, Vilno, 1829.

DAUBE, DAVID, *Studies in Biblical Law*, Cambridge, 1947.

DAVIDSON, ISRAEL, *Saadia's Polemic Against Ḥiwi Al-Balkhi*, New York, 1915.

———, *Sefer Milḥamot 'Adonai*, New York, 1934.

DELLA VIDA, G. LEVI, "A proposito di as-Samaw'al," in *Rivista degli Studi Orientali*, XIII, pp. 53–72.

DELITZSCH, FRANZ, *Jüdisch-arabische Poesien aus vormuhammedanischer Zeit*, Leipzig, 1874.

———, *Wo lag das Paradies*, Leipzig, 1881.

DOUGHTY, CH. M., *Travels in Arabia Deserta*, 2 vols., London, 1936.

DOZY, R., *Die Israeliten zu Mekka*, Leipzig, 1864.

DURAN, SIMON, *Qeshet u-Magen*, ed. Steinschneider, Berlin, 1881.

DVORAK, R., "Über die Fremdwörter im Koran," in *Sitzungsberichte der Wiener Akademie*, Philos.-hist. Klasse, Bd. 109 (Wien, 1885), p. 499.

E

EICKMANN, WALTHER, *Die Angelologie und Dämonologie des Korans im Vergleich zu der Engel- und Geisterlehre der heiligen Schrift*. New York and Leipzig, 1908.

ELBOGEN, I., *Der jüdische Gottesdienst in seiner geschichtlichen Entwicklung*, Leipzig, 1913.

ELDER, E. E., *A Commentary on the Creed of Islam*, New York, 1950.

Encyclopedia of Islam, 5 vols., London and Leiden, 1913–38.

ENELOW, H. E. *The Mishnah of Rabbi Eliezer*, New York, 1933.

Encyclopedia of Religions and Ethics (ed. J. Hastings), New York, 1908–27.

EPSTEIN, L. M., *Marriage Laws in the Bible and the Talmud*, Cambridge, 1942.

F

FALLS, THOMAS B., editor, *Writings of Saint Justin Martyr*, Christian Heritage, Inc., New York, 1948.

FARIS, N. A., ed., *The Arab Heritage*, Princeton, 1944; "Ḥanīf," *JAOS*, XIX (1939), pp. 1 f.

FINKEL, J., "A Risāla of al-Jāḥiẓ," *JAOS* (1927), pp. 326–28.

———, "Old Israelitish Tradition in the Koran," *PAAJR*, Vol. II (1931), pp. 7–21.

———, "Jewish, Christian and Samaritan Influences on Arabia," in *D. B. Macdonald Presentation Volume*, Princeton, 1933, pp. 147–66.

FINKELSTEIN, L., "The Development of the Amidah," *JQR*, XVI (1925), pp. 1–43.

———, "The Origin of the Synagogue," *PAAJR*, I (1928–30), pp. 49–50.

FISCHEL, W., "Arabische Quellen zur Geschichte der babylonischen Judenheit im 13 Jahrhundert," *MGWJ*, LXXIX (1935), pp. 302–22.

FLÜGEL, G., *Corani textus arabicus*, Leipzig, 1834.

FRÄNKEL, S., *Die Aramäischen Fremdwörter im Arabischen*, Leiden, 1886.

FRIEDLAENDER, I., "Jewish-Arabic Studies," *JQR*, I (1910–11), pp. 183–215, II (1911–12), pp. 481–516; III (1912–13), pp. 235–300.

FRIEDLÄNDER, M., *Geschichte der jüdischen Apologetik*, Zurich, 1903.

FRITSCH, E., *Islam und Christenthum im Mittelalter*, Breslau, 1930.

FUCHS, SOLOMON, *Studien über Abu Zakaria Jachja Ibn Bal'ām*, Berlin, 1893.

G

GASTER, M., *The Chronicles of Yeraḥmeel*, London, 1899.

GASTFREUND, I., *Mohammed nach Talmud und Midrasch*, Berlin, 1875.

GEIGER, ABRAHAM, *Was hat Mohammed aus dem Judenthume aufgenommen?* Bonn, 1833; translated into English by F. M. Young under the name *Judaism and Islam*, Madras, 1898.

GEROCK, C. F., *Versuch einer Darstellung der Christologie des Koran*, Hamburg, 1839.

GHAZĀLĪ, AL-, MUHAMMAD IBN MUHAMMAD, *Iḥyā 'Ulūm al-Dīn*, Cairo, 1326 A. H.

GIBB, H. A. R., *Modern Trends in Islam*, Chicago, 1947.

———, *Arabic Literature: An Introduction*, London, 1926.

———, "Law and Religion in Islam," in *Judaism and Christianity*, ed. E. I. J. Rosenthal, London, 1938, pp. 145–67.

GINZBERG, LOUIS, *A Commentary on the Palestinian Talmud*, 3 vols., New York, 1941.

———, *Legends of the Jews*, 7 vols., Philadelphia, 1909–38.

———, *Die Haggada bei den Kirchenvätern und in der Apokryphischen Literatur*, Berlin, 1900.

GLENN, M. G., *Israel Salanter*, New York, 1953.

GOITEIN, S. D., "Koran," *EJ*, X, pp. 308–23.

———, "A Deed of Privileges, Attributed to Mohammed" (Hebrew), *ḲS*, IX (1932), 507–21.

———, "Jewish Subject Matter in 'Ansab al-Asraf' of Al-Baladhori," (Hebrew), *Zion*, I (1935–36), pp. 75–81.

———, "Who were Muhammed's Chief Teachers?" *Weil Jubilee Volume* (Hebrew), Jerusalem, 1953.

———, "Zur Entstehung des Ramaḍān," in *Der Islam*, Vol. XVIII (1929), pp. 189 f.

GOLDZIHER, I., *Muhammedanische Studien*, Vols. 1–2, Halle, 1899.

———, *Vorlesungen über den Islam*, Heidelberg, 1910, Hebrew Edition, ed. Plasner, M., Jerusalem, 1951.

———, *Die Richtungen der islamischen Koranauslegung*, Leyden, 1926.

———, *Mohammed and Islam*, New Haven, 1917.

———, "Islam," *J. E.*, p. 653; "Islamisme et Parsisme," *RHR*, xliii (1901), p. 15.

———, "Die Sabbatinstitution im Islam," *Gedenkbuch zur Erinnerung an D. Kaufmann*, Breslau, 1900, pp. 86–105.

———, "Über Mohammedanische Polemik gegen Ahl al-Kitāb," *ZDMG*, Vol. XXXII, p. 372.

GORDIS, ROBERT, "The Significance of the Paradise Myth," *AJSLL*, LII (1936), pp. 86–94.

GRAETZ, H., *Geschichte der Juden von den ältesten Zeiten bis auf die Gegenwart*, 11 vols., Leipzig, 1897–1911.

GREENBERG, MOSHE, "Segullā," *JAOS*, 1952, Vol. 71 (3), pp. 172–74.

GRIMME, HUBERT, *Mohammed*, 2 vols., Münster, 1892.

———, *Die weltgeschichtliche Bedeutung Arabiens: Mohammed*, Munich, 1904.

GRÜNBAUM, M., *Neue Beiträge zur semitischen Sagenkunde*, Leiden, 1893.

GRUNEBAUM, G. VON, *Medieval Islam*, Chicago, 1946.

GUILLAUME, ALFRED, "The Influence of Judaism on Islam," *Legacy of Israel*, edited by Bevan and Singer, Oxford, 1928, pp. 132 f.

———, *The Traditions of Islam*, Oxford, 1924.

H

HAAS, S. S., "The 'Creation of Man' in the Qur'ān," in *The Moslem World*, XXXI (3), July 1941, pp. 268–73.

HALLEVI, JUDAH, *Kitab Al-Khazari*, tr. by Hartwig Hirschfeld, London, 1931.

HALPER, B., "Jewish Literature in Arabic" (Hebrew), *Hateḳufah*, XXIII (1925), pp. 262–75; XXIV (1928), pp. 359–88.

HARÎRÎ, AL-, *Durrat-Al-Gawwâṣ*, ed. Heinrich Thorbecke, Leipzig, 1871.

HARTMANN, MARTIN, *Der Islam: Geschichte — Glaube — Recht*, Leipzig, 1909.

HELLER, B., "Muhammedanisches und Antimuhammedanisches in den Pirke Rabbi Eliezer," *MGWJ*, LXIX (1925), pp. 47–54.

———, "La Légende biblique dans l'Islam. Récents travaux et nouvelles méthodes de recherches." *REJ*, XCVIII (1934), pp. 1–18.

———, "La Chute des Anges: Schmahazai, Ouzza, et Azaël, *R.E.J.*, Vol. 60 (1910), pp. 201–3.

———, "Saul . . .," *Haẓofeh*, 1926, pp. 138–39.

HERTZ, J. H., *The Pentateuch and Haftorahs*, London, 1938.

———, *The Authorized Daily Prayer Book*, New York, 1948.

HERZOG, ISAAC, *The Main Institutions of Jewish Law*, 2 vols., London, 1936–39.

HIGGER, MICHAEL, *Halakot We'agadot*, New York, 1933.

HIRSCHBERG, J. W., *Yiśrael Ba'arab*, Tel Aviv, 1946.

HIRSCHFELD, HARTWIG, *New Researches into the Composition and Exegesis of the Qoran*, London, 1902.

———, *Jüdische Elemente im Koran*, Berlin, 1878.

HIRSCHFELD, *Beiträge zur Erklärung des Ḳorân*, Leipzig, 1886.
HITTI, PHILIP K., *History of the Arabs* (3rd ed.), London, 1946.
HORODETZKY, S. A., "Michael und Gabriel," *MGWJ* (1928), pp. 449–50.
HOROVITZ, JOSEPH, "Jewish Proper Names and Derivatives in the Koran," *HUCA*, Vol. II, 1925, pp. 145–227.
———, "Judaeo-Arabic Relations in Pre-Islamic Times," in *Islamic Culture*, Hyderabad, Vol. III, 1929, pp. 161–99.
———, *Koranische Untersuchungen*, Berlin-Leipzig, 1926.
———, "Das Koranische Paradies," in *Scripta Universitatis*, Vol. I, article 6, Jerusalem, 1934.
———, "Muhammads Himmelfahrt," in *Der Islam*, Vol. IX (1910), pp. 159 f.
———, "Nabi," *ZDMG*, Vol. LVI, pp. 519 ff.
HORTON, M., *Die Philosophie des Islam*, Munich, 1924.
HUART, CLÉMENT, *A History of Arabic Literature*, London, 1903.
HUGHES, THOMAS PATRICK, *Dictionary of Islam*, London, 1885.

I

IBN HISHĀM, *Life of Muḥammad* (Arabic), Būlāq, 2 vols., 1887.
ISAAC BEN MOSES, *'Or Zarua'*, Zhitomir, 1862.

J

Jacob, G., *Altarabisches Beduinenleben*, 2nd ed., Berlin, 1897.
JANĀḤ, JONAH IBN, *Sefer Hariqma*, ed. M. Wilensky, Berlin, 1924.
JASTROW, M. A., *A Dictionary of the Targumim, the Talmud Babli and Yerushalmi, and the Midrashic Literature*, 2 vols., London-New York, 1903.
JEFFERY, ARTHUR, *The Qur'ān As Scripture*, New York, 1952.
———, *The Foreign Vocabulary of the Qur'ān*, Baroda, 1938.
———, *Materials for the history of the text of the Qur'ān*, Leiden, 1937.
JENSEN, P., "Das Leben Muhammeds und die David-Sage," *Der Islam*, XII (1922), Berlin-Leipzig, pp. 84–97.
Jewish Encyclopedia, 12 vols., New York and London, 1916.
JOSEPHUS, FLAVIUS, *Works*. Greek text with English translation, by H. St. J. Thackeray and R. Marcus, London and Cambridge, 1926–37.
JUNG, LEO, *Fallen Angels*, Philadelphia, 1926.
JURJI, EDWARD J., *Illumination in Islamic Mysticism*, Princeton, 1938.

JUYNBOLL, TH. W., *Handbuch des islāmischen Gesetzes nach der Lehre der schāfi'itischen Schule, nebst einer allgemeinen Einleitung*, Leipzig-Leiden, 1910.

K

KATSH, ABRAHAM I., "Li-She'elat Hashpa'at ha-Talmud 'al ha-Ḳoran," *Hateḳufah*, New York, Vols. XXXIV–XXXV, 1950, pp. 834–38.

Kerem Ḥemed, Vol. V, Praga, 1841, p. 180.

KHAṬĪB, (MUḤAMMAD IBN 'ABD ALLĀH), *Mishkāt al-Maṣābīḥ*, St. Petersburg, 2 vols., 1899.

Kitbe Nebiim u-Ketubim, Cailingold, ed., London, 1935.

KLEIN, W. C. (tr.), *Al-Ibānah 'an uṣūl ad-Diyānah* (The Elucidation of Islām's Foundation), New Haven, 1940.

KOHUT, ALEXANDER, *Über die jüdische Angelologie und Dämonologie: ihrer Abhängigkeit von Parsismus*, Leipzig, 1866.

KRAUSS, S., "Talmudische Nachrichten über Arabien," *ZDMG*, LXX (1916), pp. 325–53.

KUENSTLINGER, DAVID, "Eschatologisches in Sura III," *OLZ*, XLI, no. 7, 1938.

———, " 'Kitāb' und 'ahlu l-kitāb' im Ḳurān," in *Rocznik Orientalistyczny*, Lwów, 1928, Vol. IV, pp. 238–47.

———, "Ṭūr and Gabal im Ḳurān," *ibid.*, pp. 58–67.

L

LAMMENS, H., *L'Arabie occidentale avant l'hégire*, Beyrouth, 1928.

———, "Mahomet fut-il sincère," *RSR*, 1911, pp. 22 f.

———, *Le Berceau de l'Islam*, Rome, 1914.

———, *Islam, Beliefs and Institutions*, London, 1929.

LANDAU, E., *Synonyma für Gott in der neu-hebräischen Litteratur*, Zürich, 1888.

LANDAUER, S., ed. See Sa'adia.

LANE, E. W., *An Arabic-English Lexicon*, 2 Books, London, 1863–93.

LANE-POOLE, S., *Studies in a Mosque*, 2nd ed., London, 1893.

LAUTERBACH, JACOB Z., "Substitutes for the Tetragrammaton," in *PAAJR*, 1930–31, pp. 39–67.

Legacy of Islam (The), ed. Arnold Thomas and Guillaume Alfred, Oxford, 1931.

Legacy of Israel (The), ed. Bevan, A. and Singer, Ch., Oxford, 1928.

LESZYNSKY, RUDOLPH, *Mohammedanische Tradition über das Jüngste Gericht*, Berlin, 1909.

LESZYNSKY, RUDOLPH, *Die Juden in Arabien zur Zeit Mohammeds*, Berlin, 1910.

LEVEEN, J., "Mohammed and His Jewish Companions," *JQR*, XVI, pp. 399–406.

LEVY, E., *Yesodoth Hatefillah*, Tel-Aviv, 1952.

LEVY, R., *An Introduction to the Sociology of Islam*, 2 vols., London, 1931–33.

LICHTENSTÄDTER, ILSE, "Some References to Jews in Pre-Islamic Arabic Literature," *PAAJR*, Vol. X (1940), pp. 187 f.

LIDZBARSKI, MARK, "Islām und Salām," in *Zeitschrift für Semitistik und verwandete Gebiete*, Vol. I, 1922, pp. 85 f.

————, "Neue Götter," *Nachrichten von der Königlichen Gesellschaft der Wissenschaften zu Göttingen*, Philologisch-historische Klasse, 1916, Berlin, 1916, pp. 86–93.

LIEBERMAN, S., *Hayerushalmi Kipheshuto*, Jerusalem, 1935.

LIEBREICH, L. J., "The Intermediate Benedictions of the Amida," *JQR*, N.S., XLII (1952), #4, pp. 423–26.

LITTMAN, E., "Hārūt und Mārūt," in *Festschrift Friedrich Carl Andreas zur Vollendung des Siebzigsten Lebensjahres*, Leipzig, 1916, pp. 70 ff.

LYALL, CH., "The Words 'Ḥanīf' and 'Muslim'," *JRAS*, 1903, p. 772.

———, *Translations of Ancient Arabian Poetry*, New York, 1930.

M

MAAS, M., *Bibel und Koran*, Leipzig, 1893.

MACDONALD, D. B., *Aspects of Islam*, New York, 1911.

———, *The Development of Muslim Theology, Jurisprudence and Constitutional Theory*, London, 1903.

———, *The Religious Attitude and Life in Islam*, Chicago, 1909.

MAIMONIDES, MOSES, *Mishneh Torah*, 4 vols., Vilna, 1900.

———, *Moreh Nebukim*, Sabbionetta, 1553; also English tr. by M. Friedländer, London, 1942.

———, *Epistle to Yemen*, ed. Halkin, A. S., New York, 1952.

MANN, J., *The Jews in Egypt and in Palestine under the Fatimid Caliphs*, 2 vols., Oxford, 1920–22.

MARGALIYUTH, R., *Mal'ake 'Elion*, Jerusalem, 1935.

MARGOLIOUTH, D.S., *Mohammed and the Rise of Islam*, New York, 1905.

———, *The Early Development of Mohammedanism*, London, 1914.

———, *Chrestomathia Baidawiana* (*Sura III*), London, 1894.

———, "Old and New Testament in Muhammedanism," *ERE*, IX, pp. 482 f.

MARGOLIOUTH, *Mohammed and Mohammedanism*, London, 1889.

———, *The Relations between Arabs and Israelites prior to the Rise of Islam*, London, 1924.

MARMORSTEIN, A., "Iranische und jüdische Religion," *ZNW*, XXVI (1927), 141–204.

———, "Philo and the Names of God," *JQR*, XXII (1931–32), pp. 295–306.

MASSE, H., *Islam*, London, 1938.

Mechilta, ed. I. H. Weiss, Wien, 1865.

Mekilta De-Rabbi Ishmael, ed. M. Friedman, Vienna, 1870.

Mekilta De Rabbi Ishmael, tr. J. Z. Lauterbach, 3 vols., Philadelphia, 1933–35.

Mekilta, Vilno, 1844.

Midrash Abkir, Vienna, 1883.

Midrash Hagadol, ed. S. Schechter, Cambridge, 1902.

Midrash Leḳaḥ Ṭob (ed. Buber), Vilno, 1880.

Midrash Mishle Rabati, Stettin, 1861.

Midrash Rabboth, Wilna, 1878.

Midrash Sifre On Numbers, tr. by Rev. Paul P. Levertoff, London, 1926.

Midrash Talpiyot, Warsaw, 1875.

Midrash Tanḥuma, ed. S. Buber, Vilna, 1885.

Midrash Tanḥuma (*Yelamdenu*), Wien, 1863.

Midrash Tehillim (*Shoḥer Ṭob*), Warsaw, 1865.

MINGANA, A., *Syriac Influence on the Style of the Ḳur'ān*, reprint, London, 1927.

Mishnah (*The*), ed. Herbert Danby, Oxford, 1933. Also Hebrew edition, Vilno.

MITTWOCH, E., *Zur Entstehungsgeschichte des islamischen Gebets und Kultus*, Berlin, 1913.

MOBERG, AXEL, *Über eine Christliche Legende in der Islamischen Tradition*, Lund, 1930.

MONTGOMERY, J. A., *Arabia and the Bible*, Philadelphia, 1934.

———, "Ascetic Strains in Early Judaism," *JBL*, Vol. LI (1932), pp. 183 f.

MUIR, WILLIAM, *The Life of Mohammad*, edited by T. H. Weir, Edinburgh, 1923.

———, *The Coran, Its Composition and Teaching, and the Testimony it bears to the Holy Scriptures*, London, 1878.

MÜLLER, A., *Der Islam im Morgen- und Abendland*, 2 vols., Berlin, 1885–87.

MUNK, L., *Targum Scheni zum Buche Esther*, Berlin, 1876.

MŽIK, HANS V., "Die Gideon-Saul Legende und die Überlieferung der Schlacht bei Badr," in *Festschrift Joseph Ritter v. Karabaček*, pp. 63 f.

N

NAKARAI, TOYOZO W., "The Prophetic Concept of Righteousness," in *The Shane Quarterly*, Vol. XIII (1952), pp. 51–57.
NATHAN BEN JEḤIEL, *Aruch Completum*, ed. A. Kohut, Vienna, 1878.
NEUMAN, ABRAHAM A., *The Jews in Spain*, 2 vols., Philadelphia, 1942.
NICHOLSON, R. A., *A Literary History of the Arabs*, Cambridge, 1941.
———, *The Mystics of Islam*, London, 1914.
———, *Studies in Islamic Mysticism*, Cambridge, 1921.
NICOMEDIA, E., *Gan 'Eden*, Gozlowa, 1926.
NÖLDEKE, THEODOR, "Die Geschichte der Juden in Arabien," in *Beiträge zur Kenntniss der Poesie der Alten Araber*, Hannover, 1864, pp. 192 f.
———, *Neue Beiträge zur semitischen Sprachwissenschaft*, Strassburg, 1910.
———, *Geschichte der Perser und Araber zur Zeit der Sasaniden*, (trans.) from the Annals of Tabari, Leyden, 1879.
———, *Das Leben Muhammeds nach den Quellen populär dargestellt*, Hannover, 1863.
———, "Hatte Muhammed christliche Lehrer?" in *Zeitschrift der deutschen morgenländischen Gesellschaft*, 1858, pp. 699 ff.
———, *Geschichte des Qorâns*, Göttingen, 1860.
NÖLDEKE-SCHWALLY, *Geschichte des Qorâns*, Vol. I, Leipzig, 1909.

O

OBERMANN, JULIAN, "Islamic Origins," *The Arab Heritage*, ed. N. A. Faris, Princeton, 1944, pp. 58–120.
———, "Ein Werk agadisch-islamischen Synkretismus," *Zeitschrift für Semitistik*, V (1927), pp. 43–69.
———, *Practical Theology in Early Islam* (reprint), Philadelphia, 1935.
———, "Koran and Agada," *AJSLL* (1941), Vol. LVIII, Jan. 1941, pp. 23–48.
O'LEARY, DE LACY, *Arabia Before Muhammad*, London, 1927.
———, *Arabic Thought and its Place in History*, London, 1939.
'Oẓar Midrashim, ed. J. D. Eisenstein, 2 vols., New York, 1915.

P

Palmer, E. H., *The Koran*, London, 1951.

Papo, M., "Die sexuelle Ethik im Qoran," *Jahrbuch für jüdische Volkskunde*, II (1924–25), pp. 171–291.

Pautz, Otto, *Muhammeds Lehre von der Offenbarung*, Leipzig, 1898.

Perlmann, Moshe, "A Legendary Story of Ka'b Al-Ahbār's Conversion to Islam," in *The Joshua Starr Memorial Volume*, New York, 1953, pp. 85–99.

Pesiḳta D'Rab Kahana, ed. S. Buber, Lyck, 1868.

Pesiḳta Rabbati, ed. M. Friedmann, Vienna, 1880.

Pesiḳta Zuṭeta, Venice, 1546.

Pfeiffer, R. H., *Introduction to the Old Testament*, New York-London, 1941.

Philo, trans. F. H. Colson and J. E. Whittaker (Loeb Classical Library), 9 vols., London, 1929–41.

Pickthall, Marmaduke, *The Meaning of the Glorious Koran*, London, 1930.

Pirkê D'Rabbi Eliezer, ed. D. Luria, Warsaw, 1852.

Pirḳê De Rabbi Eliezer, English translation by Gerald Friedlander, London, 1916.

Plessner, Martin von, "Die Behandlung Biblischer Erzählungen im Koran," *Gemeindeblatt*, #6, 11J, Frankfurt, 1933, pp. 137–40.

Pollack, A. N., *Dibre Yeme Ha'arabim*, Jerusalem, 1946.

Pool, J. J., *Studies in Mohammedanism*, Westminster, 1892.

Poznanski, S., "New Material on the History of Hebrew and Hebrew-Arabic Philology during the X–XII Centuries." *JQR*, XVI (1925–1926), pp. 237–66.

———, *Studies in Jewish Literature in honor of Kaufmann Kohler*, Berlin, 1913, pp. 214 ff.

R

Rabbinovicz, R. N., *Diḳduḳe Soferim.* Variae Lectiones in Mischnam et in Talmud Babylonicum. 16 vols., Munich and Przemysl, 1867–97.

Rappaport, Solomon, *Agada und Exeges bei Flavius Josephus*, Wien, 1930.

Reckendorf, H., *Al-Ḳoran 'O Hamiḳra*, Leipzig, 1857.

Rittangelio, J. S., *Liber Jeẓirah*, Amsterdam, 1642.

Rivlin, J. J., *Gesetz im Koran*, Jerusalem, 1934.

———, "Muḥammad Hameḥoḳeḳ," in *Kenesset* (1933).

———, *Ḥaye Muḥammad*, 2 vols., Tel-Aviv, 1932–33.

RIVLIN, J. J., *Al-Ḳoran* (Hebrew), 1936–45.

———, "Al-Furqān," in *G. Weil Jubilee Volume*, Jerusalem, 1953, pp. 24–33.

ROBERTS, ROBERT, *The Social Laws of the Qorān*, London, 1925.

ROBSON, J., *Christ in Islam*, London, 1929.

RODWELL, J. M., *The Koran*, London, 1937.

ROSENBLATT S. (ed.), *Beliefs and Opinions*, New Haven, 1948.

———, "The Relation Between Jewish and Muslim Laws Concerning Oaths and Vows," in *PAAJR*, Vol. VII (1935–6), pp. 229–43.

ROSENTHAL, FRANZ, "Some Minor Problems in the Qur'ân," in *The Joshua Starr Memorial Volume*, New York, 1953, pp. 67–84.

———, "Sedaka, Charity," in *HUCA* (1950–51), Vol. XXIII, Part I, pp. 411–30.

ROSENTHAL, JUDAH, "Ḥiwī al-Balkhī," in *JQR* (New Series), XXXVIII, #3, p. 18.

———, "She'eloth 'Atiḳoth Batanak," *HUCA*, XXI, 1948, p. 56.

ROSMARIN, T. W., "Aribi und Arabien in den Babylonisch-Assyrischen Quellen," *JSOR*, XVI (1932), pp. 1–37.

RUDOLPH, WILLIAM, *Die Abhängigkeit des Qorans von Judentum und Christentum*, Stuttgart, 1922.

S

SAADIA BEN JOSEF AL-FAYYOUMI, *Les Œuvres Complètes de Saadia*, ed. J. Dérenbourg, Paris, 1893.

SA'ADIA B. JÛSUF AL-FAJJÛMÎ, *Kitâb al-'Amânât wa'l-I'tiqâdât*, ed. S. Landauer, Leiden, 1880.

SCHACHT, J., "Zur soziologischen Betrachtung des islamischen Rechts," *Der Islam*, XXII (1935), pp. 207–38.

———, *Der Islam mit Ausschluss des Qorans*, Tübingen, 1931.

———, *The Origins of Muhammadan Jurisprudence*, Oxford, 1950.

SCHAPIRO, ISRAEL, *Die haggadischen Elemente im erzählenden Teil des Korans*, Heft I, Leipzig, 1907.

SCHAU, ED., *Muhammedanisches Recht*, Stuttgart und Berlin, 1897.

SCHWABE, M., "Muhammad's Ten Companions" (Hebrew), *Tarbiz*, II, pp. 74–89.

Seder 'Olam Rabbah, Amsterdam, 1711.

Sefer Hajaschar, ed. L. Goldschmidt, Berlin, 1923.

Sefer Tana Debe 'Eliahu (includes *'Eliahu Rabba* and *'Eliahu Zuṭa*), Lemberg, 1867.

Sefer Yalḳut Sippurim Umidrashim, compiled by Z. W. Greenwald, 5 books, Warsaw, 1923.

SELL, EDWARD, *The Faith of Islam*, London, 1896.
———, *The Historical Development of the Koran*, Madras, 1898.
Septuaginta, ed. A. Rahlfs, 2 vols. (3rd ed.), Stuttgart, 1949.
SHIM'ONI, JACOB, *'Arbe Ereẓ-Yisrael*, Tel-Aviv, 1947.
Shorter Encyclopedia of Islam, Leiden-London, 1953.
Siddur Oẓar Hatefilloth, Vilna, 1923.
SIDERSKY, D., *Les Origines des Légendes Musulmanes*, Paris, 1933.
Sifra, ed. J. H. Weiss, Wien, 1862.
Sifré debé Rab, ed. M. Friedman, Wien, 1864.
Sifre Zutta, ed. H. S. Horovitz, Frankfurt and Leipzig, 1917.
Siphre Zu Deuteronomium, ed. L. Finkelstein, Berlin, 1935–38.
SMITH, H. P., *The Bible and Islam*, New York, 1897.
SMITH, R. B., *Mohammed and Mohammedanism*, London, 1889.
———, *Lectures on the Religion of the Semites*, 1st Series, 3rd ed., revised by S. A. Cook, London, 1927
———, *Kinship and Marriage in Early Arabia*, Cambridge, 1885.
SNOUCK-HURGRONJE, C., *Mohammedanism*, New York and London, 1916.
Soncino Chumash, London, 1947.
SPEISER, E. A., *Ethnic Movements in the Near East in the Second Millennium B. C.*, Philadelphia, 1933.
SPERBER, J., *Die Schreiben Muhammeds an die Stämme Arabiens*, Berlin, 1916.
SPEYER, HEINRICH, "Von den biblischen Erzählungen im Koran," *Korrespondenzblatt*, Berlin (1923–24), pp. 7–26.
SPRENGER, A., *Das Leben und die Lehre des Mohammed*, 3 vols., Berlin, 1861–69.
———, *Mohammed und der Koran*, Hamburg, 1889.
STANTON, H. U. W., *The Teaching of the Qur'ān*, London, 1919.
STEINSCHNEIDER, M., *Polemische und Apologetische Literatur in Arabischer Sprache*, Leipzig, 1877.
STERN, G. H., *Marriage in Early Islam*, London, 1919.
STRACK, HERMANN L., *Einleitung in Talmud und Midraš*, München, 1921.
STRACK, H. L. and BILLERBECK, P., *Kommentar zum Neuen Testament aus Talmud und Midrasch*, Vol. I, Munich, 1922.
STRAUSS, A., "Darke Hapulmus Haislāmi," in *Sefer Hazikaron lebet Midrash Lerabanim Bewinah*, Jerusalem, 1950, pp. 46 f.

T

AL-ṬABARĪ, MUḤAMMAD IBN-JARĪR, *Jāmi'u'l-Bayān fī Tafsīru'l-Qur'ān*, 30 vols., Cairo, 1331 A. H.
———, *Ikh'ilāf al-fuḳahā'*, ed. Schacht, Leiden, 1933.

AL-ṬABARĪ, *Annales*, ed. M. J. de Goeje, Series 1–3, Leiden, 1879–1901.
Talmud Yerushalmi. Korotshin ed., 1866.
Targum Yerushalmi (1), *Pseudo-Jonathan*, ed. M. Ginsburger, Berlin, 1903. (2) *Das Fragmententhargum*, ed. M. Ginsburger, Berlin, 1899.
TAYLOR, W. R., "Al-Buhkārī and the Aggada," *The Moslem World*, Vol. XXXIII, #3 (1943), pp. 196 ff.
The Pentateuch and Rashi's Commentary, ed. Abraham b. Isaiah and B. Sharfman, 5 vols., Brooklyn, N. Y., 1949.
THOMSON, WILLIAM, "Muhammad: His Life and Person," *The Moslem World*, XXXIV, #2 (1944), pp. 96–137.
Torah Shlemah, ed. Menahem M. Kasher, 14 vols., 1938–53.
TORREY, Ch. C., *The Jewish Foundation of Islam*, New York, 1933.
Tosefta, ed. Zuckermandel, Posewalk, 1880–82.
TRITTON, A. S., *Muslim Theology*, London, 1947.

V

VAJDA, GEORGES, "Jeûnes Musulmans et jeûnes Juifs," *HUCA*, XII–XIII (1937–38), pp. 367–79.
———, "Juifs et Musulmans selon le *Ḥadīt*," in *Journal Asiatique*, Paris, 1937.

W

WALKER, JOHN, *Bible Characters in the Koran*, Paisley, 1931.
WEBER, O., *Die Literatur der Babylonier und Assyrier*, Leipzig, 1907.
WEIL, G., "Oral Tradition in Judaism and in Islam" (Hebrew), *Magnes Anniversary Book*, Jerusalem, 1938, pp. 132–48.
WEIL, GUSTAV, *The Bible, the Koran and the Talmud*, New York, 1846.
———, *Biblische Legenden der Muselmänner*, Leipzig, 1886.
———, *Historisch-kritische Einleitung in den Koran*, 2nd ed., 1878.
——— (tr.), *Das Leben Mohammeds nach Mohammed ibn Ishāq*, Stuttgart, 2 vols., 1864.
WELLHAUSEN, J., "Medina vor dem Islam," in *Skizzen und Vorarbeiten*, Berlin, 1885–99.
———, *Muhammed in Medina*, Berlin, 1882.
———, *Reste arabischen Heidentums* (2nd ed.), Berlin, 1897.
WENSINCK, A. J., *A Handbook of Early Muhammadan Tradition*, Alphabetically Arranged, Leiden, 1927.
———, *Miftāḥ Kunūz al-Sunnah*, Cairo, 1933.
———, *Mohammed en de Joden te Medina*, Leiden, 1908.

Wensinck, "Die Entstehung der muslimischen Reinheitsgesetzgebung," in *Der Islam*, V (1914), pp. 62–80.
———, *The Muslim Creed*, Cambridge, 1932.
———, "Ḥanīf," *Acta Orientalia*, Vol. II, p. 191.
Wherry, E. M., *A Comprehensive Commentary on the Qurān*, Vols. 1–4, London, 1882–96.
Wieder, Naphtali, *Islamic Influences on the Jewish Worship*, Oxford, 1947.
Winckler, Huge, "Arabisch Semitisch-Orientalisch," in *Journal of American Oriental Society* (Dec. 1927), pp. 1–223.
Wolfson, H. A., "The Internal Senses in Latin, Arabic and Hebrew Philosophic Texts," *HTR*, XXVIII (1935), pp. 69–133.
———, *Philo*, 2 vols., Cambridge, 1947.
Wüstenfeld, F., *Das Leben Muhammeds nach Muhammed Ibn Ishāq, bearbeitet von 'Abd el-Malik Ibn Hischam*, edited by von F. Wüstenfeld, Göttingen, 1859.

Y

Yahuda, A. S., "A Contribution to Qur'ān and Ḥadīth Interpretation," in *Goldziher Memorial Volume*, Budapest, 1948, part I, pp. 286 f.
———, *'Eber Va'arab*, New York, 1946.
Yalḳuṭ Shim'oni, Vilna, 1898.
Yalḳuṭ Reubeni, compiled by Reuben Katz, Amsterdam, 1700.
Yellin, David, *Ḥiḳre Miḳra'*, Jerusalem, 1937.

Z

Zamakhsharī, *The Kashshaf 'an Ḥaqaiq al-Tanzīl* (ed. Lees), 2 vols., Calcutta, 1856.
Zeitlin, Solomon, "An Historical Study of the First Canonization of the Hebrew Liturgy," *JQR*, N. S. Vol. XXXVI (1946), 211–29 and Vol. XXXVIII (1948), 289–316.
———, *The History of the Second Commonwealth*, Philadelphia, 1933.
———, "The Origin of the Synagogue," in *PAAJR*, 1930–31, pp. 69–81.
Zohar, 3 vols., Vilna, 1922.
Zucker, Moses, "Berurim Betoledoth Hawikuḥim Hadatiim sheben Hayahaduth Veha'islam," in *Festschrift Armand Kaminka*, Wien, 1937, pp. 31–48.
Zunz, L., *Die Gottesdienstlichen Vorträge der Juden*, 2nd ed., Frankfurt a. M., 1892.

INDICES

Note: The numbers in ( ) refer to pages in the text.

A. INDEX OF KORANIC VERSES

References are indicated by Sura and Verse.

1:2 (18)
2:1–2 (3)
2:4 (18)
2:5 (14)
2:12 (16)
2:19 (18)
2:20 (17)
2:23 (19)
2:26 (21)
2:26 (21)
2:27 (22)
2:28 (26)
2:31 (30)
2:32 (30)
2:33 (32)
2:34 (34)
2:35 (39)
2:38 (41)
2:46 (43)
2:47 (45)
2:48 (49, 81 n., 115 n.)
2:49 (81 n.)
2:50 (81 n.)
2:51 (81 n.)
2:52 (53)
2:53 (55)
2:54 (57, 64 n.)
2:57 (60)
2:58 (63)
2:60 (65, 82 n.)
2:61 (67)
2:63 (71)
2:69 (74)
2:73 (75)
2:74 (77)
2:77 (78)
2:80 (80)
2:82 (74 n.)
2:86 (81)
2:87 (50 n., 82)
2:88 (84)
2:91 (85)
2:96 (92)
2:101 (96)
2:102 (97)
2:103 (4 n.)
2:104 (64 n.)
2:106 (105 n.)
2:109 (98)
2:111 (99)
2:118 (100, 104 n.)
2:119 (101, 104 n.)
2:123 (105 n.)
2:125 (91 n., 104)
2:127 (107)
2:129 (108)
2:136 (110)
2:137 (112)
2:144 (113)
2:147 (41 n., 42 n., 114)
2:149 (115)
2:154 (116)
2:156 (117)
2:159 (118)
2:160 (77 n., 119)
2:161 (77 n.)
2:167 (121)
2:171 (4 n.)
2:172 (11 n., 125)
2:173 (127)
2:179 (91 n., 128)
2:181 (91 n., 128)
2:182 (131)
2:183 (129 n., 132)
2:184 (130 n.)
2:185 (133)
2:186 (134)
2:187 (135)
2:193 (137)
2:196 (140)
2:206 (141)
2:209 (142)
2:211 (143)
2:213 (145)
2:216 (146)
2:217 (12 n.)
2:220 (147)
2:222 (148)
2:223 (150)
2:224 (152)
2:226 (153)
2:228 (154)
2:229 (156 n.)
2:233 (155)
2:239 (156)
2:240 (157)
2:244 (158)
2:246 (159)
2:247 (161)
2:249 (164)
2:250 (167)
2:251 (169)
2:253 (170)
2:254 (90 n., 172)
2:255 (11 n.)
2:256 (98 n., 174)
2:257 (17 n.)
2:260 (175)
2:261 (177)
2:262 (172)
2:266 (11 n.)
2:271 (181)
2:272 (11 n., 182)
2:273 (108 n., 183)
2:275 (11 n., 13 n.)
2:276–7 (184)
2:278 (11 n.)
2:280 (108 n., 186)
2:282 (187)
2:285 (82 n., 110 n.)
2:286 (188)
3:2 (110 n., 191)
3:3 (19 n.)
3:4 (193)
3:5 (195)
3:7 (196)
3:8 (197)
3:9 (198)
3:11 (199)
3:12 (16, 201)
3:13 (202)
3:14 (80 n.)
3:16 (5 n.)
3:17 (105 n.)
3:20 (63 n.)
3:23 (77 n.)
3:25–6 (203)
3:28 (204)
3:30 (172)
3:35 (205)
3:46 (160 n.)

3:47 (206)
3:54 (84 n.)
3:60 (91 n.)
3:61 (207)
3:71 (208)
3:75 (209)
3:78 (105 n., 110 n., 172)
3:84 (14, 210)
3:85 (211)
3:86 (11 n.)
3:87 (123)
3:89 (108)
3:106 (124 n., 212)
3:108 (63 n.)
3:109 (109)
3:110 (11 n.)
3:111 (41 n.)
3:114 (113)
3:127 (19 n., 214, 220 n.)
3:128 (215)
3:130 (19 n., 214 n.)
3:137 (4 n.)
3:138 (217)
3:139 (218)
3:148 (219 n.)
3:154 (220)
3:159 (221)
3:163 (115, 220 n.)
3:169 (7 n.)
3:172 (213 n., 222)
3:175 (214 n.)
3:177 (63 n., 159)
3:179 (223)
3:183 (213 n., 220 n.)
3:184 (81 n.)
3:188 (157)
3:191 (224)
3:197 (19 n.)
4:9 (11 n.)
4:10 (7 n.)
4:26–27 (154 n.)
4:46 (7 n., 146 n.)
4:94 (127 n.)
4:102 (157 n.)
4:124 (108)
4:153 (67 n.)
4:159 (122 n.)
4:175 (4 n.)
5:4 (121)
5:7 (122 n.)
5:8 (157 n.)
5:12 (11 n.)
5:48 (4 n., 110 n.)
5:69 (160 n.)
5:72 (84 n.)
6:79 (91 n., 108)
6:95 (224)
6:119 (121 n.)
6:146 (122 n.)
6:147 (122 n.)
6:162 (108)
7:18 (37 n.)
7:22 (33 n.)
7:138 (129 n.)
7:141 (91 n.)
7:156 (4 n., 76 n.)
7:158 (91 n.)
7:163 (67 n.)
8:29 (51)
8:42 (13 n.)
8:43 (52 n.)
8:56 (47 n.)
9:11 (13 n.)
9:73 (19 n.)
10:90–2 (47 n.)
10:105 (108)
11:19 (23 n.)
11:73 (100 n.)
11:100 (47 n.)
11:116 (6, 7)
13:29 (5 n.)
15:9 (4 n.)
15:53 (100 n.)
16:115 (121 n.)
16:119 (122 n.)
16:121 (90 n.)
16:124 (91 n.)
16:125 (67 n.)
17:23–41 (152)
17:36 (11 n.)
17:80 (6, 7)
17:83 (4 n.)
17:84 (4 n.)
17:111 (7 n.)
18:2 (4 n.)
18:107 (34 n.)
19:43 (152 n.)
20:13 (90 n.)
20:14 (156 n.)
20:30 (7)
20:112 (3 n., 124 n.)
20:130 (6)
20:132 (6 n.)
21:49 (51)
21:69–70 (175)
21:105 (51 n.)
21:107 (5 n.)
22:29 (138)
22:35 (121 n.)
22:46 (119)
22:76 (136 n.)
23:3 (7 n.)
23:17 (23 n.)
24:21 (11 n.)
24:57 (6)
25:1 (4 n., 51)
26:79–84 (10 n.)
26:192 (4 n.)
29:14–25 (175)
30:29 (109)
30:38 (160)
31:13 (155 n.)
31:39 (184)
32:4 (120 n.)
33:40 (90 n., 110 n.)
35:55 (19 n.)
37:29 (51 n.)
37:81–89 (175)
37:99–113 (100 n.)
38:71–75 (32 n.)
42:5 (3 n.)
42:52 (4 n.)
43:2–3 (3 n.)
44:2 (130 n.)
45:11–12 (26 n.)
45:15 (212 n.)
46:16 (20)
50:25 (152 n.)
50:38 (6, 22, 99 n.)
51:50 (110 n.)
51:57 (17)
53:3 (30 n.)
53:45 (21)
57:10–14 (11 n.)
57:17 (144, 160)
58:14 (11 n.)
59:23 (105 n.)
60:2 (136 n.)
62:2 (76 n.)
64:17 (160)
68:32 (34)
69:34 (11 n.)
72:13 (4 n.)
73:21, 30 (160)
74:2 (110 n.)
75:16 (124 n.)
75:35 (21)
76:8 (11 n.)
76:25 (6)
77:41 (19 n.)
78:3 (18)
78:12 (23 n.)
78:31–35 (19 n.)
79:30 (23)
88:5–14 (19 n.)
88:21–22 (110 n.)
89:17 (11 n.)
90:15 (11 n.)
91:15 (11 n.)
93:8 (11 n.)
93:9 (11 n.)
93:11 (4 n.)
94:14 (11 n.)
96:1 (18)
97:1 (130 n.)
97:3–4 (130 n.)
98:7 (34)
107:2 (11 n.)
107:6 (11 n.)
112:1 (5 n., 18)

B. INDEX OF BIBLICAL VERSES

(does not include biblical verses quoted in talmudic sources)

6:5 (119)
6:7 (10 n.)
7:11 (80)
8:2 (58 n.)
9:9–11 (41 n.)
9:25–26 (156 n.)
10:3–5 (165)
10:12 (119 n.)
10:14 (96, 174)
10:16 (74)
10:17 (174)
11:1 (119)
11:9 (10 n.)
11:13–21 (9)
12:30–31 (213)
13:2–13 (135 n.)
14:2 (112 n.)
14:4 (121 n.)
14:21 (121)
14:22 (12)
14:28–29 (79)
15:7–8 (143)
15:11 (79)
16:16–17 (137)
17:3 (18)
17:16–17 (94)
19:15 (187)
20:1 (135 n.)
20:10 (136 n.)
20:10–14 (134 n.)
20:18 (213)
21:1–9 (71)
23:20–21 (184)
24:1 (153)
24:10–13 (186 n.)
24:11 (91 n.)
24:16 (127 n.)
26:3 (104, 207 n.)
26:3, 4 (101 n.)
26:12 (143 n.)
26:12–14 (79)
26:18 (41 n.)
27:6 (104)
27:15–26 (116)
28:12 (17 n.)
28:15–66 (116)
28:39 (146 n.)
28:68 (64)
29:1–5 (44 n.)
29:2 (44 n.)
29:5 (146 n.)
29:28 (98 n.)
32:39 (21, 117)
34:10 (90 n.)

Joshua

9:3 f. (147 n.)

Judges

5:20 (200 n.)
6:24 (105 n.)
7:1 (167)
7:4–7 (167)
21:19 (137 n.)

I Samuel

1:13 (7 n.)
2:6 (21)
2:8 (203)
9:2 (163)
9:21 (163)
10:1 (161)
15:9 (163 n.)
17:36 (169)
22:19 (163 n.)

II Samuel

22:32 (5 n.)

I Kings

2:28 (135)
7:21 (211 n.)
8:2 (137 n.)
8:22–53 (103)
8:42–3 (103)

II Kings

19:35 (200 n.)

Isaiah

1:11 (125 n., 126)
1:17 (79 n.)
3:10 (19 n.)
3:11 (16 n.)
4:6 (58 n.)
6:3 (5 n.)
6:10 (15)
7:9 (8 n.)
8:10 (206)
37:36 (200 n.)
41:8 (100 n.)
42:19 (105 n.)
43:11 (96)
44:2 (196)
45:5–8 (174)
45:12 (99 n.)
45:23 (5 n.)
48:13 (22)
55:6 (131 n.)
55:10–11 (118 n.)
60:21 (51 n.)
66:1 (174)
66:24 (117)

Jeremiah

1:5 (76 n., 193)
5:3 (74 n.)
5:21 (16)
5:24 (17 n.)
12:1 (80)
13:23 (14)
14:22 (17 n., 118)
17:5 (220)
17:7 (96 n.)
40:15 (194 n.)

Ezekiel

5:5 (112 n.)
7:19 (211)
11:19 (74)
16:60 (41 n.)
22:12 (184 n.)
36:26 (74 n.)
36:36 (176)
37:1–14 (158 n.)

Hosea

13:4 (5 n.)

Amos

9:2–3, 6 (98 n.)

Zephaniah

1:18 (211)
3:9 (4 n.)

Haggai

2:23 (90 n.)

Zechariah

7:12 (74 n.)
8:19 (129 n.)
14:9 (4 n.)

Psalms

2:196 (8 n.)
7:15–16 (188)
15:5 (184 n.)
17:15 (183 n.)
18:32 (5)
19:13 (188 n.)
22:11 (193 n.)
24:1 (96 n.)
30:1 (101 n.)
32:10 (220)
33:6 (99)
33:9 (99)
33:15 (194 n.)
37:23 (218)
39:5 (218)
40:32 (5)

42:2 (119)
44:14 (8 n.)
49:6–18 (197)
50:12 (96 n.)
55:18 (8 n.)
68:5 (24)
68:20 (6 n.)
72:16 (224 n.)
78:4 (6 n.)
86:5 (116)
89:12 (96)
89:53 (140 n.)
96:3 (6 n.)
96:4 (119)
98:2 (5)
104:8 (51 n.)
104:19 (133 n.)
105:2 (6 n.)
105:5 (114)
105:8 (41 n.)
105:39–40 (57 n.)
105:41 (60 n.)
106:8 (55 n.)
106:23 (55 n., 90 n.)
106:48 (140 n.)
107:23 (118)
118:6 (220)
121:1–2 (96)
130:3 (188 n.)
135:7 (17 n.)
136:13 (45 n.)
136:15 (47 n.)
138:4 (5 n.)
139:7–10 (98)
139:13 (193)
145:18–19 (131 n.)

PROVERBS

6:22 (4)
15:17 (181 n.)
17:1 (181 n.)
19:17 (144 n.)
19:21 (206)
20:24 (218 n.)
21:1 (203)
21:30 (206)
28:8 (184 n.)
30:19 (118)

JOB

31:15 (193)

SONG OF SONGS

4:12 (150)

ECCLESIASTES

4:6 (181 n.)
5:1 (7 n.)
7:16 (163 n.)
10:19 (146 n.)

DANIEL

6:11 (6, 8, 111 n.)

EZRA

9:13–14 (147)

NEHEMIAH

2:13 (177)

I CHRONICLES

16:12 (114)
29:11–12 (203)

II CHRONICLES

20:7 (100 n.)

C. INDEX OF QUOTATIONS FROM THE TARGUMIM

TARGUM ONḲELOS

Gen. 22:14 (101 n.)
Lev. 15:31 (149 n.)
Deut. 29:5 (146 n.)
Deut. 32:5 (217 n.)

TARGUM JONATHAN OR YERUSHALMI

Gen. 2:7 (29 n.)
Gen. 3:21 (38 n.)
Gen. 4:26 (142 n.)
Gen. 15:7 (176 n.)
Gen. 18:2 (87 n.)
Gen. 21:33 (101 n.)
Gen. 22:14 (101 n.)
Gen. 28:10 (171 n.)
Gen. 49:1 (107 n.)
Exod. 2:23 (43 n.)
Exod. 4:20 (62 n.)
Exod. 14:19 (57 n.)
Exod. 32:20 (50 n.)
Lev. 18:21 (147 n.)
Num. 11:32 (58 n.)
Deut. 7:10 (80 n.)
I Sam. 11:13 (52 n.)
Jer. 14:22 (17 n.)
Ezek. 36:26 (74 n.)

TARGUM SHIR HASHIRIM

14:1 (83 n.)

TARGUM ḲOHELET

1:12 (95 n.)
9:7 (20 n.)

TARGUM SHENI ON ESTHER

1:3 (95 n.)

D. INDEX OF RABBINICAL PASSAGES

1. MISHNAH

2. TOSEFTA

3. TALMUD YERUSHALMI

4. TALMUD BABLI

B. M.

75b (186 n.)
86b (87 n.)
87a (205 n.)

B. B.

9b (12 n., 13 n., 181 n., 182 n., 215 n.)
10a (12 n., 160 n., 182 n.)
10a, b (160 n.)
11a (19 n.)
75a (20 n.)
121b (42 n.)

SANH.

4a (195 n.)
5b (62 n.)
7a (64 n.)
9b (187 n.)
15b (38 n.)
20b (135 n., 136 n.)
36a–36b (29 n.)
37a (29 n.)
38a (112 n.)
38b (28 n.)
42b (7 n.)
44b (156 n.)
58b (68 n.)
59b (33 n.)
63a (213 n.)
64a (147 n.)
70a–70b (37 n.)
74a (19 n., 119 n., 145 n.)
74b (150 n.)
90a (84 n.)
90b (224 n.)
90b–91a (21 n.)
92a (115 n.)
92b (158 n.)
94a (120 n.)
99a (20 n.)
99b (52 n.)
100a (214 n.)
104a (197)
105a (224 n.)
108a (21 n.)
109a (67)
110a (97 n.)

MAK.

24a (105 n., 125–6 n.)

'A. Z.

2a–2b (196 n.)
2b (201 n.)
4b (52 n.)
8a (39 n.)
44a (83 n.)

ZEB.

19b (157 n.)

MEN.

29a (89 n., 220 n.)

ḤUL.

7b (115 n.)
17b (123 n.)
39a, b (121 n.)
40a (122 n.)
42a (121 n.)
43a (122 n.)

'ARAK.

30b (185 n.)

TAM.

32a (52 n., 115 n.)

NID.

8b (154 n.)
63b (149 n.)

5. MIDRASHIM

ABOTH D'RABBI NATHAN

(cited by chapter)

1 (37 n., 148 n.)
1–2 (41 n.)
1–8 (4 n.)
12 (30 n.)
13 (78 n.)
27 (47 n.)
31 (99 n.)
33 (46 n., 100 n.)
37 (24 n.)

AGGADATH BERESHITH

(includes MIDRASH TEMURAH and MASEKETH 'AẒILUTH)

(cited by page)

8 (188 n.)
9 (193 n., 219 n.)
11 (206 n.)
15 (50 n.)
25 (91 n.)
130 (174 n.)
147 (22 n.)

MEKILTA

(cited by Parashah and section)

BESHALAḤ

1 (45 n., 58 n.)
4 (57 n.)
6 (46 n., 47 n., 91 n.)
10 (99 n.)
60 (90 n.)

KI TIS'A

1 (68 n.)

YITHRO

5 (65 n.)
9 (54 n.)

MIDRASH RABBOTH

(cited by chapter and paragraph)

GEN. RABBA

3, 2 (99 n.)
4, 7 (23 n.)
5, 7 (37 n.)
6, 1 (133 n.)
8, 3–4 (27 n.)
8, 6 (33 n.)
8, 7 (29 n.)
13, 3 (20 n.)
13, 6 (142 n.)
14, 6 (91 n.)
17, 4 (30 n., 31 n.)
18, 6 (3 n.)
19, 1 (36 n.)
19, 6 (36 n.)
20, 10 (36 n.)
21, 6 (40 n.)
22, 12 (39 n.)
26, 7 (92 n.)

6. INDEX OF OTHER WORKS

E. INDEX OF AUTHORS

F. GENERAL INDEX

(Major references are indicated by bold type.)